Day and Night

On the Sufi Path

Charles Upton

DAY AND NIGHT

On the Sufi Path

◈

SOPHIA PERENNIS

First published in the USA
by Sophia Perennis, 2015
An imprint of Angelico Press
© Charles Upton 2015

Series editor: James R. Wetmore

For information, address:
Angelico Press
4709 Briar Knoll Dr.
Kettering, OH 45429
angelicopress.com

pbk: 978-1-62138-135-8
ebook: 978-1-62138-136-5

Cover image: Doorway in Hall of Ambassadors, Alhambra
Cover design: Michael Schrauzer

CONTENTS

Introduction 1

PART ONE: BASIC CONCEPTS

1: An Outline of Sufism 11

2: The Sufi Doctrine of the *Nafs*—A Detailed Exposition 32

3: The Practice of Remembrance (*Dhikr*) 82

PART TWO: THE SCIENCE OF SPIRITUAL STATES

Preface to Part Two 105

4: Gathering (*Jam'*) and Dispersion (*Tafriqah*) 123

5: Expansion (*Bast*) and Contraction (*Qabd*) 140

6: Fluctuation (*Talwin*) and Stability (*Tamkin*) 153

7: Intoxication (*Sukr*) and Sobriety (*Sahw*) 162

8: Intimacy (*Uns*) and Awe (*Haybat*) 177

9: Absence (*Ghaybat*) and Presence (*Hudur*) 190

10: Annihilation (*Fana'*) and Subsistence (*Baqa'*) 197

Afterword: The Shame of States; the Shame of Talking 209

Appendix I: The Dangers of the Strictly Intellectual Approach to the Spiritual Path 212

Appendix II: The Vulnerabilities and Duties of "Civic Sufism" 223

Bibliography 232

It is He who taketh your souls at night, and knoweth what you have merited in the day. [Q. 6:60/6:60]

Every day doth some new work employ Him. [Q. 55:29/55:29]

If you want to be counted among the people of insight
You must pass from *statement* to *state*.
You can't become a unitarian simply by reciting the Surah of Unity
Any more than you can sweeten your mouth just by saying the word
"sugar."
                                                                    —Jami

Praise the name of thy Lord The Most High, Who hath created and balanced all things. [Q. 87:1–2/87:1–2]

By a Soul and Him who balanced it… [Q. 91:7/91:7]

◇

Despite the growing number of academic books on Sufism, original treatises in English are quite rare. When they do appear, they compel us to acknowledge that Sufism is still a living tradition best explained from within. In *Day and Night on the Sufi Path* Charles Upton provides us with a lucid glimpse of one of the spiritual paths to God in Islam. Classical Sufi teachings on the soul, spiritual practice, states and stations, and potential dangers are discussed with eloquence and rigor in a manner that is true to the tradition and relevant to the time we are in. This work is at once philosophical and poetic, systematic and with flashes of original inspiration that can only come from someone conversant in both the theoretical and practical dimensions of *tasawwuf*. It is a faithful reflection of the Divine Light that has captured the author's attention and may help to illuminate the path for others.

In a manner that is reminiscent of Ibn 'al-Arabi, the vision articulated here is receptive to the diversity of Divine disclosures while not being exclusively bound by any single one. Through the recognition of God in each moment we open ourselves to the movement of His signs in the cosmos and the soul, and in that which transcends them.

—Zachary Markwith, author of *One God,
Many Prophets: The Universal Wisdom of Islam*

Introduction

THE SUFIS SAY that you can't get Sufism from books—and yet they keep on writing books. How can we explain this apparent paradox? Books on *Tasawwuf*, if they are true and accurate, may at the very least prevent the growth of certain errors and misconceptions. Beyond that, they have the potential—God willing—of attracting to Sufism some of those who are destined by Allah to embrace the Path as a concrete reality, not just a mental image.

I am not a shaykh; I am not a "public Sufi" who runs workshops; speaking as precisely as I can, I am someone with a facility for expressing metaphysical ideas and with some insight into spiritual psychology who has been on the Sufi path for the past quarter century. I pray that my presentation of *Tasawwuf* will not be so gross as to obscure the truth of my subject, or so subtle as to counterfeit that truth, diverting the reader from Divine Reality by the very expression of it, in view of the fact that the closer we come to the Real, the more destructive any error or illusion becomes. Those who study the words and follow the prescriptions of the shaykhs may know something, but their words are without authority, except whatever momentary authority Allah may grant them out of His generosity, often without their ever being aware of it. The words of the shaykhs, however, are spoken out of His realized and established authority. The most subtle esoteric philosophy, in the absence of this authority, is of no more than academic interest, while what may seem to be a mere moral platitude, when spoken by a true shaykh, carries the power of its own realization, deeper than words, deeper even than silence. Many call themselves shaykhs who are not so in reality, but if Allah has destined you to encounter a true shaykh then you will meet him without fail; may Allah also grant you the power to recognize him, and follow his guidance.

Metaphysical knowledge is knowledge of eternal, changeless

Principles. However, if one attains such knowledge and also *identifies* with it on the basis of a subtle possessiveness, spiritual transformation becomes impossible; because one sees oneself as "already there", one cannot take even the first real step on the spiritual Path. What to the Heart is the Spirit of Allah, the vibratory Self-manifesting radiance of eternal Truth, to the *Nafs al-ammara bi'l su'*, the "self commanding to evil" or largely unconscious ego, is only stagnation and paralysis. The cure for this illness, if one has been unfortunate enough to contract it, is to shift one's attention from what one knows of Allah to the truth that one *is known* by Him, known more intimately and more completely than one could ever know either Allah or oneself. The object of this Knowledge, this *Ma'rifah*, is the human form; the Knowledge itself belongs to Allah, and *is* Allah.

One of the central subjects of this book is what are called in Sufism the *ahwal* or "spiritual states." A danger in writing about such states is that people might think of them as "interesting" and hope to "try them out"—instead of fulfilling their spiritual duties, putting themselves in the hands of Allah, making His wishes theirs, and wanting nothing but Him. But since states will likely occur in the course of the spiritual Path, it is advisable to have a sufficiently accurate and useful theory of them, otherwise they may be unnecessarily puzzling, disorienting, frightening, distracting, or enticing. (Even a perceived lack of states may, from one perspective, be considered as a state or station in itself—the station of Stability, let us say, or that of Sobriety.) States arrive when the Presence of Allah encounters subjective psychic barriers that need to be dissolved. A river that flows deeply and without obstructions may be so silent and so free of turbulence that it appears motionless—though anyone who enters it will certainly learn its power. A relatively shallow river, however, one that is filled with stones and sand bars and fallen logs, will exhibit many "interesting" patterns of turbulence, and make a lot of noise. But such a river is navigable only with difficulty. Over time, however, the force of the water may clear the obstructions, wear down the rocks, and sufficiently deepen the channel so that it becomes useful for purposes of travel, capable of swiftly and easily transporting many passengers. In my own case, I was blessed, or cursed, with what is called "the artistic temperament", indicating a degree of psychic volatility that, while useful for some things, also presents many problems; one of my goals in writing this book has been to better understand, and learn to more skillfully deal with, qualities and tendencies that otherwise might have wasted my capacity and damaged my spiritual life.

The present volume is more explicit and systematic than many others dealing roughly with the same subject, and clarity of exposition is certainly a virtue. But it also has a down side. The subject of Sufism is vast, capable of being seen from innumerable different perspectives; and this is even truer of the spiritual life as a whole. If my systematic treatment brings greater clarity, well and good—but if it goes to feed the illusion that this subject can be exhausted, or that less systematic, subtler modes of expression (the writings of Niffari come immediately to mind) are somehow inferior to more systematic treatments, then I have done my readers a disservice. Every indication of the reality of the Unseen is either a sign or an idol, depending upon how we receive it. The sign is a path to Allah because it is given by Allah; the idol begins and ends only with oneself. May the idols lurking in this book rise and fall away; may the signs it may be capable of transmitting conduct us, by the power and mercy of Allah, more deeply into His Presence—and then also fall away.

Some, especially those sensitive to (or mired in) details, may discern a number of contradictions or tautologies in this book. Is this simply sloppiness on the author's part, or is there is a rationale behind it? Sloppiness may be one explanation, but another one is more to the point: that Sufism is not an abstract philosophical system but a concrete, lived relationship with Absolute Reality; that's why you can't get real Sufism from books.

One of the main reasons this book is was written was in order to demonstrate how true Sufism, far from being a heterodox "innovation" or an intrusion into Islam of doctrines and practices essentially foreign to it, is nothing more or less than a science of practical spirituality based on an understanding of the inner teachings of the Qur'an—supplemented of course by the *hadith*—a Book which, though full of secrets, nonetheless presents these secrets quite openly, "hidden in plain sight", in *the clear Arabic tongue* [Q. 26:195].

3

Rumi compares the Qur'an to a new bride shy of being unveiled, a bride we must first marry, and only then undertake to court. To crude and grasping hands she is nothing but a burqa, opaque and forbidding; to subtle hearts she is unveiled in all her beauty and majesty:

> *Truly in this is a Message of remembrance for people of insight.*
> *Is one whose heart God has opened to surrender*
> *so that he is illumined by a light from his Sustainer*
> *no better than one who is hard-hearted?*
> *Woe to those whose hearts are hardened*
> *against remembrance of God!*
> *They obviously wander astray!*
> *God has revealed the most beautiful message*
> *in the form of a Book consistent within itself,*
> *repeating its teaching in various guises.*
> *The skins of those who stand in awe of their Lord tremble with it;*
> *then their skins and their hearts soften*
> *with the remembrance of God.*
> *Such is God's guidance:*
> *with it He guides the one who wills to be guided,*
> *but those whom God lets stray have none to guide them.*
> [Q. 39:21–23]

May Allah soften our skins and our hearts to perceive the inner beauties of the Noble Qur'an, in which one continuing theme is the Day and Night of the Heart; *ayat* expressing this theme appear below. [NOTE: Most of the Qur'anic verses reproduced in this book are from the English versions of Rodman and Pickthall, though in a few places other versions are used. In the case Rodman, his surah and verse numbers are followed by those of Pickthall, since Rodman's numbering of verses departs significantly in some places from what has become standard in English versions of the Qur'an.]

◇

> *Verily, in the creation of the Heavens and of the Earth, and in the succession of the night and of the day, are signs for men of understanding heart. . . .* [Q. 3:187/3:190]

His, whatsoever hath its dwelling in the night and in the day! and He, the Hearing, the Knowing! [Q. 6:14/6:13]

Verily, in the alternations of night and of day, and in all that God hath created in the Heavens and in the Earth are signs to those who fear Him. [Q. 10:6/10:6]

God causeth the night to enter in upon the day, and He causeth the day to enter in upon the night: and for that God Heareth, Seeth. [Q. 22:60/22:61]

God causeth the day and the night to take their turn. Verily in this is teaching for men of insight. [Q. 24:40/24:44]

See they not that We have ordained the night that they may rest in it, and the day with its gift of light? Of a truth herein are signs to people who believe. [Q. 27:88/26:86]

Say: What think you? If God should enshroud you with a long night until the day of Resurrection, what god beside God would bring you light? Will you not then hearken?

Say: What think you? If God should make it one long day for you until the day of Resurrection, what god but God could bring you the night in which to take your rest? Will you not then see?

Of His mercy he hath made for you the night that you may take your rest in it; and the day that you may seek what you need out of His bounteous supplies, and that you may give thanks. [Q. 28:71–73/28:71–73]

And of His signs are your sleep by night and by day, and your goings in quest of His bounties. Herein truly are signs to those who hearken. [Q. 30:22/30:23]

Seest thou not that God causeth the night to come in upon the day, and the day to come in upon the night? and that He hath subjected the sun and the moon to laws by which each speedeth along to an appointed goal? and that God therefore is acquainted with that which you do? [Q. 31:28/31:29]

He causeth the night to enter in upon the day, and the day to enter in upon the night; and He hath given laws to the sun and to the moon, so that each journeyeth to its appointed goal. . . . [Q. 35:14/35:13]

A sign to them also is the Night. We withdraw the Day from it, and lo! they are plunged in darkness;
And the Sun hasteneth to her place of rest. This, the ordinance of the Mighty, the Knowing!
And as for the Moon, We have decreed stations for it, till it change like an old and crooked palm branch.
To the Sun it is not given to overtake the Moon, nor doth the night outstrip the day; but each in its own sphere doth journey on. [Q. 36:37–40/36:37–40]

For truth hath He created the Heavens and the Earth: It is of Him that the night returneth upon the day and that the day returneth upon the night. . . . [Q. 39:7/39:5]

It is God who hath ordained the night for your rest, and the day to give you light: verily God is rich in bounties to men. . . . [Q. 40:63/40:61]

And in the succession of night and day, and in the supply which God sendeth down from the Heaven whereby He giveth life to the earth when dead, and in the change of the winds, are signs for a people of discernment. [Q. 45:4/45:5]

And ordained the night as a mantle,
And ordained the day for gaining livelihood. . . . [Q. 78:10–11/78:10:11]

I swear by the sunset redness,
And by the night and its gatherings,
And by the moon when at her full,
That from state to state shall you be surely carried onward.
[Q. 84:16-19/84:16–19]

By the Sun and his noonday brightness!
By the Moon when she followeth him!
By the Day when it revealeth his glory!
By the Night when it enshroudeth him!
By the Heaven and Him who built it!

6

By the Earth and Him who spread it forth!
By a Soul and Him who balanced it,
And breathed into it its wickedness and its piety,
Blessed now is he who hath kept it pure,
And undone is he who hath corrupted it! [Q. 91:1–10/91:1–10]

By the Night when she spreads her veil;
By the Day when it brightly shineth;
By Him who made male and female;
At different ends truly do you aim!
But as to him who giveth alms and feareth God,
And yieldeth assent to the Good;
To him will We make easy the path to happiness.
But as to him who is covetous and bent on riches,
And calleth the Good a lie,
To him will We make easy the path to misery. . . .
[Q. 92:1–10/92:1–10]

By the noon-day Brightness,
And by the Night when it darkeneth!
Thy Lord hath not forsaken thee, neither hath He been dis-
pleased. [Q. 93:2–4/93:1–3]

◇

A Note on Terminology

I have used the words "soul" and "self" to translate the Arabic
Nafs—which in Sufi terms generally denotes "unconscious ego"—
though sometimes "soul" is used more in its original English sense
to refer to the *Fitrah*, the totality of the essential human psyche or
basic human makeup as Allah created it. Nowhere does "self" refer
to the Self in the Vedantic sense, the Absolute Indwelling Witness or
Atman; this notion is implied in a general way in the term *Ruh*. *Al-
Ruh*, as seen from the human side, is the immortal human spirit; as
seen from the side of the Divine, it is the Spirit of Allah within us,
one aspect of which is *Al-Shahid*, the Universal Witness. (Note that
"Self" in the Jungian sense is roughly equivalent to the Sufi *Qalb*,
the Spiritual Heart.) The *Nafs*, as we first encounter it, is the great
enemy of the spiritual life; when it occupies the Heart, the Spirit

7

cannot enter it. And *al-Nafs* in the higher sense of the word, as the Soul or Self of Allah, can perhaps be defined as the totality of Allah's Self-manifestation and Self-knowledge within His own Nature, a Divine mystery that constitutes a great danger for those who encounter it—namely, the danger of unconsciously identifying one-self with Allah. This definition, however, is in one sense no more than a pattern perceived by the limited human mind. Every distinc-tion we make or discern in an attempt to understand the Reality of Allah is ultimately resolved within His Absolute Unity; conse-quently there are aspects or levels to the *Nafs* that cannot be defined in words, only grasped by direct realization.

According to a few Sufis—one being Ruzbehan Baqli in his *Sharh-e-Shathiyat*—the *Nafs* in her highest aspect is identifiable with *Al-Dhat*, God's Absolute Essence, which in Itself is absolutely unknowable. As such she is the One the Persian poet Nizami (based on Arab legend) called *Laylah*, whose name means Black Night. Laylah drives Her lover *Majnun* crazy—his name means "madman", literally "jinn-possessed"—because the Essence is both infinitely attractive and totally ungraspable, which is why Majnun can be united with Her only after death. Most Sufis, however, limit the Nafs to the lower passional self, which may become pacified and submissive, but holds no transcendental mysteries to be revealed upon successful completion of the spiritual Path.

Part I

BASIC CONCEPTS

1

An Outline of Sufism

WHAT CAN BE SAID of Sufism? Jalaluddin Rumi said, "There is no such thing as a Sufi in this world—and if there were he would be non-existent."

Sufism—*Tasawwuf* in Arabic—is Islamic mysticism. Though the Sufis have produced a vast literature of exquisite spiritual poetry— Hafiz, Rumi, and a thousand others—and innumerable master-pieces of metaphysics, such as those wrought by Ibn al-'Arabi, the Shaykh al-Akbar, the "greatest teacher," who was also a poet—there is nothing essential in Sufism that is not ultimately a *batini* (inner, esoteric) *tafsir* (exegesis), of the Holy Qur'an. And though he was not called by that name, the Prophet Muhammad, peace and bless-ings be upon him, was really the first Sufi. After Muhammad, the most widely acknowledged prototype and exemplar of Sufism, cho-sen recipient of the Prophet's inner teachings, was the fourth Sunni caliph and the first Shi'ite Imam, the Prophet's son-in-law Ali ibn Abi Talib, peace and blessings be upon him. Initiation (*bay'ah*) under a Sufi shaykh who possesses a valid *silsilah* (teaching lineage; chain of transmission) stretching back to the Prophet Muhammad, peace and blessings be upon him, as well as a degree of realization in his own right, puts the initiate in touch (virtually at least) with the immediate presence of Allah, in a deeper way than is enjoyed by those of the faithful (*mu'minin*) who are without Sufi initiation— unless Allah wills otherwise, who *guideth whom He will* [Q. 14:4].

Sufism is sometimes thought of as a collection of doctrines plus a set of spiritual methods for realizing them. This picture of *Tasaw-wuf* gives it the appearance, to some—aided and abetted by the arrogance and unwarranted assumptions of many Orientalists—of a heterodox innovation or an intrusion into Islam from some outside source. But in reality, just as all orthodox Sufi doctrine is ultimately based on the Qur'an, so Sufi methodology—including *Dhikr* ("remembrance (of God)" in the form of the invocation of the Name of God, or a formula containing it), *khalwa* (spiritual retreat, which was practiced by the Prophet himself), *wird* (litany), poetry, music (the *sama'* or "spiritual concert"), and sometimes dance—are more accurately seen as *responses* to the Grace (*barakah*) or Presence (*Hadrat*) of Allah than ways of "producing" it. God is never absent so He need not be "summoned", nor do we possess the power to summon Him; the thing in need of summoning, and of redemption from *ghaflah* ("heedlessness") is the subtle spiritual attention of the Sufi to His Grace and His Presence. This is not meant to imply that Allah Himself does not send "infusions" or "breaths" or "unveilings", withdrawing them or altering them at will, only that none of these things can be *produced* by spiritual exercises. Such exercises may center and purify the spiritual attention of the Sufi; they have no power to operate upon God.

Sufism is indeed the mystical or inner dimension of Islam; the use of the word *mystical*, however, presents certain problems. Sufism is not "mysticism" if we take this to mean the response of especially sensitive souls to the universal Life of Allah that streams through the universe; it is much too precise and methodical to be described in this manner. Nor is it "mysticism" if we use this word to denote the result, in terms of "higher consciousness," of a dedicated and self-directed struggle to apply various contemplative techniques to the work of spiritual development; as a gift of Allah it is incapable of being acquired by simple human effort, so it cannot be really defined in this way. Sufism is fully comprehended neither by the notion of a set of special "secret" doctrines—though it certainly includes modes of expression (and modes of silence) that are not to be found in any of the other Islamic sciences—nor by the notion of special *ecstatogenic* techniques, though practices that appear to be for the purpose of inducing "altered states of consciousness" are also in evidence. It might be correct to say that Sufism possesses a secret doctrine—except for the fact that there is no Sufi teaching that is not found, in one way or another, in the Holy Qur'an, a book written *in the clear Arabic tongue* that can be read by anyone who knows that language. It also would be correct to say that Sufism includes various techniques for producing spiritual states—except for the fact that, as we have already pointed out, any given "technique" will be more the effect of a state than the cause of it. According to Sufi doctrine, spiritual states or *ahwal* are gifts not acquisitions: there is no Creator, and no Opener, save Allah.

The root of Sufism is a special relationship to the Presence of God, a relationship that is conferred by initiation, by taking *bay'ah* (an oath of allegiance) with a Sufi shaykh who is both a link in a *silsilah*, a human chain for the transmission of a particular spiritual influence stretching back to the Prophet Muhammad, peace and blessings be upon him, and who himself possesses a certain degree of real mystical attainment. This Presence totally encompasses the *faqir* ("poor man", another name for "Sufi"); it is always more full of Power than he is aware of, more full of Love than he can feel, more full if Knowledge than he has yet realized. It is not a state of consciousness but the Source of all such states; It is the Presence of the Real, which is Objectivity Itself; It does not depend for Its existence upon Its recipient's awareness of It.

As for the mass of doctrine and lore and narrative and poetic composition produced and held in trust by Sufis over the ages—material that does not always seem to derive from the Qur'an, at least not directly—much of this comprises the record of the responses of the psyche of man, initially sunk in heedlessness and dissipation, to the Power of the Presence of God; it has come into being only so as to give report of, and define the inner principles of, the profound effects of the Presence of Allah upon the human Heart. These effects are different in every Heart and in every moment, yet there is a great unanimity running through them, because the human form is always the human form, and Allah is always Allah. Allah's Presence plows and harrows the soul, seeds it, fertilizes it, and finally harvests it—and, in the process of this alchemy, It inevitably reveals many separate facets and distinct ontological levels of the human being that are usually hidden from us, along with the innumerable ways in which human consciousness—and human existence itself, even apart from consciousness—responds to the approach of God, in those souls who desire it, and are willing to ask for it, and have the God-given stamina to withstand it. God is always seeking us, while we most often find ourselves fleeing from Him, which is why the Qur'an advises, *Flee unto Allah!* [Q. 51:50]. Likewise, as the *hadith* reminds us, "When his servant draws nearer to Him walking, He comes toward His servant running" [Bukhari].

Sufic modes of expression range from the entirely explicit on one end of the spectrum to the highly subtle and allusive on the other end, with subtlety and allusiveness predominating—as opposed to such works as the Hindu Upanishads, for example, where metaphysical doctrines are presented as explicitly as possible. The necessity for subtlety and allusiveness in expression arises from the nature of the Holy Qur'an and the character of the Prophet who perfectly mirrors it. The Qur'an is a comprehensive revelation, encompassing everything from the most outer rules for comportment and behavior and political action to the most inner and esoteric sciences. It is addressed to the whole Muslim community, but nonetheless contains subtleties that only a few will discern or understand, and then only if Allah has opened this understanding to them. A book addressed exclusively to mystics can be explicit about metaphysical and contemplative doctrines; one addressed to a whole community must express many things *sub rosa*, in allusive or symbolic language, or through explicit outer or *zahiri* prescriptions that also have various inner or *batini* meanings and effects. If Allah, the Hidden Treasure, is revealed only by his Veil, the created universe—whose secret synthesis is the Human Form—and by His second Veil, the Holy Qur'an, then the esoteric doctrines of the Qur'an are necessarily projected on the curtain of the explicit commands and prohibitions that form the basis of the shari'ah—though sometimes that curtain parts for an instant to reveal, as in a flash of lightning, an inner truth from the Heart of the Book. And then the curtain closes again; if it did not, we would first be blinded by the Light of Truth and then vaporized by its Power. So the first reason for the subtlety and allusiveness of Sufi expression is to protect from injury those who are unready for the full Light. And the second reason, inseparable from the first, is that subtlety exercises and sharpens the intellect and the spiritual intuition in a way that explicit doctrine cannot; at the same time it demonstrates that the intellect cannot grasp such subtleties until the Heart is purified. The book you are presently reading, however, is more explicit than most; this is due to the fact that, as the Hour draws ever nearer, the inner doctrines are progressively unveiled: first, because as the traditional modes of the transmission of these doctrines continue to break down in many places (though certainly not all), such unveiling becomes necessary, since it is better for the inner truth to be exposed—for all the damage this will inevitably cause—than for it to be forgotten, and secondly because these latter days, the days of the *fitan*, the Tribulation, are a time of Divine Judgment—and Truth, Allah as *Al-Haqq*, comprises the Scales of that Judgment.

Sufi doctrine and practice stretch all the way from the sciences of repentance, such as al-Ghazali's practical methods for overcoming gluttony and lust, to the sciences of *Ma'rifah*, the most profound subtleties of metaphysical discernment and mystical consciousness such as appear in the works of Ibn al-'Arabi and many others; in this, it mirrors the Holy Qur'an itself. And this is precisely why *Tasawwuf* possesses a comprehensiveness that few other systems of spiritual understanding and development can boast: it is addressed both to the grossest and most materialistic of human tendencies which simply need to be reined in by obedience to explicit rules, and also to the subtlest potentialities of the human Heart, as well as to everything else in between, all the levels of self-discipline, devotion, spiritual striving, and psychological insight that manifest and demand to be satisfied when imperfect man encounters perfect God, when he comes into the presence of Allah as *Al-Quddus*, the Holy, and as *Al-Salam*, the Flawless. The goal of Sufism, and of Islam itself, is to produce not only reclusive saints or heroic spiritual warriors, but *al-Insan al-Kamil*, the Complete Man, whose model is the Prophet Muhammad himself, peace and blessings be upon him.

In the first generation or two after the Prophet's death, the Sufis had no name of their own, but after the current of history began to sweep Islam further away from the purity of its origins, the early Muslim ascetics were transformed into the Sufis, and Sufi "orders" began to be established around great saints and teachers, to concentrate the inner teachings and the spiritual practices of Islam. A Sufi order is roughly analogous to a Catholic monastic order, except for the fact that the normal practice of Sufis is to meet in "lodges" known as *zawiyyahs* (Arabic) or *khaniqas* (Persian) or *tekkes* (Turkish). Generally speaking, Sufis are not cloistered like monks (in the words of the Prophet, peace and blessings be upon him, "there is no monasticism in Islam") and are usually married (in the words of the Prophet, "marriage is half the religion" [Bukhari]). And also unlike Catholic monastic orders, Sufi orders are independent; they are "chartered" by no authority outside their own masters and lineages, though traditional Sufi orders nonetheless live by generally accepted Muslim norms. Sufism as a whole is not a sect as are Sunni and Shi'ite Islam; Sufi orders, though they are nominally either Sunni or Shi'ite (most being Sunni), are institutions unto themselves. Sufism thus represents a kind of independent, though not separate, "estate" within Islam: that of the "organized mystics."

The word "Sufi" is said to be derived from the Arabic word for "wool" (Arabic root *swf*) from which the rough garments of the of the poor and the ascetics were made—or from the word for "purity" (*safa*)—or (according to some) from the Greek word for wisdom (*sophia*). A more likely derivation, however, is from the *Ahl al-suffa* or People of the Bench (or "sofa"), the contemplatives attached to the Prophet's household. The Sufi is commonly known in Arabic as a *faqir*—"poor man"—or, in Persian, a *darvish*, "thresholder", which means essentially the same thing, being used to denote the kind of beggar who stands at the doorway hoping for a handout, but which may also allude to the one who occupies the "threshold" between this earthly world and the realm of the Transcendent—the spiritual Heart. A Sufi is poor in the sense of Jesus' words when He said, "blessed are the poor in spirit, for they shall see God"; he is a poor man because he recognizes his own intrinsic poverty, which is the poverty of all things other than God. According to Sufi doctrine, only God possesses *being* in His own right; all other things possess it only as a gift of That One. In themselves, they are nothing.

The essential practice of Sufism is to remember God and forget oneself and one's claims—which does *not* imply a rejection of vigilance with regard to one's behavior and states. The essential form this practice usually takes, beyond the practices common to all

Muslims (such as the daily prayer) is known as *Dhikr*, "remembrance." *Worship preserveth from lewdness and iniquity, but verily remembrance of Allah is more important* [Q. 29:45]. *Dhikr* is the occasional group vocal recitation, and the constant, individual, silent recitation, of God's name, or a formula containing it, or another Name referring to a particular aspect of God.

The Sufi's Master (*shaykh* in Arabic, *pir* in Persian) is, to him, the very presence of God. He can be this for his followers not because he has become Godlike in his human nature, but because he has become nothing. He is an open door through which streams the Divine Light. One Sufi master has said: "If the master is not perfect the darvish will worship him, and to worship one's master is the same as worshipping oneself." It is the Master who admits the prospective darvish to his order and his presence; gives him (God willing) both the right and the power to invoke the Name of God; and transmits to him the *barakah* of his spiritual *silsilah*, which stretches back usually to Ali but sometimes to the first Sunni Caliph Abu Bakr, and from there to the Prophet, and from the Prophet to the Angel Jibra'il who revealed the Qur'an, and from Jibra'il to Allah, the Absolute Reality.

Sufism possesses a vast metaphysical literature, embodying a complex and sophisticated understanding of the ways and planes and dimensions of being through which the Absolute Reality of Allah manifests itself, and an equally vast literature on spiritual psychology and the various "states" and "stations" through which the Sufi passes on his path to God—or, rather, his path *in* God. "States" are gifts of God which can be neither merited nor produced at will; "stations" are spiritual achievements of the Sufi himself, based upon his ability to actualize the virtues—virtues like Humility, Zeal, Courtesy, Trust-in-God, etc. States may announce stations; they may even be considered virtual stations in themselves; but only the labor to assimilate the freely-bestowed grace of a state can turn it into a station. God may plant the grain, water it, harvest it, thresh it, winnow it, grind it, bake it into bread, slice it and serve it; He may even place it in our mouths. But it is up to us, at the very least, to chew, swallow and digest it.

But there is more to it than this—because, from another point of view, *everything* is a gift of God: not only our existence as creatures, but also our actions, our striving, our aspiration; only Allah is the Doer. Aspiration and striving on the spiritual path are certainly necessary—the fact is, however, that they do not belong to us, but to Allah. We do not own even our own existence; how then can we own our actions? *You cannot will unless Allah wills* [Q. 76:30].

The notion of States and Stations in Sufism is not some later innovation derived from non-Islamic influences, but was revealed in the first surah of the Holy Qur'an received by the Prophet Muhammad, peace and blessings be upon him. Speech and listening come before writing and reading—and the motion from speech to writing, from inspiration to memory, from potential to crystallization, was recapitulated by the descent of the Holy Qur'an upon the Prophet Muhammad, peace and blessings be upon him. When Jibra'il revealed to Muhammad the surah known as *The Clot*, commanding him to *Read!*, his first answer was, "but I don't know how to read!" He could certainly *hear*, however, otherwise he would not have responded. At that moment, *hearing*, for him, began to be transformed into *reading*. His response to the present Word of Allah in that unique moment, when to *hear* was to *obey*, opened him to the vision of the *Umm al-Kitab*, the eternal Mother of the Book, the celestial Qur'an, woven of the archetypes of all things, of which the written Qur'an is simply an epitome translated into human language. It was Muhammad's perfect submission to the States that came upon him, to time and motion and change understood as the Living Speech of Allah, that lifted him to the Station of Eternity, where no change can come:

> *Read: In the name of thy Lord who createth,*
> *Createth man from a clot,*
> *Read: And thy Lord is the Most Bounteous,*
> *Who teacheth by the pen,*
> *Teacheth man that which he knew not.* [Q. 96:1–5]

Here the development of the human being from fertilized egg to full adult form, and the motion from hearing and listening to reading and writing, are presented as strictly equivalent. In a single flash, on that day, in that moment, Muhammad understood the relationship of speech to writing, of hearing to reading, of the immediate response to the Command of Allah to the full assimilation and establishment of that Command, inscribed on the human Heart. In the science of *Tasawwuf*, this motion from the spoken to the written word is understood as the passage from *hal*, "state" (the singular of *ahwal*), to *maqam*, "station." First Allah reveals a truth to us, not to head but to Heart, not mentally but totally. This unveiling, because of the contrast between the new knowledge and our old condition, results in a *state*: rapture, dread, heart-melting love, bewilderment—the list is endless. But once this knowledge has become part of our character—once our nature is not simply impacted by it but conformed to it—it becomes a *station*; our character has been qualified by a Name of Allah. First the Name "Allah" is heard by the inner ear, the subtle spiritual intuition; then it is written on the Heart. It is said that *hal* is a gift and *maqam* an acquisition; I would only add that *hal* is imperfect obedience and *maqam*, total obedience. When obedience has become perfect, both the sense of a Command issued, and that of a slave who complies with this Command, are obliterated. In this book we will speak more often of the *awhal* (states) than of the *maqamat* (stations), though sometimes you will find that the two terms have become interchangeable. It is said that any state can become a station—and yet those whose station is Intoxication or Absence or Annihilation will likely appear, from the human point of view, to be imbalanced or mentally ill. Stations such as Gathering or Stability or Sobriety or Presence, on the other hand, are much more capable of being lived, as relatively constant conditions, with the fullness of our humanity. This is one of the points where the actual truth of the matter, as we warned above, evades any purely systematic treatment.

Sufi ontology—the science of the nature of Being—takes many forms. Ibn al-'Arabi speaks of the Five *Hadharat* (modes of God's Presence): the "human domain" *al-Nasut*, which is the corporeal dimension, also known as *al-Mulk*, the material world; the "domain of royalty" or angelic world, *al-Malakut*, which has direct sovereignty over the *al-Nasut*, one mode or level of the *Malakut* being the *'Alam al-Mithal* or Imaginal Plane (also known as *al-Khayal*) which we experience as the world of visions and dreams; the "domain of power" (*al-Jabarut*), the celestial or archangelic world; the "domain of the Divine", *al-Lahut*, the realm of the Logos or the Personal God; and the *Hahut*, the domain of the Divine Essence, the Formless Absolute. From another point of view, the world of events (inner and outer) can be seen as the ensemble of God's Acts, the world of intelligible realities as His Names or Attributes, and Allah Himself as a perfect synthesis of those Names; this Synthetic Unity is known as *al-Wahadiyyah*. Beyond this lies only the Absolute Essence, *Al-Dhat*, which cannot be conceived of and should not even be contemplated; this Absolute Transcendent Unity of Allah is also known as *al-Ahadiyyah*, God's Uniqueness. Yet, in a way, the Essence can be known—though not by us. God's Essence is known only by God; when we are annihilated in our limited selfhoods, then God knows Himself *in us*. As Abu Bakr al-Siddiq said, "To know that God cannot be known is to know God." But Allah does not simply lie at the apex of this hierarchy. If we saw him strictly in terms of His *Tanzih*, his "incomparability" or Transcendence, that might be true—except for the fact that if He were strictly transcendent we could never know Him, not only because He would be inaccessible to us but because we, and the universe, would never have come into existence. But because Allah also possesses comparability, *Tashbih*, all things, including ourselves, stand as signs of His Presence; each of the Five *Hadharat* is a mode of that Presence.

The complement to Sufi ontology is its anthropology, which deals with the inner structure, or potential development, of the human person. This anthropology takes many forms; perhaps the simplest hierarchical scheme would be the following: first material nature, which today we would call a person's genetic inheritance; then *al-Nafs*, "soul", most usually in the sense of the passions and the unconscious ego; next *al-Qalb* or Heart, the essence of the human being (though not everyone realizes this essence), which may also be seen as the point of established spiritual attention, both intrinsic and intentional, oriented to the One, or as the central point of the psyche where it is intersected by the ray of the Spirit. Next comes *al-Ruh*, the immortal human Spirit itself, the overflow of God's life and love and knowledge which creates us, and recreates us, in each separate instant (*waqt*) of spiritual time. Next, according to some authorities, comes the inner consciousness (*Sirr* "Secret") which is deeper than the Spirit, and finally the innermost consciousness (*Sirr al-Sirr,* "the Secret of the Secret"), which is known to God alone and *is* God alone. And the Secret of these secrets is: that from one point of view the *Sirr* is actually—and unexpectedly!—a different face of the Nafs, the *single soul* [Q. 4:1] from which everything is created, which is none other than the Soul of Allah, the latency of all things within Him, before He brings them into existence. But, as we shall see, the Nafs as the realm of the permanent archetypes of all things in Allah, the *ayan al-thabitah,* is a far cry from the Nafs as the great and terrible enemy of the spiritual life; in essence they are one, but in effect they are as far apart as can possibly be imagined.

The two final stations of the Spiritual Path are *Fana'*—Annihilation (as a separate selfhood) and *Baqa',* Subsistence in God. Our goal is to become nothing—as the moth consumed by the candle is annihilated in the light and flame to which it was attracted, as the lover in the act of love is lost and annihilated in his Beloved. And if, after that, we still subsist, it is by God's Will and Grace alone—as indeed it always was. The Nafs believes it is self-created, or at least acts as if it does. But when the Nafs is ultimately subdued and annihilated, then if we exist, we exist not as we think or believe or fantasize or fear or desire ourselves to be, but as God *knows* us to be. Who He knows us to be is who we really are, from pre-eternity to post-eternity; who we think we are has never existed, and never will.

A Deeper Look at *Nafs, Ruh,* and *Qalb*

In order to understand the basics of the Sufi path, a more thorough theoretical knowledge (which is all this book can provide) of *al-Nafs, al-Qalb* and *al-Ruh* may be useful. These principles are central to the "esoteric anthropology" of the science of *Tasawwuf,* the Sufi understanding of the various faculties of the human psyche, which are precisely the ontological hierarchy, the various levels of Being ordained and written by Allah, as they appear within the human microcosm. This hierarchy can legitimately be divided into many levels—three, five, seven or more—but the simplest and perhaps the most useful (since for the conceptual framework of the Path to be excessive is as bad as for it to be deficient) is the threefold hierarchy of Nafs, Qalb and Ruh, which (speaking provisionally, and rather simplistically) are the unconscious ego, the conscious attention oriented toward Allah by a Power transcending consciousness, and indwelling Divine Spirit that Allah breathes into us, thereby creating us. As we have seen, certain Sufis speak of levels beyond these three, such as the Secret (*al-Sirr*), the Secret of the Secret (*Sirr al-Sirr*), the Arcane (*Khafi*), and the Most Arcane (*Akhfa*), but these three are enough for our purposes here. Some Sufis identify *al-Qalb* as the site of the Knowledge of God, *al-Ruh* as the Love of God, and *al-Sirr* as the pure Witnessing of God; here, however, we are positing *al-Qalb* as the organ capable receiving spiritual States, which include aspects of both Love and Knowledge, and *al-Ruh* as the synthesis of Love, Knowledge and pure Witnessing, the power of Allah within us that produces States and also transcends them. The *Sirr*, the *Sirr al-Sirr* and the others may transcend the Ruh, but they are nonetheless virtual within it; consequently it is possible to speak of the Ruh as the Presence of God, on all levels, within the human microcosm.

Al-Nafs

The Nafs is who we are when we have not yet reached certainty as to the reality of Allah or begun to intuit His Presence. As the unconscious ego, the Nafs is not exactly our self-image, though it is certainly the origin of that image. Nor is it simply the instincts or the passions since it is also highly intelligent, in a negative and deceptive way, especially when it undertakes to teach us how to indulge these passions and then justify that indulgence to ourselves and others. When western psychology speaks of the "subconscious" or the "unconscious" it is referring largely to the Nafs, but since such psychology often recognizes no higher potential within the human being than the body plus the mass of partly-unconscious reactions that make up its rather limited idea of the psyche, it does not really understand what the Nafs is, and consequently cannot present a very accurate picture of it.

When the Heart begins to open to the Presence of Allah, the Nafs appears as a separate power within the human makeup, one that acts to block this opening. Consequently, at one point, we can say that a battle begins between the Ruh—the Spirit—and the Nafs for possession of the city of the Heart, a battle known as the Greater Jihad. But even after this battle is won and the Ruh triumphs over the Nafs and takes up residence within the Heart, the Nafs is not simply negated or left behind. Rather it is progressively transformed, first from the "Self Commanding to Evil" or *Nafs al-ammara bi'l su'* (the passions) to the "Accusing Self" or *Nafs al-lawwamah*, (the nagging conscience) then from the Accusing Self to the "Self-at-Peace", the *Nafs al-mutma'inah*, whose constant prayer is (in the words of Jesus), "not my will but Thine be done"; it is pacified and educated until the Divine potential within it is unveiled. (We will have much more to say about the Nafs and the science of its transformations below.) When the Heart is being purified of the influences of the Commanding and Accusing Nafs through the action of the Spirit, this purification may manifest as a psychophysical toxicity, experienced as a psychic or subtle-material energy in the process of being released. It is often released through dreams.

Al-Qalb

But have We not established for them a sacred secure precinct, to which fruits of every kind, Our gift for their support, are gathered together? But most of them have no knowledge. [Q. 28:57/28:57]

The Heart is the site of our true humanity. It is the secret chamber where the *Fitrah*, the human essence, meets its Lord. We are only truly ourselves in the Presence of Allah; in our own "presence" we are nothing but ghosts feeding upon phantoms.

The Heart is the central point of the psyche, the point where it is intersected by the ray of the Spirit, *al-Ruh*. It can be described as *the unconscious root of our conscious attention*, our attention to Allah. It is the essence of consciousness because human awareness is only fully unfolded and realized when it is fixed upon God. But it is also beyond the limitations of human awareness since it is founded first on Allah's consciousness of us, not our consciousness of Him. The Heart is always turning; the tri-literal root in of *al-Qalb* in Arabic, QLB, essentially means "to turn, turning, that which turns." It turns because it is always seeking Allah; when the Qur'an says *wherever you turn, there is the Face of Allah* [Q. 2:115], it is referring to and addressing itself to the Heart. The Heart turns so that it may progressively become aware of the truth that there is no place, no state, in which Allah is not present in one of his infinite Names. Nonetheless the Heart's seeking of Allah, in time, is nothing but a later and lesser reflection of Allah's own seeking of the Heart, in Eternity— and whatever He seeks, He has already found. The Heart, however, may or may not be awake to this fact; and if it is not awake, if it remains asleep and dreaming, then it cannot properly be called a real Heart, only a potential or a virtual one.

Within the Heart is the Eye of the Heart. When this Eye is open, it sees and contemplates only the Spirit, *al-Ruh*, and *is* that Ruh; at this point Allah is no longer "another." As Rabi'ah al-'Adawiyyah said in one of her poems, "When the Heart is fully awake, it needs no Friend."

Al-Ruh

The Ruh, though it is often defined as the animating spirit of the individual, can also legitimately be seen as the Presence of Allah within the human form. It is like a flood of warm, brilliant light— immensely subtle, immensely powerful—in which Love and Knowledge are perfectly united. (I say "like" a flood of light so that no-one, in these post-New Age days, will think that to deliberately *visualize* such a light is to invoke it in any real way. The Spiritual may express itself in terms of the imaginal, but the imaginal, operating on its own, in the absence of the Divine *Barakah*, can in no way command the presence of the Spiritual.) It is inexpressibly sweet, tender, fragrant, and intoxicating; at the same time it is awesome, tremendous, ruthless, overwhelming—and also something more, something indescribable. It is indescribable because it is not an experience, consequently it affects the soul both consciously and unconsciously, both intellectively and existentially. It enlightens what pays attention to It and darkens what ignores It, because It is Knowledge; It elevates what submits to It and abases what resists It, because It is Love. In the presence of the Ruh, self-transcendence, "dying before you die", becomes easy; it is hardly even felt as a sacrifice. The Ruh first dawns as the *Sakinah*, Spiritual Tranquility; further deepens as *Mahabbah*, the Love of Allah; and culminates in *Ma'rifah*, the Knowledge of Allah—a Knowledge that is alluded to in the following verse of the Qur'an: *Lo! the righteous shall drink of a cup whereof the mixture is of Kafur (Camphor), A spring wherefrom the slaves of Allah drink, making it gush forth abundantly.* . . . [Q. 75:5–6] If we say that Knowledge is higher than Love, however, we must always remember that it is never without Love because it is the perfection of Love. A Love that is not yet Knowledge is partial and affected with longing; a Love that has reached its consummation in Knowledge is serene and complete.

And if Love uncovers Knowledge, Knowledge also deepens Love. In the words of the *hadith qudsi*, "Who seeks Me, finds Me; who finds Me, knows Me; who knows Me, loves Me; who loves Me, I love him; whomever I love, I kill; whomever I kill, I Myself am his blood price" [found in the *Akhlaq-i Jalali* of Al-Dawani]. It is possible to say that Allah *sends* His Ruh; it is equally possible to say that it is not sent, but simply unveiled as an eternal reality: when the Heart is purified of the veils of the Nafs, the Ruh is revealed. The Presence of Allah is stable and constant in Itself, but it is subject to our own fluctuations. And when it is unveiled it appears not simply as a passive object of your active awareness, since God's present intent that it enter your Heart is unveiled along with it. It is true to say that purification opens the Heart to Knowledge, but it is truer still to say that Knowledge itself (not *learning*, but actual Knowing) purifies the Heart. The root of every transgression is illusion. When illusion is dispelled the roots of the transgressions are exposed, and Knowledge, like water, washes them away.

The notion that Love both initiates Knowledge and deepens it may appear "counter-intuitive" to many people, especially today. When *Mahabbah* first dawns we may feel as if we were being led away from Knowledge and toward some vast inarticulate Power that could never really be understood. Where, we ask—or at least the philosopher inside us asks it—have all the clear principles gone, the articulate insights, the *formulations*? But all this is only a deception of the Nafs. *Mahabbah* leads away from reliance on mental knowledge and toward real, Existential Knowledge, toward *Ma'rifah*. This does not mean that mental knowledge is "wrong", or that it is never based on the light of *Ma'rifah* reflected, albeit obliquely, off the mirror of the Heart. It's just that mental knowledge can never lead to the full realization of its proper Object; only Love can do that. Rumor of and speculation about the Beloved, no matter how accurate they may be, have no place or purpose when the Beloved is here before us, and within us. "Heaven and Earth (mind and universe) cannot contain Me, but the Heart of my loving slave can (and does) contain Me" [*hadith qudsi* repeated by the Sufis, probably first found in Al-Ghazali]. When Divine Love touches and opens the affections, thought and will submit to this Love, effortlessly and immediately, until the Presence of God is revealed within the Heart. When the will submits to this Love it goes beyond asceticism and self-sacrifice; it is unveiled as the power of the Divine Will itself. When thought submits to this Love it goes beyond both conceptual clarity and intellectual intuition and becomes fully-embodied, complete Knowledge—the *Ma'rifah* of Allah.

Mahabbah is not a sentiment. In some ways, on some levels, it is more like an excitement, a rapture, a fascination, bristling with indescribable Knowledge. All other loves—human love, love of nature, love of beautiful character traits and profound ideas—are only distant reflections of it, though *Mahabbah* embraces and perfects these as well. In addition, to be strictly accurate, it is necessary to say that *Mahabbah* in its real essence it is unlike any description of it, seeing that the closer language comes to Truth, the more vulnerable it is to illusion. Human language is invaluable as an indicator, a pointing finger. But to the degree that it substitutes an imagined presence for a concrete Reality, it represents a great spiritual danger. This is why the Qur'an, in the surah of *The Poets*, describes these craftsmen of language as ones *upon whom the devils descend*, who *say that which they do not*. [Q. 26:221; 226]

The Ruh is the very Reality of Allah as offered to our humanity, the Power and Mercy that creates us from moment to moment. Allah unveils His Ruh when He will and to whom He will; we have no power to engineer Its appearance. But this does not mean that we can simply trudge through our lives as sullen, unspiritual lumps, impotently wishing that Allah might bless us but incapable of taking any concrete steps to open ourselves to His influence. The Ruh dawns upon the Heart to the degree that the Heart is purified of the Nafs—and yet it is the very intuition that the Ruh exists, is about to dawn, or is in fact dawning, that in itself accomplishes this purification. And we have every right, if not an actual duty, to anticipate Its coming, because in reality It is already here. While the Ruh is not in evidence we must struggle against the Nafs; it is this struggle alone that keeps the Heart open to the Ruh and capable of discerning It when It appears. (We must be careful, however, that this struggle doesn't become simply another way for us to stay within the field of the Nafs and its power, and so remain vulnerable to it.) But when the Ruh actually does dawn, this struggle is pacified; we begin to move out of Accusing Self, the *Nafs al-lawwamah* or the troubled conscience, and into the *Nafs al-mutma'inah*, the Self-at-Peace, the soul perfectly submissive to Allah. The Ruh has the power to overcome the Nafs not because it lends invincible power to our struggle against ourselves, as if the *Nafs al-lawwamah* could triumph over the *Nafs al-ammara* (the Commanding Self, the passions) by pure self-will and not end up actually turning into the *Nafs al-ammara* in the process—no. The Ruh overcomes the Nafs because it is immensely more beautiful, more fascinating, more compelling; in the presence of a living peacock, or an eagle in its swiftness and power, who would want spend time contemplating a dead rat? Yet we must never underestimate the *resistance to Beauty* that may lurk within us. In the presence of *Al-Jamal*, the Divine Beauty, we feel our own ugliness, and the ugliness of *al-Dunya* (in Christian terms, "the Darkness of This World")—and the Nafs' way of helping us hide from this ugliness is to influence us to take refuge in it. We also sense our impotence to invoke or possess this ravishing Beauty, and so may experience its vitality, its lambency, its endless kaleidoscopic changes, as the ultimate tease; this is part of the Divine Rigor, *Al-Jalal*, that hides within Beauty.

This rigor of beauty is perfectly expressed, on the romantic human level, by the Andalusian poet Ibn al-Qabturnuh (in Lysander Kemp's translation):

Day and Night on the Sufi Path

I remembered Sulayma when the passion
of battle was as fierce
As the passion of my body when we parted.

I thought I saw, among the lances, the tall
perfection of her body,
And when they bent toward me I embraced them.

In al-Qabturnuh's poem, love on the physical plane (*al-Mulk*) is transformed into love on the imaginal plane (*al-Malakut*). But the Divine Love of *al-Ruh* is much higher than this. In the words of Rumi (in my own "transcreation", based on the translations of Ibrahim Gamard and A.G. Rawan Farhadi appearing in *The Quatrains of Rumi: Ruba'iyat-é Jalaluddin Muhammad Balkhi-Rumi*, Sufi-Dari Books, 2008):

Whoever meets You without smiling like a rose
Is void of life and understanding—empty like a drum.
He who does not leap for joy at the call of God Most Glorious
And the vision of his messengers,
Is a pagan forever.

Soul of my soul! Come live at my core.
Like reason and wisdom, crown the heads of true men!
You are the luck and good fortune of all in both the worlds;
Like luck and good fortune, keep wandering across the earth!

My soul and Yours are One in essence,
Our outer appearances One, our inner secrets also One.
Though I speak of "mine and Thine" to instruct the heedless,
Within You and me there *is* no "You and me"—
That's the real truth.

Love is formidable; it cuts to the bone. Every resistance to Allah is annihilated by it, because Allah IS Love. Love creates everything and destroys everything. How could everything not flourish in the presence of it? How could anything, any self-identity, stand in the face of it? It is the ultimate Generosity and the ultimate Jealousy. What was it that terrified us so profoundly that we begged to be turned into machines to hide from it? What was it that ravished us so completely that we were even willing to be born and die so as not to miss any of its gifts, or any of its chastisements? Or any of its lessons? It was Love.

We were afraid that Love would hurt us, which is the same as saying that we believed that hatred would protect us and heal us. But the wounds of Love are only proportional to our own hatred. Love Himself could never hurt us, because Mercy is without any admixture of correction or chastisement, except insofar as we resist it. Resistance makes Submission look like the process of being broken by a hard taskmaster, but Submission itself knows that what the Qur'an says is true: that the words *Allah*, "the Deity", and *Al-Rahman*, "the All-Merciful", refer to the same Reality.

Nonetheless, Allah is ruthless in His Generosity—terrifying to those crabbed and contracted parts of ourselves that want to live without insight and without love. The ocean of gratitude is only a single drop in His Ocean; nothing but Annihilation has room for a Generosity like that.

In the presence of the Ruh, the practice is to melt into the Light of God, and be simply and gratefully annihilated in Him: no body—no world. This Presence makes it possible to follow the prescription of one contemporary Shaykh, which is not to fight the Nafs, but to gently lay it aside. Yet after we have been totally annihilated, and then wake up in the knowledge that *He* still beholds us, or something that *once was* us—*what then*? What, exactly, is He beholding?

◇

The Nafs is the Dungeon with the vicious dogs; the Ruh is the high Tower that looks out over the whole land; the Heart is the central Throne.

The Nafs is the Treasure that the Cobra guards; the Heart is the Keyhole in the Lock and the Lantern that illuminates it;

The Ruh is the Key. It opens the Lock, kills the Cobra, takes the Throne, and reveals the Hidden Treasure.

Thought, Feeling, and Will

From a different and more limited perspective, but nonetheless a useful one, the human psyche—considered as the *Fitrah*, the Pri-

29

mordial Human Nature—can be considered as composed of three main elements or powers: thought, feeling and will. While we are under the power of the Nafs these powers are inverted, and at war with each other. After we have realized the Heart, they are correctly hierarchicalized and operate in harmony, as they did before Adam was expelled from the Garden. And as soon as the Ruh dawns, they are perfectly united: to Know God is to Choose Him and to Choose Him is to Know Him; to Choose God is to Love Him, and to Love Him is to Choose Him; to Love God is to Know Him and to Know Him is to Love Him, all in a single motion, a single act of submission. And we are no longer even the ones doing the submitting.

In the correctly ordered soul, the will submits to the rational mind and the feelings submit to the will. The rational mind itself is informed either by the norms of the shari‘ah, the teachings and principles to be found in Qur’an and *hadith*, or by immediate commands and infusions from Allah directed to the Heart, to which the mind listens and submits. The rational mind uses these teachings, laws, principles and commands to formulate rules of behavior and plans of action, which the submissive will then follows and enacts. And the submissive feelings reverently follow the dictates of the submissive will, thus lending it all their stored-up power. So the original structure of the *Fitrah* is all submission, all Islam.

On the other hand, in the unregenerate psyche under the power of the *Nafs al-ammara bi’l su’*, the *Fitrah* is corrupted. The rational mind ignores or rebels against what the Heart knows from Allah, and (later on in the succession of the ages) what the Qur’an has revealed, and what the shari‘ah prescribes and prohibits. And as soon as the mind is darkened by this *ghaflah*, this "heedlessness", the structure of the *Fitrah* inverts. Now the feelings rule, and the will submits to them instead of to the rational mind; we do not do what we ought to do, or what it would be prudent for us to do, but only what we want to do at the moment. And the rational mind, which now comes last, is reduced to the status of a slave to the will—or rather the *self*-will—which is itself now no more than a slave to the feelings. All the rational mind is allowed to do at this point, and actually forced to do, is *rationalize* the impulses of the will, make excuses for them, as well as devise various cunning schemes so that the will, dominated by the feelings, can do whatever it wants. This is the inversion of the *Fitrah* that expelled Adam and Eve from Paradise.

To recapitulate: In the Commanding Nafs, the feelings rule the will and the will rules the rational mind; the Heart is asleep.

When the Heart awakens, the rational mind (following the Heart, as the Heart follows Allah) rules the will, and the will rules the feelings.

When the Eye of the Heart opens and the Ruh dawns, when it conquers the city of the Heart and takes up residence there, then the rational mind, the will, and the feelings act as one, and *are* one.

◇

Tasawwuf is made up of whatever you cannot do for yourself in the spiritual life. This, however, does not mean that there is no work involved: the work is to say "yes", and this yes-saying is more complex and subtle and rigorous than you can possibly imagine—though Sincerity has the power to simplify it. *Tasawwuf* is the arrival of more and greater Life than you can possibly understand—so of course you resist it. The work is to learn how not to resist it, how to make room for it; and the only way to make room for it is for the Nafs—the one resisting, the one struggling not to resist—to submit to being annihilated, until it becomes all Heart. "Heaven and earth (mind and world) cannot contain me, but the Heart of my loving slave can contain me" (*hadith qudsi* repeated by the Sufis, probably first found in Al-Ghazali). The Prophet Muhammad, peace and blessings be upon him, once said: "Die before you are made to die." This is the real essence of Sufism, its whole practice, and its final end. [NOTE: The famous *hadith* of the Prophet Muhammad, peace and blessings be upon him, "die before you die" or "die before you are made to die" is apparently not to be found in the *hadith* collections. It may in fact be a paraphrase of a *hadith* recounted by Tirmidhi: "Live in the world as if you were a stranger, or be like a traveler. Regard yourself as one of the residents of the grave (before you die)!"]

2

The Sufi Doctrine of the *Nafs* — A Detailed Exposition

THE WORD *Nafs* means "soul", most usually in the sense of the unconscious ego and its impulses. The word generally has a different nuance than what is called "soul" in western Christian terms, which includes notions analogous to the Islamic *Qalb* (Heart) and *Ruh* (Spirit). Since *Nafs* is most commonly used to specifically denote the "lower soul", the passions, sometimes called in Christian terminology "the Old Adam", certain Sufis translate the English word "soul", and its equivalent in other European languages, not as *Nafs* but as *Ruh*—a word I have translated here as "Spirit."

In the course of the spiritual Path, the Nafs is purified and refined. Various Sufis have spoken of different stages of this purification, some referring to three stages, others to as many as seven. The simplest and most universal scheme, however, is made up of three stages. First the Nafs appears as "the Commanding Nafs", the lower passional soul which rules us on the basis of our own whims, desires and self-will, until we submit instead to God's rule and become true *Muslims. Lo! the (human) soul enjoineth unto evil, save that whereon my Lord hath mercy.* [Q. 12:53]

Next it takes the form of "the Accusing Nafs," the troubled conscience, which recognizes the evil of the Commanding Nafs, struggles against it but is ultimately powerless to overcome it. *Nay, I swear by the (self-) accusing soul. . . .* [Q. 75:2] (The Accusing Nafs is powerless because it uses its obsession with self-willed repentance precisely to prevent *real* repentance.) And the final development is the "Nafs-at-Peace", the individual self in perfect submission to the

Will of God. *But ah! thou soul at peace! Return unto thy Lord, content in His good pleasure!* [Q.89:27–28] Some authorities identify the Nafs-at-Peace with the Heart; at any rate, it opens onto the Heart, which is only firmly established as Heart when the Spirit, Ruh, has finally disciplined the Nafs and pacified it. These three stages of the Nafs can also be seen as three separate principles, which simply means that one doesn't always simply follow the other; there is often a considerable period when all three "struggle for dominance" before the Heart is occupied by *al-Ruh* and the *Nafs al-mutma'inah* is fully established.

The work of subduing and refining the Nafs is also the work of developing the virtues; every virtue is the expression of a Name of God existentially actualized within the Heart.

◇

Once upon a time the prophet Muhammad (peace and blessings upon him), after returning with his warriors from battle, said to them: "Now we return from the Lesser Jihad to the Greater Jihad." "What is the Greater Jihad?" they asked. "The war against the soul (*al-Nafs*)", he replied [Al-Khatib al-Baghdadi, on the authority of Jabir ibn Abd-Allah]. When the Prophet defined the Greater Jihad in these terms, he laid one of the essential foundation stones of Sufism. As we have already seen, however, the Nafs is regarded not only as a enemy to be conquered, but also as a deceiver to be outwitted, a resource to be tapped, a servant to be enlisted, and ultimately as the inner mystery of God, in all modes and on all levels. The Greater Jihad, and even the lesser one, is really the battle for Love—and the moment you realize this, the battle is won—because when Love takes the field, it meets no opponent. Jalaluddin Rumi [*Mathnavi* I:1131] said, "God has no opposite." Love is not the *opposite* of hate and the enemy of it; where Love is, there can be no enemy.

The Nafs, from one perspective, is the entire "natural." human psyche, which, like an iceberg, is composed of a relatively small visible portion—the "conscious" ego (which, however, is never consciously recognized *as* ego), and a much larger invisible mass—the "unconscious." But the concept of the Nafs in Sufi psychology differs from that of the soul or psyche in most other psychological or religious doctrines in that the psyche only "constellates" as the *Nafs al-ammara bi'l su'*, the "soul commanding or inciting to evil," after one has committed one's life to the spiritual Path. Before that the psyche will produce pleasant or unpleasant, constructive or destructive effects. It may be "maladjusted" in social terms or relatively better-adjusted; it has certain virtues, certain vices, certain potentials, and various tendencies which are not well-formed enough to clearly belong to either camp. But when God has become the conscious center of one's life, then—as in a time of civil war— the various citizens of the psyche are forced to take sides. The Commanding Nafs only reveals itself as "commanding" when we have begun to disobey it. Since the Nafs in its first stages represents all that comes between us and God, all that perverts our will so that we do not obey Him, or darkens our intellect so that we cannot intuit His Reality, a war without quarter against this Nafs becomes imperative—the "war against the soul." But from another point of view, things are not quite so simple.

The position of humanity in the hierarchy of being is unique, a position which Islam defines by saying that we are both *'abd*, God's abject slave, and *khalifah*, God's fully-empowered representative. In a certain sense, we bear the responsibility for the maintenance of the cosmic order. As it says in the Qur'an, *We offered the Trust to the heavens and the earth and the hills, but they shrank from bearing it and were afraid of it. And man assumed it* [Q. 33:72]. The Trust is our human duty to act as mirrors for God in the created universe—and while we are in the grip of the Nafs, which causes us to believe that we are self-created, and therefore that we have the right to be self-determined, we cannot fulfill this function. But we can't literally destroy this Nafs, nor can we conquer it. We can't conquer it because the "we" in question is itself part of the Nafs, the part that is entirely capable of perverting spiritual struggle so as to build up an apparently separate identity instead of annihilating it. Nor can we destroy it, because the Nafs is created by God Who wills its existence, and a war against the Will of God is lost before it begins. And beyond this, on a deeper level, the Nafs as we experience it as part of the human makeup is really an aspect of the Nafs of Allah, the prefiguration of all created things within the Divine nature—and creation is a manifestation of *Al-Rahman*, the Mercy of God. In the words of the Holy Qur'an, *Your Lord has written Mercy on His Nafs*. [Q. 6:54]

So is God then a tyrant and deceiver, who has put us in a hopeless double-bind by commanding us, on pain of hellfire, to quash the passions, to kill the Nafs—something which He knows to be impossible because He Himself opposes it? Certainly, the tyrannical and deceiving Nafs will tend to falsely represent Him in these terms. Nonetheless, it is true that God has commanded us, in one sense, to struggle against the current of His Self-manifestation in order to reach Him, just as a salmon must swim upstream against the current of the river to reach its Source.

The Nafs is the trace in our nature of God's original creation of the universe, of his command *kun*, "be!", addressed to all the things that have come into being [Q. 2:117]. If we follow this current, which is the "natural man" within us, we will live only to express ourselves, to develop and enhance our existence, and end by burning ourselves out in dissipation and flight from God, like sunlight that becomes ever dimmer in its flight from the sun. What could be more *natural*? This is, in fact, what the whole cosmos is doing, according to the theory of an expanding universe originating in a "big bang." It is simply following the law of entropy, dissipating itself, burning itself out in order to manifest, on the material plane, certain possibilities latent within the Divine Nature, and thereby fulfilling its function, as expressed in the famous *hadith qudsi* in which God says: "I was a hidden Treasure and longed to be known, so I created the universe that I might be known" [Bukhari; Muslim].

The universe outside humanity, though it does indeed mirror God, mirrors Him in a fragmentary way, as does a human psyche when in the grip of the Nafs. The material universe, composed of whirlpools of galaxies and throngs of living species and swarms of elementary particles, of energies and their fields, and the human consciousness made turbulent by passions and attachments, are like a lake on a windy day. The light of the sun reflected in such a lake appears as a million dancing sparks of light. But when the wind sinks, and the lake becomes calm, then the sun is reflected as a single unified form. The sun here is a symbol of the Spirit, *al-Ruh*; the turbulent lake, of the Nafs before it is pacified; the calm lake on a bright and windless day is the *Nafs al-mutma'inah*, the "Nafs-at-Peace" become transparent to *al-Qalb*, the spiritual Heart, and to the light of *al-Ruh* shining through it. This ability of the human Heart to reflect God in His entirety—and on the basis of this perfect mirroring to contemplate the material universe as ultimately composed of nothing but the "signs" of Allah—is the *Amana*, the Trust which That One has laid upon us. *We offered the trust unto the heavens and the earth and the hills, but they shrank from bearing it and were afraid of it. And man assumed it* [Q. 33:72]. It is the reason why He created us and why He has sent prophets to instruct us and religious revelations to enlighten and save us. As we have seen, the Heart in Sufism is the "central" point of the psyche where it is intersected by the breath of *al-Ruh*, the Spirit, the radiant Presence of Allah. The Heart is thus the border between the realm of psychic multiplicity (*Tafriqah*, Dispersion) and that of Spiritual Unity (*Jam'*, Gathering). As it is said in the *hadith qudsi*, "Heaven and earth cannot contain Me, but the Heart of my believing slave can contain Me." "Heaven and earth"—the expanding, entropic universe—is precisely *the heavens and the earth and the hills* in flight from the Trust. The universe is indeed God's manifestation, but the power which manifests Him also necessarily veils Him by appearing to be something other than He. Nonetheless what is Dispersed in the *Zahir*, the Outer World, is Gathered in the *Batin*, the Inner World. It is because the human Heart has the capacity to consciously open to the Inner World, and thereby gather together and transfigure its experience of the Outer World, that humanity was created and chosen as bearer of the Trust. We can fulfill this function because we are a true *microcosm*: whatever exists in the outer universe is reflected somewhere in the *Fitrah*, in the human form. *I will show them My signs on the horizons and in their own souls until they are satisfied that this is the Truth. Is it not enough for you, that I am Witness over all things?* [Q. 41:53].

For the Nafs to become pacified so that the spiritual Heart is fully unveiled, we must struggle to subdue it, in the course of which struggle we will learn that no-one struggles against the Nafs nor has the power to subdue it but Allah—and that He subdues it by *seeing* it. He is the sole Doer of all things done—a truth the Nafs is at great pains to hide, first by falsely claiming that it itself is the Doer, and secondly by maintaining that this Doer is actually you yourself. But as soon as you reach entire certainty as to the truth that only God can and does struggle against the Nafs, the battle is ended, the war is won— because to continue to battle against and suppress the Nafs is to keep giving it power, since to posit yourself as the Doer, the warrior in the Greater Jihad, is (and this is the supreme irony) to identify with and act *as the Nafs*. And if the war against the soul were never-ending, how could it ever become the Soul-at-Peace? Initially the Nafs must be fought against; later, as the Path unfolds, it is to be instructed and trained and pacified; ultimately it is to be killed by Allah and made immortal, at which point it becomes the total Knowledge of God as witnessed by God through the Eye of the Heart. From the human perspective, God can only be known through the Nafs-at-Peace, this being a limited and subjective form of knowing. But the Nafs can be known in its entirety only by and through God. The *Ma'rifah* of Allah is (from one point of view) the realization of Allah as *Al-Sha-hid*, the universal Witness, before whose Eye the human psyche is purified of all subjective self-involvement: *Is it not enough for you, that I am Witness over all things?* [Q. 41:53]. And when this *Ma'rifah* of Allah is perfected—when God ceases entirely to be an object of human witnessing, at which point all that exists in universal creation is Gathered into the human form, on the Day *when the wild beasts are herded together* [Q. 81:5], and the human form established as the sole object of God's witnessing—then the soul is transformed from a self-referential obscurity into a total and unified manifestation of Being in all modes and on all levels, as Witnessed by the One Who is beyond even Being itself. This is the higher *Ma'rifah*, the *Ma'rifah* of the Nafs.

God has two mercies: *Rahman*, His general mercy, by which He creates the universe, and *Rahim*, His particular mercy, by which He leads all things back to Himself. *Rahman* is general because it says "yes" to everything; *Rahim* is particular because it says "yes" to beliefs and actions which bring us closer to God and "no" to beliefs and actions which drive us further away from Him. By *Rahman*, God grants the wish of all possible things within His Being to be actualized; He bestows upon them the individual life and reality

they long for. The joy of sexuality and the fear of death are the measure of the depth of this longing. But the desire for separate existence, which begins as a mercy, ends under the sign of wrath:
departing from God, or rather from the knowledge that God is the
only Reality, created beings end up in the outer darkness, subject to
evils and sufferings of all kinds, and they cry to God for relief. In
response to this cry, God unveils *Rahim*, which manifests in terms
of religions, and sacred laws, and prophets, and saints, and the spiritual Path. All creation cries to be saved, and *Rahim* mercifully
dawns to show the Way back to God, the Sovereign Good, the Only
Reality. The mercy of creation is general because it encompasses all
things. The mercy of divine revelations such as the Qur'an is also
general to a degree because it is addressed to an entire community—yet within it are the seeds of a particular mercy, one
addressed to "myself" alone and fully manifest only as *tariqah*,
the Spiritual Path. And even though the work of this Path is the
conquest of the Nafs, the Annihilation of "myself," nonetheless,
without the appearance of "myself", the spiritual crisis which heralds the dawn of God's particular mercy, and ultimate the return of
all creation to Him, could not take place. Though revelations are
given to entire religious communities, no community as a whole
ever became a saint.

Religion, *al-Din*, is God's wish that we abandon attachment to
His general and creating mercy, and commit ourselves to His particular and saving mercy. Only humanity and the Jinn are confronted
with this choice. The animals, the plants, the minerals, the angels
are fixed under *Rahman*. Only humanity and the Jinn can consciously choose, by God's grace, to shift their center-of-gravity from
Rahman to *Rahim*—and they alone need to; this choice is the
essence of the spiritual Path. We are required, in other words, to
break identification with one of God's mercies and avail ourselves of
the other. According to the doctrine of Ibn al-'Arabi, this means that
we must stop living on the basis God's *Will* to send us out into creation, manifest as our God-given instincts—a Will that is essentially
nothing but God's perfect fulfillment of both His desire to be
known and our own desire to exist—and grant His *Wish* that we
abandon our own desire and return to Him, a Wish that is nothing

but His compassionate response to our own cry for help. In terms of the spiritual psychology of the Sufi way, we must purify the Heart so that the army of the Spirit may take possession of it from the army of the Nafs. All this is epitomized in the passage from the Qur'an, *There is no refuge from Allah except in Him* [Q. 9:118]. But it must be made clear that it is never a question of actually rejecting *Al-Rahman* in favor of *Al-Rahim*; to realize God as *Al-Rahman* is to know oneself not as self-created but as a manifestation of God's creating Mercy, and thus as totally dependent upon Him, breath by breath—and to realize one's total dependence on God is to open oneself to *Al-Rahim*, the Mercy of the spiritual Path. [NOTE: Though the Jinn are also confronted with the choice between *Al-Rahman* and *Al-Rahim* since they too possess free will, their choice plays no part in the choice confronting humanity. Though the Holy Qur'an was sent to instruct both men and Jinn, the lessons the Jinn are required to learn are not for us; those Jinn who are Muslims worship and are instructed by the Spirit of Allah just as we are, but they possess a different *tariqah*.]

The Nafs, then, being the product of God's *Rahman*, is not evil in essence, though it is certainly the *source* of evil, which is why it is said in the Qur'an, *I seek refuge in the Lord of Daybreak from the evil of that which He created* [Q. 113:1–2]. And in a larger sense, we can say that if God had not created the universe by His general mercy, His particular mercy would have no field of operation—just as a salmon, though it must fight against the current to swim upstream, would have no river to travel in if the water were not flowing downstream. And just as that fish, even though he is struggling against the current of the river, is also using it, so the goal of the alchemy of the Sufi path is to transmute the Nafs from a mortal enemy into an obedient servant—not, of course, a servant of oneself (that is, of *itself*), but rather of its Lord. This is why Sufis say that first you have to repent—thus transforming the Commanding Nafs into the "Accusing Nafs", the *Nafs al-lawwamah* or remorseful conscience, the field of the Greater Jihad—after which you will eventually have to repent of that repentance: the goal of war is not war without end, but victorious peace. This is the point at which the Accusing Nafs, the sign of the struggling ascetic, is transformed into the Nafs-at-

Peace, the sign of the *'arif*, the knower of God. When God takes the field, He finds no battle to be fought, He meets no enemy—because only God is.

Nonetheless the war against the soul, against the Commanding Nafs, is a total war, and the enemy, even though in essence she is a product of Allah's mercy and a mystery from His Essence, is effectively merciless, profoundly destructive and infinitely more powerful than the puny "spiritual" ego (*al-Nafs* masquerading as *al-Qalb*) that wants to be wise or good or even self-annihilated by its own efforts and on its own terms, without God's help and the grace of one's shaykh. The war is total in the sense that it must command our total commitment; nonetheless to make the "total effort" to come to grips with the Nafs and combat its effects is extremely unwise. To fight the Commanding Nafs on the basis of one's self-will is doomed to failure, if for no other reason than that the self-will of the spiritual ego is itself an aspect of the Commanding Nafs—the aspect personified by the Sufis as Iblis, the Muslim Satan. When Allah first created Adam and before he had sent him to earth as His *khalifah*, he commanded the angels to make obeisance to him. All the angels obeyed except Iblis, who—at least according to the Sufis—declared that, as the perfect lover of God, he would never bow down to anything other than God Himself:

> *When thy Lord said unto the angels: Lo! I am about to create a*
> *mortal out of mire,*
> *And when I have fashioned him and breathed into him of My*
> *Spirit, then fall down before him prostrate,*
> *The angels fell down prostrate, every one,*
> *Saving Iblis; he was scornful and became one of the disbelievers.*
> *He said: O Iblis! What hindereth thee from falling prostrate*
> *before that which I have created with both My hands? Art*
> *thou too proud or art thou of the high exalted?*
> *He said: I am better than him. Thou createdst me of fire, whilst*
> *him Thou didst create of clay.*
> *He said: Go forth from hence, for lo! thou art outcast,*
> *And lo! My curse is on thee till the Day of Judgment.* [Q. 38:71–78]

40

Adam here is a symbol of the Nafs in the guise of *al-Fitrah*, the primordial human nature that reflects all the Names of God in a single form:

> *And He taught Adam all the names, then showed them to the angels, saying: Inform of Me the names of these, if ye are truthful.*
> *They said: Be glorified! We have no knowledge saving that which Thou hast taught us. Lo! Thou, only Thou, art the Knower, the Wise.*
> *He said: O Adam! Inform them of their names, and when he had informed them of their names, He said: Did I not tell you that I know the secret of the heavens and the earth?*
> *And I know that which ye disclose and which ye hide.* [Q. 2:31–33]

By his refusal to make obeisance to Adam, Iblis rejected the *Ma'rifah* of the Nafs, which would have required the Annihilation of himself as the knower; by so doing he transformed his *Ma'rifah* of Allah from a high spiritual station into the *primal transgression*—the worship of Allah on the basis of ego—and himself into the enemy of the human race until the coming of the Hour.

But the impossible battle of "me" against the Nafs still has to be fought. The Nafs must try to annihilate itself, try to attain God, simply because the spiritual traveler has to begin somewhere, and at the beginning of the Path the traveler is virtually all Nafs. This hopeless attempt at attaining self-transcendence through self-will has the effect of transforming the primitive passions of the Commanding Nafs, based on the struggle for security, pleasure and power, into self-criticism and spiritual aspiration: the Accusing Nafs. In the course of this struggle, the very energies of the lower passions are tapped for the purpose of traveling the spiritual Path. This transformation does not take place by self-will, however, but by the grace of Allah—yet insofar as we still believe we are self-determined, we must make full use of this fundamentally illusory self-determination, or no progress will be made.

According to the *hadith qudsi*, "My Mercy takes precedence over My wrath" [Muslim; Bukhari; An-Nasa'I; Ibn Majah]—which, in terms of the individual, means that submission is higher than struggle; the Accusing Nafs is superseded by the Nafs-at-Peace. Thus the goal, and one might say the "environment" of the Greater Jihad, even in the midst of the fiercest conflict, is peace, submission, surrender—and absolute submission can only be made to the Absolute itself, a truth indicated by the fact that the Arabic words *Taslim*, "submission," and *Salam*, "peace," come from the same root, as does the very name *Islam*. And the ultimate end of submission is not simply submission of the will or the affections to God, this being Annihilation in God's Acts and Attributes, but submission of one's very sense of separate existence—Annihilation in His Essence. In Sufi terms, this is *Fana*', Annihilation-in-God, whose seemingly-opposite but actually complementary aspect is *Baqa*', Subsistence-in-God. To subsist in God is to know oneself as absolutely contingent upon the Absolute. It is to come to the end of self-determination and self-definition. In *Fana*', the Nafs is killed; in *Baqa*', it is recognized as immortal; it is simply no longer identified as "me." When, in the Qur'an, God says *Allah is the Rich, and ye are the poor* [Q. 47:38], *and God is the Rich to whom all praises are due* [Q. 31:26], He is attributing all Being to Himself, and none at all to us—except *His* Being. The ego, then, the Nafs identified as "me", is fundamentally a mis-perception, a substitution of a limited human self-witnessing for the Absolute Witnessing of Allah. It is our human duty to witness God up to the limit of our capacity, but only God can fully witness the Human Form. When *Al-Shahid*, the Absolute Witness, is completely unveiled, Man's knowledge of God is replaced by God's knowledge of Man—God, to Whom nothing is "other", Who sees all things as Himself. This why *La ilaha illa Allah* is interpreted by the Sufis to mean, not simply that God is the only deity, but that God is the only Reality: *Everything is perishing except His Face* [Q. 28:88].

The Isolation and Transformation of the *Nafs*

Sufism, in practice, is the constant attention to God—the awareness that He *is*, and that He is *here*; *We are nearer to him than his jugular vein* [Q. 50:16]. And in order to practice this kind of attention, you must be able to differentiate between the "Heart" and the "soul", between *al-Qalb* and *al-Nafs*. The Nafs is whatever you identify with, whatever you think you are, whatever you think the world is—anything other than the presence of God in the Heart. In the simplest terms, the Heart is that in us which attends to God, while the Nafs is that which blocks or interrupts this attention; so it behooves us to be able to identify the Nafs when it appears. How can we do this?

The first thing we need is a set of moral and ritual standards, such as is provided by the Islamic shari'ah. It's not that obedience to these standards by itself will necessarily advance us on the Sufi path—but without standards like this we will not be able to catch the Nafs in action. The shari'ah is God's command that we do this and avoid that—and whatever wants to make us *do what we should avoid* or *neglect what we should do* is the Nafs. The shari'ah is the line; the Nafs is whatever crosses the line. Without the line we will not be able to pinpoint the Nafs, to recognize its own particular quality.

It's also important that the rules we follow come from an objective source outside us. We might be able to invent ethical rules for ourselves that, from one point of view, are very wise and very practical. But if *we* are the authority that enforces them, then—for all their wisdom and practicality—they are at least partially an expression of the Nafs, which means that they can't be reliably used to discover and isolate the Nafs.

The Nafs is that which tempts us, through threats or enticements or distractions, to violate the shari'ah. But it also tempts us to betray the *tariqah*. Certainly it pressures us to transgress moral rules and ritual obligations. But once we have begun the practice of *Dhikr* or constant attention to the Presence of God, it also influences us to let our attention wander away from God through every sort of obsession and distraction, every imaginable negative emotion or self-indulgent mental pleasure, including false fantasies of so-called "heavenly" realities. We *begin* the work of isolating the Nafs through watching for whatever tempts us to disobey moral rules, but we *develop and refine* our understanding of it by watching for whatever distracts us from the constant remembrance of God. And *Dhikr* not only provides a more sensitive gauge for the activities of the Nafs than moral standards do; it also begins to establish a more objective standpoint in us—the Heart—from which we can spy on the Nafs' antics without being observed. God is Objective Reality; the more real God is to us, the more objective we ourselves become.

We are advised not to fight the Nafs but gently lay it aside, and concentrate the Heart, by means of the Ruh, on Allah; the Greater Jihad could even be defined as the careful avoidance of any conflict with the Nafs that takes place on the Nafs's terms. We cannot lay the Nafs aside, however, until we can see it, and as long as we identify with it, as long as we think of it as "me", it remains invisible to us. But as soon as we begin to exist as Heart rather than as Nafs, the Nafs starts to becomes visible. We recognize it as that thing that is always desiring, and fearing, and talking, and thinking (obsessively and half-consciously thinking, not deliberately pondering), and fighting, and fleeing, and grasping things, and pushing things away—*all that*. It becomes like a snake that can't strike as long as we are gazing at it steadily; but as soon as we blink, or let our attention wander, it seizes its opportunity, strikes, and becomes "me" again. When you identify with the Nafs you are in the state of ego, and ego, by definition, is never aware of itself. But as you begin to become aware of the Nafs, you dis-identify with it, and so begin to move out of ego—at which point the question arises: If the Nafs is not "me", then what is it? And what is "me"?

To begin with, the Nafs blocks the influx of the Ruh into the Heart. Later, it falsifies this influx, diverting it from its true goal. It either makes us obsessed with moral purity or spiritual practice, or leads us to indulge in emotional states and imaginary experiences we falsely believe to be angelic or Divine. And when it finds that it can no longer block the Spirit from entering the Heart, or divert it in various false and useless directions, it learns how to *abduct* the Spirit, to claim It for its own.

You can't fight the Nafs hand-to-hand; it's far too strong, far too cunning. As we have seen above, the Nafs that influences us, or all but forces us, to do evil is called the *Nafs al-ammara*, the "commanding self"; the Nafs that struggles against itself is the *Nafs al-lawwamah*, "the Accusing Self." It does little good to say, "I WILL be good, I WILL defeat the Nafs"—and then, when you fail, to cry "Damn me, I did it again! Why can't I control myself? I'm corrupt! I'm evil!" You can't fight the Nafs through self-will, because self-will *is* the Nafs. And if you claim that you are corrupt, then you will be corrupt. The *Nafs al-lawwamah* appears humble, and believes itself to be humble, due to its habit of excruciating self-accusation. But there is an element of arrogance hidden within it. To berate yourself for your imperfections implies, 1) that you are entirely capable of reaching perfection by your own power but, 2) you have simply chosen not to do so. Neither proposition, however, has a word of truth in it: there is no Might nor Power except in Allah, and *you cannot will unless Allah wills* [Q. 76:30]. To "repent of repentance" is to repent of the arrogance that is inseparable from self-accusation—an arrogance that slights Allah by implying that your weakness is stronger than His Strength. Because your will is free He will allow you to wallow in that weakness if you so choose, but as soon as you fully turn to Him He'll sweep it away, like a gale force wind dispersing a wisp of smoke. Forget the arrogance of self-hatred: *just turn.*

The real use of the Accusing Nafs is not to fight the Commanding Nafs, but to establish the mark by which the action of the Commanding Nafs—and later, the Accusing Nafs itself—can be detected. You still might have to kick yourself from time to time, force yourself to do what so much of you doesn't want to do and refuses to do—but this kind of struggle ultimately cannot be won, because it is a struggle against yourself. Will-power must ultimately give way to submission; forcing yourself to do something or avoid something must develop into *Taslim*, surrender to God—and there can be no surrender without Love (*Mahabbah*). Instead of standing behind yourself and whipping yourself forward, you must learn (God willing) to look ahead, to Him—to *Al-Hadi*, the Guide—and joyfully follow His lead.

So if you can't oppose the Nafs directly and expect to win the battle, what can you do? What you can do is to watch it, discern it, understand it. (The one who watches, discerns and understands is essentially the Heart.) The time will come when the action of the Nafs will appear to you in its true guise—and when it does, when you can confidently say, whenever it rears its head: "There! That's the Nafs again, I'd know it anywhere"—*whether or not you can always overcome it*—then the battle is already half won. And *perfect* awareness of the Nafs does in fact overcome it, because the Nafs can only overpower you when you identify with it, and when you identify with it, it disappears as a separate entity: you start to think it's you. The veil of the Nafs has fallen over the Heart.

But perfect awareness of the Nafs cannot come until it is pacified, and one way to pacify it is to make a bargain with it. Don't fight the Nafs—just temporarily put it aside, and let the influx of the Spirit enter the Heart. And when the Nafs protests, simply explain to her: "What you really want is the Spirit, but you can't have that just yet. If you try to grab for the Spirit on your own, you will drive It away. And if the Spirit enters the Heart, and then you show up at the Heart's table uninvited and ready for a hearty meal, you will eat up all the Spirit in one gulp, go into an unbalanced ecstasy, and wake up the next day with a bad headache and no memory of what happened the night before. If you want your share of the Spirit, you need to hold back until it fully enters the Heart and becomes established there. Then (and only then) can you have your share of it. Certainly you want to be satisfied and spiritualized and pacified; Allah wants that too. But you can't be pacified if you want to grab His Spirit and possess it. First you'll need to stand back, take a breather, and let the Heart do its work. Rest assured that when the Spirit is fully established there, you will receive your invitation." The Nafs that is willing to accept this bargain has begun to be transformed into the *Nafs al-mutma'inah*, the "Self-at-Peace."

And once the Spirit is fully established in the Heart, the Nafs WILL catch its overflow. Because the truth is, the Nafs wants nothing but Allah—but she doesn't know that yet; if she did, she would not struggle against Him. As His Absence is progressively revealed as an aspect of His Presence, her struggle begins to appear, unexpectedly, as a form of prostration to Him: the same turbulence, the same emotional energy, can be pressed into the service of either. The passionate turbulence of the Nafs longing for the world and the flesh pulls us ever closer to destruction; its turbulence when longing for God (though this desire can never be satisfied on its own terms) draws us ever closer to peace—to a spiritual tranquility in which turbulence and conflict and self-contradiction are left far behind. Only when the Nafs is pacified by Allah's *Sakinah* can the she prostrate to *Mahabbah*, and ultimately become the object of *Ma'rifah*. From the veil that hides the Spirit she will then be transformed into the mirror that reveals It, until she is ultimately indistinguishable from the Spirit itself. Every one of her impulses will become a virtue; every one of her attacks, a protection; every one of her wiles, a wisdom; every one of her twists and contortions, a reflection of one of the Names of God in the mirror of the human form. The end of the first phase of the Sufi path is the *Ma'rifah* of Allah, which lies under the sign of *Tanzih*, the Divine Transcendence. The second phase culminates in the *Ma'rifah* of the Nafs, which is the site of *Tashbih*, the Divine Immanence. But you must never let the Nafs convince you that its glamours, its half-truths and its various brands of psychic information are *Ma'rifah* of the Nafs! *Ma'rifah* of the Nafs is through the *Ruh* of Allah alone; it is the complete *Ma'rifah*. *Ma'rifah through* the Nafs—or perhaps we should call it "attempted *Ma'rifah*"—is incomplete and bound up with delusion; ultimately, it leads to the Fire.

We have observed above that the desires of the Nafs for this or that object are really veiled forms of the Nafs' true desire—her desire for *al-Ruh*, the Spirit of God. But how can she consummate this desire? The unpacified Nafs cannot encompass the Spirit any more than a gnat can devour an elephant. Only the Heart has room for the Spirit of God, according to the *hadith* "Heaven and earth cannot contain Me, but the Heart of my believing slave can contain Me." (Heaven here is *al-'aql*, the individual mind, the conscious Nafs; earth is the unconscious Nafs.) The Nafs cannot possess God—but she can be possessed *by* Him. And how is she possessed by Him? She is possessed by being *seen*. One contemporary shaykh has said: "The Nafs confuses the mind and inflames the passions because *she doesn't want to be seen.*" Allah, of course, sees and knows the Nafs from all eternity because she is His Nafs, the One Soul of All from which He created all things. But the Nafs considered in terms of the human form, the Nafs we must contend with on the spiritual Path, is initially involved in a self-defeating struggle. Hungry for the Spirit, she grasps after this or that object of passion or curiosity which she mistakes for the Spirit, and in so doing hides herself from Him. If she were to realize that she can only possess the Spirit by allowing herself to be possessed by Him, and that she can only do this by letting herself be seen, she would become quiet, having been transformed into the *Nafs al-mutma'inah*, the soul-at-peace. And only *Mahabbah* can accomplish this; only Love can pacify the Nafs. Divine Love is the doorway to *Ma'rifah*; it sees everything exactly as it is because it accepts everything as it is—not that it doesn't want things to change, or want the sickness of the Nafs to be healed; it's simply that True Love does not deny what's real out of fear or shame.

In the book *Children at Risk* [1992] by James Dobson and Gary L. Bauer, the authors tell the story of certain children—budding sociopaths—who are adept at charming and fooling their parents and guardians, allowing them to transgress many human norms without getting caught. (The same sort of child is portrayed in the 1956 motion picture "The Bad Seed.") The recommended treatment for these children is simply for the therapist to hold them down, gently but firmly; this usually precipitates a violent tantrum. The at-risk child does not want to be restrained, even if there is nothing in particular that he or she is planning to do at the present moment, but neither does he or she want to be *seen*. It is the role of the therapist first to peel off the child's surface charm to reveal his or her rebelliousness, and then to allow this rebelliousness to exhaust itself, revealing the true humanity of the child, the *Fitrah*, hidden first under seductive charm and then under rebellious violence. If the child can allow his or her humanity to be seen by the therapist, that child has taken a real step toward *becoming* human in the true and effective sense of that word. Likewise, if we can allow our humanity to be fully seen by Allah, then we will become what is called *al-Insan al-Kamil*, the Complete Human Being.

It certainly appears as if the Nafs, in creating all her dramas, wants to draw attention to herself in any way she can; she is notoriously narcissistic. But at the same time, like any drama queen, she is trying desperately *not to be seen as she really is*. And since Allah only sees things as they are, not as they wish to appear to the eyes of the world, the fundamental fear of the Nafs is the fear of letting herself be seen by Him.

Nafs, Ruh, and Body

Rumi says, in his *Fihi ma-Fihi*: "The spiritual path ruins the body, but subsequently restores it to health. It ruins the house to reveal the treasure, and with that treasure it builds better than before."

Before the beginning of our journey on the spiritual Path, the body is ruled by the Nafs. The life that maintains the body ultimately derives from Allah as *Al-Hayy*, the Ever-Living—not only by virtue of His original creation of the body in His Names *Al-Khaliq* (the Creator), *Al-Bari'* (the Producer) and *Al-Musawwir* (the Fashioner), but also by the ongoing power of His knowledge of and attention to the body in His Names *Al-Shahid* (the Universal Witness), *Al-'Alim* (the Omniscient) and *Al-Muhsi* (the Knower of each Separate Thing). But this continuous influx of Divine Life, which shines into the Heart of the human individual by virtue of the Spirit, is initially mediated by the Nafs and only reaches the body through the Nafs. It is the Nafs that turns the Will of Allah into self-will, the Love of Allah into the whole range of personal emotions, and the Truth of Allah into the thoughts that course through our brains second-by-second, year after year, all of which result in the unconscious belief that we have in fact created ourselves, and so have the absolute responsibility to maintain our own existence. As the Holy Qur'an asks: *Were they created by nothing? or were they the creators of themselves?* [Q. 52:35/52:35]

The identification of the Nafs with the body begins at conception. At first this relationship is almost entirely physical, but it becomes progressively more psychic as the foetus forms, the baby is born, and the growing child develops. The characteristics that the individual is destined to embody pre-exist within Allah, as do all characteristics of all individuals and all entities in the universe; all are drawn from the One Soul of Allah; He needs only to say to them *kun!*, "be!" [Q. 2:17], and they emerge from virtual existence into real existence. If they had any other origin, they could claim to exist in the same sense that Allah exists, which is impossible. The emergence of the *individual* Nafs is based on the identification of the Nafs of Allah with a particular human body. This identification is necessary for the individual being to be conceived, develop in the womb, be born and grow to maturity. If the process of this identification is interrupted in the womb, the result is either a miscarriage or the birth of a defective foetus. If it is interrupted later, when the Nafs has become more psychic and less purely physical, the individual becomes psychologically fixated at a particular stage of development, or exhibits some other form of psychic imbalance. Only when the Nafs has done its work, by Allah's will and design, by producing a "natural" human being who is complete both physically and psychologically, can the spiritual Path be entered on, and the Nafs—or rather the individual Nafs, based on the identification of the eternal Nafs of Allah with a particular human organism—be progressively deconstructed, so the Nafs may be known again as the Nafs of Allah, in the face of which the separate Nafs of the individual is effectively nothing. *And Allah's is the Invisible of the heavens and the earth, and unto Him the whole matter will be returned* [Q. 11:123]. This is not to imply that an individual must be physically perfect or in a state of complete psychological integration in order to embark on the spiritual Path; many psychological complexes and fixations can only be overcome by the deconstruction of the separate Nafs over the course of that very Path. But the individual must have reached enough stability and individuality for him or her to be able to consciously intend to sacrifice that individuality—or rather the unwarranted claims it makes to self-determination and self-creation—in submission to Allah.

As our identification with the Nafs is progressively deconstructed, Allah begins to take direct charge not only of our consciousness, but of all the affairs of our lives, even the ongoing functioning of our bodies. But during the transition from our being ruled by Allah through the Nafs—that is, through the illusion of self-determination—and our acceptance of His direct rule, through *al-Ruh*, of all aspects of our daily lives, all the way down to our physical motions and organic functioning, a point is reached where we feel the reins of our life slipping from our grasp, but have not yet reached the full certainty that they now rest in the hands of Allah—

as in fact they always have. This phase may manifest as a sense of uncertainty and paralysis of the will. And even after we have reached certainty or *yaqin* as to the Reality and Presence of Allah, and His complete sovereignty over our lives, we may still feel that Presence as a crushing weight, paralyzing all our efforts and even making it difficult to move our bodies. The Prophet himself experienced states like this when the surahs of the Qur'an descended on him; these states were sent by Allah to demonstrate His Absolute Sovereignty over even the Complete Man, whose stress in the presence of *Al-Jalal*, the Divine Majesty, made him fit to be a model for us in our own *adab* toward Allah. As Abbas Husain tells us, "So crushing was this experience that he said that he would burst out in a cold sweat even if it were winter. If he were sitting on a camel, the camel would sit down." In our own case, since we are not prophets, one purpose of this heavy weight is to crush out the last vestiges of the self-will and illusory self-determination of the Nafs, so that all our affairs down to the simplest daily activities may fully come under Allah's rule. It is nearly impossible to act in the world without some trace of the sense that "here I am acting; here I am walking down the street, doing my taxes, cleaning my house"—except perhaps for those pure contemplatives or *batinis* who have severed all ties of responsibility to the outer world; consequently the heightened Presence of Allah during moments of Divine influx may continue to be felt as a great physical heaviness. Allah, in the Holy Qur'an, had to remind even the Prophet that His direct action through Muhammad was on a different plane than the Prophet's normal day-to-day activities: *It was not you who threw when you threw, but God threw* [Q. 8:17]. In other words, there is a difference between the perfect obedience of the Nafs to Allah, a station that the Prophet never departed from, and its complete Annihilation in Allah. This perfect day-to-day obedience, however, can only come as a result of such Annihilation, which is already virtual within the Nafs as its true nature. The Annihilation of the Nafs, by virtue of which Allah completely takes over all our human functions, is followed by—or is inseparable from—the Subsistence of the Nafs within Him, not as the self of the individual, but as Allah's very own Soul. The *Insan al-Kamil* or Perfect Man is the one who has fully realized the Human Archetype that has been at rest within Allah from all eternity, the complete synthesis of all His Most Beautiful Names. The Perfect Man doesn't act like one who has been overwhelmed by a superior force and doesn't know what he is doing; he acts like a man. Yet all his actions are the actions of Allah and no-one else; this is one of the meanings of the Sufi term "Sobriety after Drunkenness." [NOTE: When we say that Allah takes direct charge of the ongoing functioning of our bodies, we don't mean to imply that those who submit to Him will never become ill; the New Age/Christian Science identification of perfect sanctity or enlightenment with perfect physical well-being is a serious falsification of the spiritual life. It's simply that those who are submitted to Allah are conscious that they are living from Him, not from themselves.]

While the Nafs rules the body, it sets up its own system of habitual muscle tension and endocrine imbalance; these make up the measurable, outward expression of various blockages, depletions and excesses in the flow of subtle psychophysical energy. This system reflects the passions and worldview of the Nafs, its impulses, fascinations and fixed ideas. But when the Heart awakens, when the Spirit of Allah begins to take direct control of your psychophysical functioning, then the energy-system invented by the Nafs is progressively deconstructed. In the course of this deconstruction you may feel that God is *twisting* you this way and that, but the fact is, He is *un*twisting you, untying the psychophysical knots that underlie and constitute the ego, one by one. Your sense of identity expresses itself as a complex (but quite specific) "posture", both physical and psychic. This is the form imposed upon you by the Nafs, as well as by the various life-experiences you encountered and internalized on the basis of the Nafs. But the Ruh carries Allah's knowledge of your *true* form, which at one point will come into conflict with this artificial, imposed form; that's when the contrived posture mediated by the Nafs will attempt to re-assert itself against Allah's Knowledge of you and Will for you. This will result in suffering. The cure for this suffering is to extend *Taslim* beyond the mental and emotional levels, until your submission to the Will of Allah becomes physical as well as spiritual and psychological. The postures of the *salat* are a kind of symbolic training in this level of submission. If you can physically prostrate to Allah while maintaining your conscious intent to submit to Him, then you are preparing yourself for the day when He will place His hands not only on your mind or your feelings but on your body too, to deconstruct it, pacify it and reform it; this is one of the more concrete meanings of the Sufi advice to "be like a corpse in the hands of a Washer of the Dead."

Taslim on the physical level is non-resistance to the flows of energy within the body, in every state and every moment, seeing them not as the product of secondary causes derived from the organism or its environment or its history, but as the direct action of Allah. In terms of the practice of *Dhikr*, resistances to the flow of energy are recognized on the in-breath and released on the out-breath.

Responsibility

To the degree that the Nafs opposes it, assuming responsibility causes pain. It also results in a degree of legitimate self-respect, felt as an inner warmth that helps you fulfill the responsibilities you have assumed—though we must watch out that this self-respect doesn't turn into pride and self-esteem, which are no help at all— but still the element of pain, great or small, is always present. The Nafs offers her various sins—pride, concupiscence and all the others—as a way of sedating you against this pain.

One Sufi teacher, when asked how Sufism deals with the paradox of free will vs. determinism and/or predestination, replied as follows: "At the beginning of the Path, if you claim that only God is acting and you are merely His puppet, you are *kafir*. At the end of the path, if you still claim that action in any sense derives from you, you are equally *kafir*. First fulfill your duties; only then will you begin to see (insha'Allah) that no one is really acting but God." A point will most likely come—in the course of the Path, in the course of your life—when you feel that the responsibilities laid upon you are too heavy to bear. This may be because the realization is beginning to dawn, half-consciously, that action belongs only to Allah; the reason your responsibilities are experienced as a crushing weight is because you have been acting in the place of Him, and have taken on burdens that, in the last analysis, only He can carry. At this point Allah may give you the grace to consciously realize this, allowing you to abandon your life and its responsibilities fully to Him. This, however, is precisely when the Nafs will try to intervene; her proposal to you may go something like this: "I like the 'abandon your responsibilities' idea—but Allah, as we both know, is invisible and capricious; there's no telling what He might do at any given moment. I, on the other hand, am much more reliable and predictable, which is why you keep on committing the same sins over and over again. So I suggest that it would be a better course of action for you to abandon your responsibilities to me." When the Nafs suggests that you submit yourself to her, shirking your responsibilities, you can take this as a reminder to submit to Allah, thereby placing yourself and your responsibilities in the most reliable hands.

Effort

True spiritual effort is the process of overcoming both the laziness of the Nafs and its self-will, thus readying the Heart to be fully occupied and dominated by Allah, and the Eye of the Heart to be opened for the witnessing of Divine realities.

Throughout this book we have emphasized, based on the verse *You cannot will unless Allah wills* [Q. 76:30], that only Allah is the Doer, and that all things we possess, and all that we are, are gifts from Him. And one of the greatest of these gifts is *effort*. Effort is received and learned partly through the states of Gathering and Dispersion, Fluctuation and Stability; it is perfected in the station of Sobriety. *You cannot will unless Allah wills* does not mean that you should make no effort; it means that effort neither begins nor ends with you: it is a gift of Allah, and returns only and inevitably to Him. It is our responsibility to accept this gift with gratitude, not reject it out of a sense of false humility and helplessness that is really nothing but laziness, cowardice, ingratitude and despair. It is said that we should perform every one of our actions for Allah, and dedicate it to Him. But what exactly does this mean? If we do not grasp the reality of effort, such dedication will amount to no more than a formal courtesy—better than nothing, certainly, but nowhere near

54

as effective as a true and concrete understanding of what action is, and Who is acting. In reality, to dedicate every action *to* Allah is to see every action as coming *from* Allah—the formal support for this vision being the *basmalah*. If we truly understand that we can do nothing, and yet clearly see ourselves doing and accomplishing things, we will learn how to see Allah as the present source of our whole power to act. We may be sitting at our desk operating our computer, but the Will of Allah is (so to speak, and if I may be permitted a metaphor that might have the appearance of bathos or impiety) the electrical current that flows through the computer and allows it to function. Before we sit down to work, first we have to turn the computer on and let it boot up; this may be compared to an acknowledging that "there is no Might nor Power except in Allah" [Bukhani]. Beyond this, we must also progressively realize that Allah has designed and built the computer, its operating system, and all the software, as well as the body and mind of the one sitting there operating it. He is equally the Source of the food we eat, the air we breathe, the thoughts and intentions on the basis of which we act. Before we act and *while* we act we must acknowledge Him as the Source of all our effort, even that required to do the simplest things. We must first "plug in", so to speak, before we try to do anything; then our actions will be in line with His Wish and capable of drawing upon His Power. If the first breath we draw when we wake up in the morning is drawn in His Name, if we recognize it as an echo of the *nafas al-Rahman*, the Breath of the Merciful by which He has created us and through which He holds us in existence, second by second, then we may (insha'Allah) continue to draw our life, our intent, and our guidance from Him alone—He Who is *Al-Hayy* (the Living), *Al-Muqtadir* (the All-Determiner) and *Al-Hadi* (the Guide)—throughout the Day and into the Night. And if we see Him as the Source of our actions, then those actions will become not self-assertions but offerings; as soon as we perform them they will pass out of our hands, and return to the Source that sent them.

Acting in line with the will of Allah requires a discernment of the quality of the moment. *Every day doth some new work employ Him* [Q. 55:29/55:29] means that each *waqt* or moment of spiritual time, based on Allah's will for that moment and no other, is the occasion for a different response from us, a different approach to submission. And one aspect of our awareness of the changing occasions through which the Will of Allah manifests is an intuition of what might be called "God's time"—an intuition that we develop mainly in the station of Fluctuation. According to a *hadith* recounted by Tirmidhi, "Patient deliberation is from Allah and haste is from Satan"; this can be seen as the complementary opposite of the western aphorism, "The mills of God grind slowly, but they grind exceeding fine." The goal is to blend our actions with the flow of *spiritual* time, Allah's Time, so that they move in concert with His Action, without either "foot-dragging" or "jumping the gun." If we learn how to stay within His Time then we have effectively submitted to His Will, and opened ourselves to the Power necessary to follow and enact that Will. Haste and procrastination are weakness; *occasion* is Power. If we know how to intuit occasion, then we have effectively realized the truth that only Allah is the performer of every action.

But since we are human, and consequently tend to trust (often unconsciously) the Seen above the Unseen, we will most likely fall into the habit, from time to time, of seeing ourselves as the authors and starting-points of our own actions—this being the root of all idolatry, transgression and rebellion. The name of this bad habit is "self-will"; all the gods of the Pagans, all the idols of the scientists and the politicians, are nothing but imaginary projections of this same self-will. And if we fall into self-will, then Allah will make us suffer; He will do this because, in effect, we have asked Him to. He will send this suffering not to "punish" us because He is angry with us, but simply to return us to the Remembrance of Him, to an acknowledgement that there is no might nor power except in and through Him, that all power of action comes from Him, and that all things return to Him. In the words of the Qur'an [Q. 10:22–23]:

> *He it is Who maketh you to go on the land and the sea till, when ye are in the ships and they sail with them with a fair breeze and they are glad therein, a storm-wind reacheth them and the wave cometh unto them from every side and they deem that they are overwhelmed therein; (then) they cry unto Allah, making their faith pure for Him only: If Thou deliver us from this, we truly will be of the thankful.*

Yet when He hath delivered them, behold! they rebel in the earth wrongfully. O mankind! Your rebellion is only against yourselves. (Ye have) enjoyment of the life of the world; then unto Us is your return and We shall proclaim unto you what ye used to do.

If only suffering reminds us of Allah, then we will forget Him again; one of the lessons learned in the course of the spiritual Path is how to make *everything* a reminder—*even our forgetfulness.*

When we take Allah's power into our own hands and use it—this being a mistake that only His closest friends know how to avoid—then idols multiply in our closet; our actions produce residues, and we begin to act on the basis of the promptings of these residues, the momentum of past actions, rather than by the power and guidance of Allah operating in the present moment. In terms of action, the purpose of Remembrance, of *Dhikr*, is to return us to this present moment, this *waqt*, which is our only point of connection with that power and guidance. And once we have turned back to Allah, then the residues of past actions begin to be released, seeing that *unto Allah all things are returned.* [Q. 3:109] *And those who put away false gods, lest they should worship them, and turn to Allah in repentance, for them there are glad tidings.* [Q. 39:17]

These residues are released through suffering—not through pain itself, but through our willingness to let pain *be*, recognizing it as coming from Allah, and thus to let pain *go*, watching as it returns to Allah. (The English verb "to suffer", interestingly enough, means both "to undergo pain" and "to allow.") In reality, all things come from Allah and return to Him *simultaneously*, in the twinkling of an eye. But since we have the habit of filtering everything through the illusion of our own self-existence, based on our human habit of self-will—which is in turn based on our *ghaflhah*, our heedlessness, the inconstancy of our attention and our Remembrance—it seems to us as if Allah first generously provides us with His gifts, then wrathfully tears them away from us, and then ultimately summons them all back to Himself, thus producing the Day and Night of the Heart. But when the turning Heart has fully turned toward Allah—when Heart, Nafs, Ruh, everything we are, are annihilated in Him—then Day and Night are no more.

◇

Self-will may initially seem like it's energizing you, and *Taslim* as if it were draining you—but at the final accounting, it turns out that tasks performed on the basis of self-will require energy, while those performed on the basis of submission provide energy. When you use your will-power *against* submission, effort accumulates until it becomes a crushing weight that you will eventually be unable to bear. When you use it *in line with* submission, effort diminishes, till it finally gives way to the free flow of Allah's Life and Power. Nor should self-will be understood only as self-assertion; passive resistance to the Will of God—that is, the denial of reality—is also self-will.

If you must use will-power, then instead of using it in an attempt to draw nearer to God, use it for obedience to the shari'ah and the guidance of your shaykh; that way you stand a chance of wearing it down, until ultimately (insha'Allah) nothing is left but the Will and Power of the One.

Don't beat your head against a locked door—use the Key.

The Passions

When the will is fragmented and the mind chaotic, the passions of the *Nafs al-ammara* will tend to present themselves as various kinds of peace. Even anger, since it temporarily unifies the will, the mind and the affections—or appears to—may be experienced as a form of relief or repose, and this is even more true of low, intoxicating passions like sloth or lust, not to mention actual chemical intoxicants. But as one Sufi authority has said, "it is impossible to find repose in something intrinsically lower than yourself." Every passion, since it is necessarily fragmentary, is lower than the *Fitrah*, the human essence; this is why our humanity can never find rest in vice and self-indulgence, only in God. In response to the constant and heartfelt Remembrance of God, He will (insha'Allah) send us His *Sakinah*—Tranquility of Heart. *Behold, it is only by the Dhikr (remembrance) of Allah that the heart finds tranquility* [Q. 13:28]. This is the one true peace, the serenity which teaches the Heart that it can only find rest in what transcends it and encompasses it. Paradoxically, however, the dawning of the *Sakinah* may be announced by a profound restlessness, often including insomnia. This is because Allah is withdrawing from you everything you formerly found rest in, so you can rest in Him alone. The Nafs will do its best to try and disturb this rest, but in so doing it will only expose itself as being the furthest thing from any kind of genuine peace. Nor can we overcome this disturbance by fighting against it; it can only be dealt with by Allah Himself through His *Sakinah*. The first work of the God's Divine Tranquility is to put us at peace with the pain of His Absence, to pacify us so that we no longer need to flee from this pain—and as soon as we stop fleeing from it, His felt Absence is revealed as one face of His Presence: if Allah were not right here with us, how could we feel the acute anguish of separation from Him? In reality, the Nafs wants nothing but Allah—but she doesn't know that yet; if she did, she wouldn't fear being seen by Him. As His Absence is progressively revealed to be His Presence, her struggle against God begins to appear, unexpectedly, as a form of prostration to Him: the same turbulence, the same emotional energy can serve either flight from God or submission to Him, depending on our intent. If we choose God, this turbulence will be pacified; if we choose flight, it will be petrified.

Those who have been granted the *Sakinah*—sometimes after great struggle with the Nafs, which will do everything it can to create the kind of psychic pain that tempts us to seek relief in the passions—will no longer be attracted to the false peace of the passionate soul; their Nafs will be progressively transformed from the "Commanding Nafs" into the "Nafs-at-Peace." After this there are undoubtedly more struggles to come; they are not struggles with the Nafs, however, but with *Al-Jalal*, the awesome Majesty of God. After the battle to pacify the Nafs, with God's help, comes the battle which leads to *Fana'* and *Baqa'*, to the death of the Nafs as "me" and its resurrection as "Another." When all that we have identified as being "myself" is now seen as Another, the One witnessing this Other is no longer myself either—now could it be?—but Allah in His Name *Al-Shahid*, the Universal Witness. This is one of the several meanings of the *hadith* "He who knows himself knows His Lord"; to know one's Lord is to know one's Knower. [NOTE: This *hadith*, universally repeated by the Sufis, is found in few collections; one source is the *Mizan al-Hikmah*, apparently quoting from the *Ghurar al-Hikam* and the *Safinat al-Bihar*.]

The Nafs knows that it has to die; consequently it is angry and afraid. What it does not know (nor can you tell it) is that it can never die, because the ego—the Nafs as "me"—when revealed in its true essence, is the Divine All-Possibility, the synthesis of all the Names of Allah—the Nafs of God. But if you tell the Nafs that it is the universal manifestation of Allah, it will take you literally and then do its best to set itself up *as* Allah, such that it will have to be overthrown and broken down all over again. And if you tell it that it is nothing, it will only rebel and assert itself to prove you wrong. So the only thing to do is stop taking the Nafs as the central point of reference for everything, stop obsessing about it—this obsession being precisely the self-referential narcissism of the Nafs itself—and let Allah turn your Heart to Him, in Gathering and Intimacy. At the dawning of the *Sakinah*, the Nafs forgets itself, and gazes in rapture on the Beauty of God. Thus it is pacified, and becomes the *Nafs al-mutma'inah*. It no longer thinks about the fact that it must die, nor does it yearn for the immortality that it doesn't realize it already possesses. In its rapture before *Al-Jamal*, the Divine Beauty, it forgets these irrelevancies.

The Problem of Self-Esteem

Since the Nafs is the source of self-definition, it has everything to do with the development of self-esteem, and the various illusions and struggles that are inseparable from it. There are two kinds of self-esteem, two different *self-estimations*: positive and negative. You esteem yourself either as admirably living up to the standards of the world or as ignobly sinking below them. In either case, however, the criterion you judge yourself by is This World, *al-Dunya*, not Allah. So self-esteem is all idolatry.

There is, however, a good use for positive self-esteem—especially when you are in the habit of indulging in negative self-esteem so as to avoid responsibility. Either an excess or a deficiency of self-esteem will act as a veil between you and Allah; nonetheless, the debt represented by negative self-esteem can sometimes be satisfied by "paying it off" with positive self-esteem, until the result is *no* self-esteem at all—zero on the books. This is the ideal. When our self-esteem reaches zero, then we have stopped estimating ourselves by the standards of the world and turned that function over to Allah as *Al-'Adil*, the Only Judge.

This method of paying off the debt of negative self-esteem with the coin of positive self-esteem can, however, only succeed if we consciously dedicate all our actions to Allah and allow Him to be the Judge during the whole process—otherwise we might collect great masses of positive and negative self-esteem that never encounter each other. We could end up like a person with a dual personality, one half crass billionaire and the other half hopeless pauper; it is entirely possible for arrogance and self-hatred to co-exist in the same psyche. But if we accept all estimations of who we are and how well we are doing as Allah's business, not ours—if we recognize all negative estimations only as Justice, and all positive ones only as Mercy—then we will be free of the unnecessary burden of self-esteem.

Morality as Purification from the Dunya

Before it is annihilated, the Nafs sees only the Dunya, exists only in relation to the Dunya; they are strictly equivalent. Therefore to break with the Dunya, with "the darkness of this world", is to break the stranglehold of the *Nafs al-ammara*, and vice versa. The Dunya is our tendency to identify with, to become associated with, to effectively be possessed by, various things, persons and situations on the basis of the passions of the Nafs, not the gifts or commands of Allah; and when such association is in force it seems the most "natural" thing in the world. In Islam, all human acts are classified either as obligatory, recommended, indifferent, discouraged or prohibited, and the largest category by far—especially in the modern world—is "indifferent." But as the Nafs is progressively purified and its power to veil the Heart diminishes, more and more acts, thoughts and associations that were once "indifferent" now become "prohibited." Take *levity* for example. Initially it seems like a harmless diversion, a form of playful relaxation. (Levity—meaningless silliness—is of course poles apart from intelligent wit, one of whose main functions is to shame and deconstruct the ego through irony and satire.) But when the Heart is fully awake, levity is revealed as a way of denying the meaning inherent in things, persons and situations—and to deny meaning on any level is to repudiate the signs of Allah, Who *created the heavens and the earth with the Truth* [Q. 39:5]. To many in the West the Prophetic *sunnah*, with its minute rules governing daily gestures and actions, seems like little more than a way of placing one's life under the power of some weird, archaic, obsessive-compulsive disorder; and it certainly can become that for some people, in either the West or the East. But in essence it is much more than this: it is a way of helping us understand that *no* act is neutral or meaningless, that whatever we do expresses Truth (or its distortion) and comes from Truth.

When the Spirit of God takes possession of the Heart, it expels the Dunya, and this can sometimes be an extremely shocking process. Certain things are suddenly denied to you that previously you could apparently always possess, or handle—or ignore—with impunity. Certainly the Nafs is capable of perverting this process by transforming it into the passion called *scrupulosity*, where you obsess over unimportant matters in the moral dimension and end up making life miserable for yourself and the people around you. But when a particular act or association or identification is denied to you by Allah, you can't obsess about it anymore because you can't get *near* it; it has been removed from you, often without your conscious participation, by a Sovereign Power that absolutely transcends you. When you submitted your will to Allah, to the degree that you did so in real sincerity, you gave Him leave to rearrange your life. He always retains that power, of course, but to be overpowered against your will and to pray for and accept guidance are two very different things. Some of the most shocking and unexpected transformations we experience in life actually arrive in direct answer to our prayers.

It is impossible to know beforehand all that will be required in allowing Allah to turn your Heart to Him, and all the aspects and levels of the Dunya that must be released before this turn is complete. Morality, with its many commands and prohibitions—necessary though they are—is too coarse a net to catch all the changes destined to happen. The Sufis say that you must be "like a corpse in the hands of a Washer of the Dead" not only because a corpse cannot resist, but also because it can neither anticipate nor remember. All spiritual change happens in the *waqt*, the eternal present moment of spiritual time, not by virtue of any attempt to assess our past progress or map our future development. From time to time Allah may elect to unveil these to us, or a part of them, for His own purposes, but to pry into them is only a waste of spiritual potential, besides being the height of discourtesy. *But God measureth the night and the day:—He knoweth that you cannot count its hours aright, and therefore, turneth to you mercifully.* [Q. 73:20/73:20]

Approaching the *Sakinah*

The primitive elements of the *Nafs al-ammara bi'l su'* are knots of associative ideas bearing no intrinsic relationship either to spiritual perception or to practical action, and manifesting on the level of the body as various habits of physical tension. Later these knots will build themselves into specific beliefs and identities, into those largely unconscious structures that constitute our world-concept and self-concept (the Dunya and the ego who witnesses it), but when they start out they are like rudimentary cell colonies whose only organizing principle is association—which is to say, the building-blocks of the *Nafs al-ammara* are aggregates of more-or-less automatic mental activity that have not yet risen to the level of "meaning." In their later development they will presume to claim our attention and allegiance by presenting themselves as a true picture of what the self is and what the world is; this is the stage when they become transformed into idols, idols maintained by the arrogance of our self-will and rebellion against God. But before that happens they are nothing but random aggregates of meaningless mental static. Consequently, when we renounce idolatry and self-will and make progress in the practice of submitting to the Will of Allah in every moment and every state—when, that is, we renounce belief and conjecture and submit to Reality—our self-concept/world-concept begins to be resolved into its constituent elements, which appear again in their true guise as knots of reactive tension and agitation, composed primarily of shifting mental images and sub-vocal speech, psychic impurities that do not possess enough meaning to justify either our belief in them or their own existence. Divested of their cloaks of falsely-assumed significance they present themselves as they really are: as insignificant, unnecessary, relatively unpleasant, and therefore easily released. As we continue to let go of these residues they are progressive replaced by the deepening sense of the Presence of Allah in the Heart; this is one of the several legitimate ways of describing the development of Spiritual Tranquility or *Sakinah*. The release of mental knots and residues is a practice; nonetheless the arrival of the *Sakinah* is a gift of God because the practice itself is a gift of God—a gift that arrives specifically through the shaykh.

To Die Before you Die

"You Sufis are always talking about 'dying before you die.'
What's that like?"
"It's like dying."

◇

When we are assaulted by the *Nafs al-ammara bi'l su'*, the "soul commanding to evil", we will ultimately realize, insha'Allah, that we have no power against this Nafs; that's when—if we are people of faith—we will turn to Allah for help. The certainty that Allah has the power to pacify the Nafs, along with the certainty of our own powerlessness, are preliminary signs of the *Ma'rifah*, the knowledge, of Allah—though the greater part of this *Ma'rifah*, like most of the subjects dealt with this book, cannot be fully expressed in words. But even greater than the *Ma'rifah* of Allah is the *Ma'rifah* of the Nafs. This in no way implies, however, that the Nafs is somehow greater than Allah; such a notion is both blasphemous and absurd. It's simply that *Ma'rifah* of Allah, if "I" am the knower, still retains a trace of the Nafs—of "me", that is—whereas in the case of *Ma'rifah* of the Nafs, the only Knower is Allah Himself, Who knows it with a complete and perfected *Ma'rifah* in which the last traces of "me-as-

64

knower" have been annihilated. The *Ma'rifah* of the Nafs does not exclude the *Ma'rifah* of Allah, but perfects it; the Prophet Muhammad, peace and blessings be upon him, alluded to this higher *Ma'rifah* when he said "he who knows himself (his Nafs) knows his Lord." But so radical a transformation as the annihilation of "me-as-knower" and the unveiling of Allah as the Absolute Knower could not happen as simply and easily as this bare schematic definition might lead us to believe. Given that Allah witnesses only Himself, the *Ma'rifah* of the Nafs must manifest as *Al-Jalal*, the Divine Majesty, as the apocalyptic destruction of everything other than Allah, the systematic annihilation of all that claims separate self-existence, all the world powers, all the secondary causes, everything that says "this is that" and "I am this." In terms of the inner world, the *Ma'rifah* of the Nafs is nothing less than the arrival of the Hour.

◇

As we have seen above, the Nafs inflames the passions because she doesn't want to be seen, given that nothing is more *distracting* than things like as lust and anger and envy and pride. But what happens when the Nafs *is* seen, not after she has become tame and peaceful and presentable, but right in the middle of her sins?

At this point we are no longer imploring God's help to overcome the passions of the Nafs, nor pacifying it with the practice of the virtues, but rather seeing those passions as the Names of God stolen and by the Nafs and perverted—stolen through identification. (Ego-identification with the Names is the exact opposite of the penultimate goal of the Sufi path, which to let the soul be qualified by those Names, this being the realization of the virtues.) When the Nafs renounces anger, anger appears as *Al-Jalal*, the Majesty of God; when she renounces lust, lust appears as *Al-Jamal*, the Beauty of God. So the worst things in us are also the best things. By the power of Allah, right in the middle of its sin, the Nafs may suddenly repent in spite of herself, and become the mirror of all the Most Beautiful Names.

But this can obviously only happen through tribulation, through *fitan*. No more hoping to meet the mark of righteousness, even with God's help—seeing that, in the words of Rabi'ah al-'Adawiyyah, "thine existence is a sin wherewith no other sin may be compared"—and yet still not despairing: that's the real *fitan*. And then, of course, in the lull between tribulations, we still have to try and be good. And we still have to struggle to escape our sufferings, to fix them, to heal them, with the help of whatever help we hope might do the trick, because we have responsibilities to ourselves and to others, responsibilities we have no right to shirk. That's our human duty; we can't just wallow in our sufferings. But ultimately none of these therapies will succeed—they won't be enough. Only *Taslim*, only the complete sacrifice of self-will to Allah, only "dying before you die," will be enough. But until we exhaust all our human attempts to conquer our vices and end our suffering, and let Allah win the battle for us, we will never be confronted—existentially, not merely intellectually—with this ultimate fact.

Fear, when we dis-identify with it and begin to witness it through the Eye of the Heart, is the punishment and the cure for fear; likewise anger is the punishment and the cure for anger. Fear and anger are the rebellion of the Nafs against Allah, but they are also Allah's just chastisement and correction of the Nafs for that very rebellion. Seeing the Nafs ultimately not as the enemy of God but as His deepest Will, and seeing this without thereby claiming the right to break the law because you are now "beyond good and evil"—this is truly formidable, and indescribable.

When all the things you've built up your life and personality in an attempt to hide from come to the surface, there's finally nothing you can do about it but know that *there is no refuge from Allah but in Him* [Q. 9:118]. When you acknowledge that only God is the Doer, that you can do nothing, you might first take this simply as a proposition you believe to be true. But what's it like to really know, really feel, that you can do nothing? It can totally terrifying, a feeling of complete helplessness, because you aren't just losing your Promethean arrogance, your pride in being a "self-made man" who is "captain of his fate, master of his soul"; it goes deeper than that. When you turn to the source of energy you've always drawn upon to perform the simplest actions, the thing that allows you to say "here I am washing the dishes, here I am mowing the lawn", it's no longer there. It's gone. What can you do now? How can you live? You flip

66

the switch but the lights don't come on. The source of power you've always used to perform your simplest daily activities is no longer there. This produces a feeling of total helplessness, like suddenly waking up as a quadriplegic. And that helplessness most likely turns into fear. *What can I do now? How can I live?* To the degree that you have based your life on self-will, the dawning of the Will of Allah will initially be experienced as a kind of paralysis.

At such moments of radical helplessness we either despair or, insha'Allah, throw ourselves upon God's mercy. And when we pray, we can't even ask God—or shouldn't ask Him—to restore our power to "lead our own lives"; all we can really do is renounce all self-willed action forever, and with it all ambition and self-satisfaction, even those little moments when we say, "Ah! Now the carport's all swept. Good job." We give all that to God, really understanding, maybe for the first time, that we really can do nothing, that no-one acts but Him.

But then, somehow, we keep on functioning, and so the moment when we sincerely turned all our actions over to God because we had no choice, and in the realization that it was He who had brought us to this extreme condition so we could do just that, is slowly forgotten, or at least put on the back burner. Life goes on. It goes on, but it isn't really the same. Because to the degree that we truly turned our power and our ability and our right to act over God, it really is He who is performing our simple daily actions.

But we don't always see this. We imagine that when God acts for us and through us we will necessarily experience ourselves as being picked up and wielded by a great Power, like a swordsman who loses himself in the heat of battle, then returns to himself to find the field around him strewn with the bodies of his enemies: *It was not you who threw when you threw, but God threw* [Q. 8:15]. But it's not always dramatic like that. If we have really renounced self-willed action, whether or not this renunciation takes place during some crisis of our lives, then God has already stepped in to perform the actions we can no longer lay claim to.

Some Sufis call this "Annihilation in the Acts", and see it as an early stage of *Fana*. Our qualities and our essence are not annihilated in God's Qualities and Essence; we still look and feel like our same old selves. But our actions are annihilated, obliterated in His Acts. We no longer own them or take credit for them. They keep on happening, but we are not performing them. And we may not always realize this—possibly not until another crisis wakes us up to our condition. When you die you can't do anything in the world anymore; when you die before you die, the actions go on but you're not the One performing them.

The feeling of fear and helplessness we often experience when we are beginning to die before we die is often accompanied by a lot of anger—the anger of frustrated self-will. Anger is one of the two most common ways of hiding from the fear; you feel that you could at any time make the supreme effort and sweep the enemy from the field. And the other main way of avoiding fear is lust. When sexual desire arrives, the struggle to hold on to life is transformed into the urge to give life. Anger is the feeling that, temporarily at least, you are invincible. And lust is (or includes) the feeling that you are *safe*. When animals go into mating behavior they lose all their fear; their instinct for self-preservation is submerged by their instinct to propagate the species. The feeling that anger makes you invincible, the feeling that sex makes you safe, are obviously illusions. But they are necessary illusions, implanted in us by God, otherwise home and family would never get defended and the species would never get reproduced. *By a Soul and Him who balanced it, And breathed into it its wickedness and its piety . . .* [Q. 91:7–8/91:7–8]. As such they are the main motivations of the Nafs—and when the Nafs feels threatened by God's command to die before you die, it turns them on full blast. But feeling the fear, feeling the helplessness, though this is certainly very unpleasant, is the better way. They are what God has sent us and what He wants from us, until we renounce ownership of action and let Him act in our stead. When anger and lust are renounced as ways of dealing with fear, only *Taslim*, only the sacrifice to Allah of the last traces of self-will, has the power to overcome that fear, through the Annihilation of the very one who fears. On the level of God's Acts, which has to do with all our questions and worries about *what might happen*, this is "dying before you die."

The ultimate cure for anger is to reach *yaqin*, "certainty", as to the truth that Allah is the only Power; the ultimate cure for lust is to know for certain that Allah is the only Beauty.

◈

Beyond Annihilation in the Acts lies Annihilation in the Names, and beyond that, Annihilation in the Essence. Annihilation in the Names develops out of the practice of the virtues, until you recognize those virtues as God's Attributes, not yours. And Annihilation in the Essence is complete Annihilation. There is nothing you can do to produce this outcome. Dying before you die is not a goal to be pursued in itself; rather, our goal is to come closer to God, to gain an ever-deepening sense of His Presence, His Reality and His Power, and an ever-increasing willingness to submit to His commands. First the moth hears the legend of the candle; then he sees its light; next he feels its warmth; finally he is burned to death in its flames. And the more clearly you see God, the more completely you can give up the futile attempt of *trying* to die before you die, and simply let God kill you—and turn you around—and transform you—and make you known to Him. The *Ma'rifah* of God is your business, with His help; the *Ma'rifah* of the Nafs is His business, with no help from you at all. At the point of its death the Nafs may actually try to *will* and *manage* its own dying; this produces immense pain. The only way of ending this pain is to let God do what He will with you, to become "like a corpse in the hands of a Washer of the Dead."

Furthermore, before you can die before you die, the Nafs may actually try to kill you; one of the increasingly common false conceptions of *Fana'* it is capable of producing is the notion of "suicide for Allah." Sometimes this notion is unconscious, leading us to take unnecessary risks without realizing what we're doing; sometimes it is conscious enough (though its causes remain unconscious) to express itself as a perverted ideology, such as that of the suicide bombers. Those who have been brought near to Allah unconsciously, in an imbalanced way and with only a fragment of their human nature, who have developed a deep earnestness or obsession in terms of the will while allowing the Nafs to obscure their intellect and pervert their feelings, may end by contracting this terminal disease. Such an outcome is possible because the Hour is drawing near, which means that Allah is inevitably drawing nearer to all of us, whether or not we are coming closer to Him, or even if we are actively fleeing Him. And it is a matter of indifference to the Nafs whether it causes you to die as a "heroic martyr" in a blaze of evil glory, or as a degenerate alcoholic in a pig-sty somewhere—just as long as it can make you believe that your life belongs to you, to do with as *you* will, not to Allah, to do with as He will. It does this by portraying your helplessness to resist its commands (which is actually the height of cowardice) as a heroic and virtuous submission to the Divine Will—but, *alhamdulillah*, it is relatively easy to tell the difference between the two. The criterion is as follows: Allah may command you to sacrifice your life, and will always command you to sacrifice your self-will, but He will *never* command you to degrade either yourself or others. Those who degrade and destroy themselves in His name are in fact slandering Him, a breach of *adab* that He certainly cannot be expected to take kindly to—as those who have committed it will inevitably learn, to their eternal dismay, on the Plains of Akhirah.

The Secret of the *Nafs*

We all participate intrinsically in the Essence of Allah—which is not saying much, since this is also true of a criminal, a dog, a pig, a snake, or a stone. Without this participation we would not exist, since only Allah possesses Being and Existence in His own right. This is not to say that our limited, created existences can ever be united with His Infinite Being, since in ourselves we are nothing. But since He possesses an eternal Knowledge of our earthly lives and our post-eternal destiny, we were part of His Infinite Knowledge before we ever existed; as objects of this Knowledge we have always subsisted within Him in the mode of Annihilation. This original participation is the source and essence of the Nafs, which influences us to rely upon our pre-eternal Subsistence within Allah while ignoring and rejecting His call to draw near to Him through conscious submission to His Will, thus allowing Him to open the Eye of the Heart. When Iblis [Q. 38:71–78] disobeyed Allah's command that he prostrate to Adam in pre-eternity, he chose to act according to his *intrinsic* Subsistence within Allah—which choice, since it was based on self-assertion, was a denial of the very Annihilation by which he sub-sisted—rather than the path of Islam that Allah *willed* for him; in so doing he became the origin and archetype of the *Nafs al-ammara bi'l su'*, the "soul commanding to evil." The Nafs-as-ego, because she represents our unconscious identification with Allah, is under the sign of His Wrath, and remains under this sign until *Fana'*, the Anni-hilation of other-than-Allah, when she ceases to play the role of ego and is unveiled as the Nafs of Allah Himself.

On the one hand, the arrogance of the Nafs reflects its sense of its own divinity; on the other, it arises out of *defensiveness*—a defen-siveness based on shame: If it is God, or virtually one with God, then why is it always so frustrated, so filled with unsatisfied crav-ings? (This shame is the sign of the Accusing Self, *the Nafs al-law-wamah.*) And because the Nafs is ashamed, shame is one of its most potent weapons. If you were able to feel your true degree of disgust at the promptings of the Nafs without denying or avoiding or run-ning away from that unpleasant but highly useful feeling, you would no longer be under its power. Knowing this, the Nafs will do everything it can to turn this disgust into shame. Disgust at the actions of the Nafs is *true* shame and results in purifying remorse and the birth of self-respect; the shame inculcated by the Nafs is *false* shame, the kind of shame that makes it impossible for you to look at the true state of affairs because—the Nafs is quick to tell you—it is too shameful to ever face.

The *Nafs al-lawwamah* or Accusing Self can be defined as a strug-gle between true and false shame. If true shame wins, the Accusing Self is transformed into the *Nafs al-mutma'inah*, the Self-at-Peace, totally submissive to the will of Allah, "like a corpse in the hands of a Washer of the Dead", and entirely willing to be not as it thinks it is, but as Allah knows it is. If false shame wins, the Nafs becomes once again the *Nafs al-ammara bi'l su'*, the self commanding-to-evil. And because the commanding self is ashamed, it tempts us to shameful activities to help us hide from that feeling. An alcoholic who wakes up ashamed of last night's self-indulgence can either let that shame help him become disgusted with alcohol, or he can make the shame go away in an instant simply by taking another drink. And in order to bury its shame even more deeply, the commanding self will often

invent a whole ideology where all that is shameful is falsely portrayed as admirable, much as a tyrant will present oppression of the
weak and helpless as a form of heroism, or oppressive liberal culture
define all kinds of sexual expression as healthy and any form of
inhibition as shameful. The dog eats its own vomit; the true man
cleans it up, and then does his best not to ingest something nauseat-
ing in the future. The shame you identify with in order to hide from
it is transformed into the false attractiveness of vice; the shame you
dis-identify with turns into convulsive disgust, allowing you to spew
it out of your mouth. [NOTE: Please understand that we do not
here expose the deceptions of the *Nafs al-ammara bi'l su'* so that
you can learn how to *argue* with it. At this point, the saying "pride
in reasoned argument is the work of Shaytan" applies: you can no
more argue with the Nafs than you can argue with a bad smell. A
bad smell is only dealt with by a sweet perfume, or better personal
hygiene, or a good housecleaning, or a fresh wind.]

The Nafs guides you into shameful acts, but it will never judge
you for these acts—it claims—because it is your friend. It is tolerant
and accepting and forgiving, and it teaches you to be equally tolerant and accepting and forgiving of it. But of course it *will* judge you
and shame you for them later on—because if you weren't ashamed,
why would you want to follow the Nafs in the first place? *Then shall
the mighty ones* [these, taken together, are the *Nafs al-ammara*] *say to
the weak, "What! was it we who turned you aside from the guidance
which had reached you? Nay, but you acted wickedly yourselves"* [Q.
34:31/34:31]. Without shame, and the Nafs' promise that it will
always help you deny that shame, the Nafs would lose all its attraction for you. And, of course, one of the primary ways of denying
shame is to dump that shame on others; you will never be free of
false, toxic shame if you fall into this self-destructive habit. This con-
tradictory labyrinth of shame and its denial is the disease the Sufis
are prescribing for when they speak of "repenting of repentance."

The other reason, outside of shame, that someone would want to
hide him- or herself, is fear. The Nafs knows that, if it is ever seen for
what it is, the Nafs-as-ego must die; consequently it is afraid. It is
afraid that the Eye of the Heart will open and burn it to ashes—in
other words, that the Presence of Allah will dissolve your self-con-

cept. But it certainly doesn't want to feel this fear, so it works overtime to repress it. Its strategy for repressing fear is to alternately terrorize you and grant you "rewards", like an abuser or expert brainwasher who is adept at producing the "Stockholm syndrome" in his victim, in making a lull in abuse feel like mercy, and abuse itself seem like a form of love. The victim of the Stockholm syndrome will defend his abuser; the Nafs teaches you to defend your vices, and the shame of them, as if you were protecting your self-respect.

It is our partial and limited understanding of the Nafs, prevented from becoming a complete understanding by the barrier of fear and shame, that turns the Nafs into the ego, into "me." Whatever we identify with we must necessarily be ignorant of; whatever we take as an aspect of "me" disappears from the field that this "me" is able to witness; it becomes part of the unconscious self. The full knowledge of the Nafs belongs to God alone. When this knowledge is unveiled and the self-referential ego dissolved, the Nafs is "me" no longer; it is revealed as the perfect synthesis of all the infinite possibilities or "permanent archetypes", the *ayan al-thabitah*, within the embrace of the Divine nature—the *single soul* out of which all things are created: *O mankind! Be careful of your duty to your Lord Who created you from a single soul* [Q. 4:1]. And the synthesis of this totality of Divine possibilities, which constitute the *Umm al-Kitab* or Mother of the Book, is the *Fitrah*, the Primordial Human Nature. As we have already seen above, the Qur'an relates that after Allah created Adam but before He sent him to earth, He commanded him to tell all the angels their names [Q. 2:33]; the angels themselves didn't know these names, but Adam did, because Allah had made him the repository of the eternal prototypes of all creatures. The *Fitrah* is the Nafs not as it is known by any human individual, but by God alone. And God knows only God.

In the words of the *hadith qudsi*, "I am according to My servant's opinion of Me" [Bukhari; Muslim; Tirmidhi; Ibn Majah]; this is something that cannot be said of anything other than Allah. In society, in history, in the whole corporeal universe, the nature of things is *not* based on our opinion of them. Our opinions are only valid if they conform to the objective nature of the things we investigate or experience; they are not what we imagine them to be, based on the fears and desires of the Nafs; they are what they are. The false imaginations of the Nafs *are mere names. . . . A mere conceit and their own impulses do they follow* [Q. 53:23/53:23]. In the face of these relentless fantasies, the Prophet Muhammad (peace and blessings be upon him) prayed: "O Allah, show me things as they really are" [al-Razi].

It is otherwise with Allah, because Allah is *Al-Wasi*, the Infinite—which means that every opinion that any of His servants holds of Him represents one of His actual Names—each containing all the others—given that His Names are not *parts* of Allah but His specific *relationships* with the many and varied creatures He has created—otherwise He would not be *Al-Ahad*, the One. He is so far beyond and so totally free of limitation by all conceptions of Him that *any* conception of Him, among those His Mercy has provided to humanity, must draw upon one of His Names or aspects. And because He is the infinitely Generous, *Al-Karim*, and the infinitely Merciful, *Al-Rahman*, He pours His Reality into each of these conceptions of Him to the full extent of their capacity. If, however, our conception of the basic nature of Reality is sufficiently veiled and constricted, it will invoke Allah in his darker names, such as *Al-Qabid*, the Constricter, *Al-Khafid*, the Abaser, *Al-Darr*, the Punisher, and *Al-Muntaqim*, the Avenger. You may be an atheistic materialist who believes in mechanistic determinism, or a postmodernist who thinks that "life is random", but even these conceptions, since they represent your fundamental view of the nature of Reality, are (in one sense) Names of Allah—extremely dark Names, designed to confront those who serve them with the consequences of these shrunken conceptions, ultimately (insha'Allah) in order to purify their Hearts of them by means of *Al-Jalal*, the Majesty of God.

Well and good. Yet there is still more to the mystery of Allah's Self-revelation, since to see all things in their objectivity, as they really are, untainted by the subjective imaginations of the Nafs, is to see them as signs of the Divinity: *Wherever you turn, there is the face of Allah* [Q. 2:115]. Once the Nafs has been pacified and the objective reality of creation unveiled, the Universe appears as the face of the Absolute Reality, Who continues to say to us: "I am according to My servant's opinion of Me." Consequently, on a higher level, this *hadith* applies not to Allah exclusively, but to all the forms and events of the Universe insofar as they are recognized as signs of Allah—and even (or especially!) *to the Nafs itself*, given that this "one soul" contains the seeds of all created things. If you see the Nafs as an enemy, it will be an enemy; if you see it as a teacher, it will be a teacher; if you see it as a friend, it will be a friend. The Nafs may *pose* as a teacher and *masquerade* as a friend, but this is not what is meant; these are only some of the many methods it employs in its endless attempts to destroy you. Only under the influence of the Spirit of God will the Nafs be revealed as teacher, as friend, and ultimately as the Hidden Treasure that Allah chose to reveal when He created the universe; only the Spirit can know the Nafs as that Treasure. If we turn to the unpacified Nafs *instead* of to the Spirit, hoping to be taught or befriended, the consequences will be terrible— and nothing can pacify the Nafs but *Mahabbah*, the Love of God.

The Mercy of Allah that creates us and redeems us comes to us through *al-Ruh*; He wishes us to embrace it. The Nafs is the Wrath of Allah that tries to destroy us; in His Mercy, He commands us to resist its influence. In the last analysis they are both fully Allah, but only *al-Ruh* opens the *way* to Allah; the Nafs is "the ladder of the *'arif*" (according to al-Hallaj)—*'arif* means "gnostic, the knower of God"—only under the influence of the Spirit of God; in the words of the Qur'an, *there is no refuge from Allah but in Him* [Q. 9:118]. *Al-Ruh* is Allah's gift to us in creating and saving us; the Nafs is a mystery He reserves for Himself alone. The antinomians of various religions who claim that the "elect" are no longer bound by religious law, or the followers of Nietzsche and similar philosophers who exalt the "will to power", as well as various psychics, poets, visionaries and drug-takers, are all getting wind of the vast treasure that is the Nafs and dream of plundering it; but the Nafs will plunder them instead. The Nafs tempts us to anger, to lust, to greed and arrogance, to pride and self-love. All these are transgressions that block our access to the Presence of Allah, idols that we worship in His place. But to Him they are by no means transgressions. *His* Anger is Justice; *His* Lust is His legitimate delight in creating universes and embracing what He has created; *His* Greed and Arrogance—eternally and perfectly satisfied—are His lawful ownership and dominance of all things, His status as *Rabb al-Alamin*, Lord of the

Worlds. And His Pride and Self-Love are His essential nature, given that Beauty necessarily delights in Beauty, just as Truth triumphs in Truth. So all those things that are sins for us, for Him are the very expressions of His Divinity; this is the secret of the Nafs. When we have died to this Nafs, when we are no longer attached to Nafs-as-ego, then the eternal mystery of the Nafs is revealed.

> *By the soul* (Nafs), *and the proportion and order given to it;*
> *And its enlightenment as to its wrong and its right*
> *Truly he succeeds that purifies it,*
> *And he fails that corrupts it!* [Q. 91:7–10; Yusuf Ali]

But until then the Nafs will test us with *Al-Jalal*, the Divine Rigor. What could be more maddening than being in the closest possible touch with Infinite Power and not being able to use it, with Infinite Pleasure and not being able to enjoy it? All vice and transgression come from an unconscious sense of one's closeness to Allah—from the feeling that, since we subsisted within Him in pre-eternity, we now have the right (of course!) to act and be as He is, to avail ourselves of His infinite treasures. But if you unconsciously believe that you *are* Allah, then will never be able to submit to Him—and Submission to Him is the only way you can be returned to your pre-eternal station of Subsistence within Him. You can never take possession, by self-will or cunning, of what is already yours. It must come to you as free gift, it can never come to you as plunder—and this is true even of Submission itself. Even the power to submit is not yours; it comes only through the Spirit of God. When the Holy Qur'an tells us that *There is no refuge from Allah but in Him* [Q. 9:118], it is saying that there is no refuge from the Nafs but in the Spirit.

Day and Night are one in Allah, and they turn together in harmony in the universe He has created. But in the Nafs—and in *al-Dunya*—they are separate and at war. The Nafs simultaneously flees from life into death and from death into life. It seeks death so as to avoid meeting Allah in the Day of Life, and throws itself into life so that—it tells itself—it will never have to meet Allah in the Night of Death. Truly the Nafs in this condition is *among the losers*, and the chief of them! But, in the Mercy of Allah, it will ultimately be able to avoid neither the Day nor the Night, neither Life nor Death. Day and Night were created by Allah for only one purpose: to chastise the Nafs, and educate it, and pacify it, and return it to its original station, the station of the Hidden Treasure.

The *Fitrah*, the primordial human nature, is who we really are in the sight of Allah, and as such may be identified with the *Nafs al-mutma'inah*. When the Qur'an says *your Lord . . . created you from a single soul* [Q. 4:1], it is referring to the Nafs in this sense. The Nafs becomes the Nafs commanding-to-evil, whose child is the ego, when our own partial and changing views of ourselves replace Allah's eternal and perfect Knowledge of us. Partial self-knowledge, when we rely upon it instead of upon Allah's Knowledge, creates imbalance, and imbalance always results in vice and transgression—at the very least the vice of heedlessness, which is the root of all the others. But when the self that asserts itself, that wants to live merely as its own idea of itself, that essentially believes that it has created itself, is educated and pacified by the Spirit of Allah, until it is willing to be who He knows it to be and nothing else, then we are returned to the *Fitrah*, the original human essence—to the state of Adam before the fall. If we aspire to this Divine Pacification and the Divine Knowledge it brings, we should be as vigorously responsive to the alterations of Day and Night on the spiritual Path as a warrior to the commands of his General, and as passively receptive to them as a corpse in the hands of a Washer of the Dead.

To recapitulate: The Nafs in the highest sense is the Nafs of Allah—but the Nafs is also "me." This is its great danger. Because if the Nafs is both a face of Allah and the principle of my separate identity, then am I not, in my separateness, in some sense Allah? And if, by virtue of my intrinsic Annihilation, I subsisted within Allah in pre-eternity, do I not now have the right to possess myself of all His treasures whenever I feel like it? As we have already pointed out, such thoughts do occur; the Nafs herself sends them, and then tries to convince us that they are the simple truth. This is the religion of the Nafs which it is always preaching: the religion of "Allah-without-Islam." When Sayiddna Musa, peace and blessings be upon him, was on Sinai receiving Torah, the Children of Israel practiced this religion in the valley below him, with the Golden Calf—and we all know what happened to them. But is not sexuality a direct extension of the eternal Bliss of Allah? Is not greed an extension of His Wealth, anger an extension of His Justice? Yes and no. In one way these passions are aspects of our *Fitrah*, our primordial human birthright. The lion is beautiful in his anger, the bull beautiful in his lust; the pig is even beautiful in his gluttony, according to the sensibilities of some people . . . but we are not pigs, or bulls, or lions; we are men. Pig, bull and lion, eagle and nightingale, rock, tree and star, possess *intrinsic* Islam, and so are guiltless whatever they do. But the *Amana*, the Trust laid upon Man and no-one else, requires of us conscious, deliberate Islam. It is our duty and our pledge not to conform ourselves to nature, but to conform our nature to the Book, both the written Book and the *Umm al-Kitab*, the Mother of the Book from which it is derived, that contains the seeds of all things—the *Batin* whose *Zahir* is the universe. And if, by the grace of Allah, we can do this, then pigs, bulls and lions, eagles and nightingales, rocks trees and stars—all the passions, and all the roses too—will turn toward us and submit to us, because they will see us as qualified with all the Most Beautiful Names of God. The Nafs claims to *be* God but she cannot *see* God; only in the mirror of the human Heart illuminated by the Spirit, and in full submission to it, can she gaze upon her true form, and remember Who she is.

The Nafs is not Allah by her domination and deception, but only by virtue of her Annihilation. Yet that Annihilation was always intrinsic within her, as the essence of her. According to the doctrine of *Tawhid*, the Transcendent Unity of Being, a Nafs could not exist eternally opposed to Allah in the presence of Allah, because Allah is *Al-Ahad*, the Only Being, the One. Yet within Allah, possessing no separate Being other than His Being, is the One Soul, the One Nafs out of which He made all things. And that is who we are.

The *Nafs* and Time

Ma'rifah of the Nafs is the perfection of detachment from the Nafs—and if the Nafs is the trace of how we were in our pre-eternal union with Allah, by the same token it is essentially the past. Your identity is entirely composed of the past; *right now* you aren't anyone at all. The past trying to re-assert itself, trying to be the present and claim the rights and reality of the present, is the Nafs-commanding-to-evil. The Spirit of Allah enters the Heart only in the present, not the past.

The Accusing Nafs is the future attempting to claim the rights and reality of the present; as a mixture of self-willed spiritual aspiration and fear of spiritual failure, it is the invasion and obscuration of the present moment by images of what might be when the Spirit of Allah enters the Heart, or else fails to enter it. But the Spirit enters the Heart only in the present, not the future.

Yet the Nafs is more fundamentally the past, since even the future desired by the Accusing Self is based on the memory of our pre-eternal union with Allah. To fight the Nafs is to allow it to affect and obscure the present; to set the Nafs aside and place our attention on Allah is to let the memories and aspirations of the Nafs, naturally and inevitably, flow away into the past.

The past is not annihilated, nor is the future non-existent; it's simply that they belong to Allah, not to us. The Nafs as pre-eternity is the reality of all things while they were still *in the loins of Adam* [Q. 7:172], and Adam as he was in Allah's perfect conception of him, before he entered time. Our attempt to possess the perfect and eternal past by dragging it into time is what transforms the Nafs from the treasure-house of the potentials of all things within the Divine Essence into the *Nafs al-ammara bi'l su'*. To let the past return to the Eternal Past of our original nature, and the future to the Eternal Future of our spiritual destiny, is to open the Heart to the Spirit in the present moment, and allow both past and future, untroubled by the turbulence of fear and desire, to unite in the Eternity of God.

The practice is: to let the past be what it is; to stop trying to make something out of it; to simply let it pass.

Ma'rifah al-Nafs

The Nafs is the past, however, only in terms of passing time. In her own nature she is always here; she has nothing to do with passing time, only with eternal time. The Nafs contains the entire experience and suffering of the world, the knowledge, the memory and the pain of all the ages, because she is the illusion of "other-than-

Allah." By the power of His Unity and His Love He carries her effortlessly, not as a burden to be bourn but as His intrinsic Knowledge, eternally one with Himself. He knows her not as illusion but as Reality—*Al-Haqq*.

When the Nafs arises, in all her power and cunning
    and despair,
Love her. Sweeten the roots of darkness.
Make her the mirror of Love,
The mirror of Allah.
When He gazed deep into Himself, and saw the universe,
And asked them Who their Lord was,
That was her.

She is sick now, sick with forgetfulness and jealous
    of her power;
Help her heal.
Help her remember.

The Nafs—unexpectedly—has a younger sister,
A sweet girl who remembers their Mother.
She is the Nafs too, like their Mother was.
She is full of love because she remembers her Mother,
Though her sister forgets.
She is no different from her sister,
Nor are these two any different from their Mother,
Nor their Mother from them.
So love them with the same Love
Because they are from the same Love—
    the Love of Allah.

Love them. There is no other work.

When you (as *al-Qalb*) begin to gain the power to see the Nafs, you are in the process of disentangling yourself from her—and to see someone exactly as she is is the first step toward loving her. This love, however—like all love—comes from Allah, not from you. When you are separated from the Nafs, then you can turn away from her towards God Alone, towards the One Who radiates Love like the sun sheds light. You can prostrate to that Love, and bathe in it. And she will be there in prostration beside you. In the light of His Love, Allah—as always—will witness the Nafs exactly as she is. Consequently every time you turn back to her you will see her less and less with your own seeing and more and more completely with His—with a seamless, perfect Witnessing that is totally objective, impartial and disinterested, totally accepting and liberating, totally suffused with Love and fundamentally inseparable from it. Love is the power that made everything want to exist; Love is the fire that consumes all the worlds. In the face of that Presence, the fires of lust, the fires of anger, all the passions that the Nafs brewed up in her secret laboratory of despair, are blotted out and annihilated in the perfection of the fire itself.

3

The Practice of Remembrance (*Dhikr*)

The Nature of *Dhikr*

THE INVOCATION OF THE NAME, the central practice of Sufism, possesses the virtues of simplicity, spiritual depth, and the ability to find a place in many different contexts, including solitary meditation, group practice, and the activities of daily life.

For the Invocation of the Name to become second nature, continuing even in sleep, is the proximate goal of the practice of it; nonetheless, the practice of *Dhikr* must not become merely automatic or mechanical. According to one Sufi authority, the *Dhikr* is not just some kind of internal tape recorder. One must both silently pronounce the Name, and also remember what it means. The word *Allah* must make present to us the *Reality* of Allah, otherwise we have turned the Name itself into an idol. And this encounter with the meaning of the Invocation cannot happen without a willing and conscious engagement of the Heart, which is both the spiritual center of the human psyche and the center-of-gravity of our conscious intent. The Heart, as a reality intrinsic to the human form, exists whether or not we are aware of it. And yet if we are not aware of it, it possesses only a virtual reality; in terms of our true spiritual condition, it is as if we had no Heart. If it did not pre-exist as a spiritual potential, we could never realize it: a Heart cannot be "constructed" by the will and the conscious mind operating in a vacuum. And yet without a conscious and ongoing intent to focus upon it, this spiritual potential can never be actualized, and thus cannot properly be called a "Heart." The Heart is the unconscious root of our conscious attention; because God has first remembered us in the act of creating us, He has made it possible for us to remember Him.

The Practice of Remembrance (Dhikr)

The Invocation of the Name of God is an ongoing act of willing and conscious attention, but it is also more than that. If it were not, if it depended upon nothing beyond raw self-will, it could never be constant, and would end by doing more harm than good. It is sometimes said that "God and His Name are One"; in other words, it is possible for me to become conscious of God's Presence through the invocation of His Name only because God's Name *is* His Presence. If the Name were not also the Presence, all our attempts to become aware of God's Presence by means of it would be futile; we would remain submerged in our own subjectivity. The Name is an objective factor, beyond our own habitual mental and emotional states; if it were not, it could in no way take our consciousness beyond these states, and place it in the objective Reality of God's Presence. (In Sufism, the sign of the Name's objectivity is the fact that in order to be fully effective the Name must be conferred by a spiritual Master.) And yet, without the conscious and ongoing work of paying attention to both the Name and Its meaning, that objective Reality would remain veiled for us. This is another instance, or application, of the principle of the reciprocity between God's grace and human effort. That God is objectively present, whether we attend to Him or not, is "Grace"; that we can only receive this Grace by having faith in It, and then by attending to It, and finally by reaching Certainty and Stability with regard to It, requires work. Invocation takes effort—and yet the whole of our effort is carried upon the great wave of ease and effortlessness and inevitability which is the sovereign Power of God—because, in the last analysis, God is the only Doer; we ourselves can do nothing. So *Dhikr* is both laborious and effortless, both conscious and totally beyond our consciousness, both something we do and something that is done for us and within us. Because of this dual quality of effort and effortlessness, the practice of Invocation is most naturally carried by the one human physical function in which the voluntary and the involuntary come closest to being perfectly united: the rising and falling of the breath.

If God were not consciously attending to us and thus "invoking *our* name" in the dimension of Eternity, we would be completely unable to invoke His Name in the dimension of time—if for no other reason than that we would never have come into existence in the first place. Thus the Invocation of the Name is both our willed and deliberate action, and also God's action within us. And while our action is always incomplete and imperfect, God's action within us is forever complete and perfect, eternally and instantaneously. The central work of invoking the Name of God, therefore, must be for us to *remember that He remembers us*, to progressively leave behind our imperfect acts of attention to Him, and place ourselves in the presence of His perfect Act of Attention to us—to *know ourselves as known*. In the words of Muhammad, peace and blessings be upon him: "Pray to God as if you saw Him, because even if you don't see Him, He sees you" [Bukhari; Muslim].

The Name of God makes present to us the Reality of Allah, and one way it may do this is by gathering and synthesizing the knowledge of Him that He has imprinted upon our Heart by means of the spiritual states He has sent us, each of which comes paired with an "intrinsic practice" proper to that state. For example, the recognition that God recreates the whole universe in every instant is naturally paired with the corresponding practice of letting oneself be completely transformed by Him, instant-by-instant, "like a corpse in the hands of a Washer of the Dead." The understanding that He is only imperfectly objective to me while I am perfectly objective to Him is paired with the practice of giving up trying to encompass God in knowledge while recognizing that He encompass me, and always has. And the feeling that God is absent (Absence being one of the modes of His Presence) is paired with a fierce longing to see His Face, ending in a resignation to His Will in either Presence or Absence, including a sacrifice of all one's willful attempts to command that Presence, in the recognition that they are only human conceptions of Him, and thus nothing but idols—at which point these idols are overturned and God's Presence unveiled. And these are only three examples of the innumerable modes in which He presents Himself to us in each spiritual moment, no two of which are alike. Some of these intrinsic practices are capable of being partly expressed in words; others are far too subtle for any such expression. But unless the Invocation takes us beyond these "contemplative unveilings" to the naked Presence of the Unveiled, it will degenerate into a rapid mental review of various bits of acquired philosophical knowledge, or an emotional melodrama of our love-affair with God, and the veil will fall again. What we already possess out of what God has given us is nothing; what He has yet in store for us is everything. And Who He Is in Himself is beyond even this everything. Love is beyond gratitude because gratitude veils Intimacy; Love is beyond hope because hope rejects Presence. "When I came to Love," said Rumi, "I became ashamed of everything I had ever said about Love." Because God and His Name are One, only God has the power, and the right, to speak that Name. Spiritual states and their intrinsic practices comprise the shadow of lover cast upon the face of the Beloved—but when Love arrives, that shadow is nowhere to be seen. Love (*Mahabbah*) is the door to Knowledge (*Ma'rifah*), and final Knowledge comes only by *Fana'*, Annihilation.

The Alchemy of the Emotions in *Dhikr*

The purpose of *Dhikr* is not to build a fantasy-palace of spiritual comfort with walls so thick that the clamoring of the Nafs is drowned out, leaving the soul in a state of complacency and self-satisfaction which is mistaken for spiritual peace (*Sakinah*); such an attempt is itself a deception of the Nafs.

We are asked to take our attention off the Nafs and place it upon Allah. But when the Nafs is at its most ferocious, when it is truly the *Nafs al-ammara bi'l su'*, this may not be possible. And it is even less possible for us to fight this Nafs blow by blow, hoping to pacify it by force; it is infinitely more powerful than we are. When the Nafs is in full war-cry it may assault us with intensely negative feelings: stark fear, violent anger, gnawing grief, abject despair. The practice in this case is: to be simultaneously aware of the Divine Name, which (in virtual terms) is the real Presence of Allah within the soul, and of the reactions of the Nafs to one's awareness of that Presence. In this simultaneous awareness, however, there is no essential division; to divide one's attention, giving part of it to Allah and another part to the Nafs, would be to set up the Nafs as a partner with Allah, this being the sin of *shirk*. In His Presence, the attention is not divided but unified, since He is the One (*Al-Ahad*), the Real (*Al-Haqq*). The

Presence of Allah is the Witness (*Al-Shahid*), and the Witness encompasses all that is witnessed, with no essential division between them. In that Presence, if we fully embrace it through self-forgetfulness, the egoic patterns and deep feelings which arise are not something ultimately other than God, something we always have to keep a separate lookout for, but are progressively revealed as the energies of *Al-Jalal*, the Majesty of God, which swim like sharks, or roll like waves, through the depths of the Divine Nature. The self-forgetfulness required is not lack of vigilance, which is immersion in the ego, or psychological repression, which is nothing but the self-imposed division of attention between what is acceptable to the ego and what is not; rather, it is the willingness to sacrifice one's self-concept. And as they move, those waves of Wrath are slowly—or swiftly—transformed into waves of Mercy.

Remembrance of God transmutes will, thought and feeling. Because it is a constant and never-ending practice performed under vow of obedience, it pacifies and strengthens the will. Because it is based on a Name which refers to and makes present a real Object, it transmutes thought. In the course of *Dhikr*, by which we remember that God *Is*, ordinary dissipated thought is transmuted into the question, "*if* God is, then Who and What is God?" The asking and answering of this question continues, constantly changing, in the light of God's presence, until "I-and-You" is transcended. In Sufism this spontaneous asking-and-answering, on a level deeper than dis-cursive thought, where question and answer are not successive but simultaneous, is termed *fikr*, contemplation. In the words of Ruzbe-han Baqli, "Thought for the ordinary man is plunging in the sea of illusion, while contemplation for the elect is being immersed in the ocean of understanding."

On the level of feeling, remembrance of God brings to conscious-ness the psychological knots or habitual patterns of psychophysical tension of which the individual Nafs is composed. We have created these psychological knots in part to prevent ourselves from feeling our true feelings. These patterns of tension operate on the level of the emotions by making us dissipated and manic, or congealed and depressed, or both. On the level of the will, they make us lazy and/ or driven; on the level of thought they render our minds formless

and chaotic, but also filled with hard fixed ideas—all for the purpose of hiding from us what we really feel, and what we might really
know. They are very good at what they do.

One of the primary ways that *Dhikr* cuts through this mass of
ghaflah, this "heedlessness," is by alchemizing the emotions. The
practice is to use whatever emotions the *Dhikr* brings up—fear,
anger, sorrow, elation, mellowness, shame, disgust—any and every
emotion which arises in a given moment, to deepen and empower
the *Dhikr.* Thus "the obstacles become the Path." The law here is:

> Emotions are Energy;
> *Dhikr* is Vigilance (*Muraqabah*).
> Vigilance invokes Energy;
> Energy either feeds heedlessness
> or further empowers Vigilance.
> Energy in the absence of Submission
>   (*Taslim*) is heedlessness.
> Energy, when met with Submission,
> is Vigilance.

In *Dhikr*, the will is dedicated to constancy of practice and the
Heart to constancy of attention. Once this dedication is established,
the emotions arise spontaneously and offer themselves to be transmuted. Initially they appear as distractions; ultimately they are
transmuted into fuel. The emotional and psycho-physical knots are
the fuel; the remembrance is the fire. The practice is to feed the fire.
Feed those knots to the *Dhikr* and it will burn brighter and hotter,
bringing more and more psycho-physical knots smoking and bubbling to the surface.

> The Fire is kindled;
> Hear it seethe and crackle.
>
> Suffering is the Fire:
> *Dhikr* fans the flames.
>
> *Dhikr* is the Fire,
> Suffering the fuel that feeds it.

Day and Night on the Sufi Path

My wandering attention
Lights like a fool on
This or that perishing thing—

Dhikr calls it home:
Home to the Fire.

My heart is the altar,
Dhikr the Fire,
My living flesh the sacrifice.

Every nest on this world's tree:
Thrown into the Fire.
No perch. No resting-place.
No home.

Don't let the Fire starve.
Never let it die.
Bring more suffering.
Bring more fuel.
What would not wish
To pass through that Fire
And become immortal?

Come, fear of death.
Come, terror of failure.
Come, grim loneliness.
Come, weight of the world.

To feel pain is to bear;
To bear is to suffer;
To suffer is to allow;
To allow is to prevail.

The Fire speaks the Name.
The Fire is the burning Name
Of Him Who speaks it.

Beaten on the anvil of it
I take the single shape
That is His will.
Sweet Fire. Pungent knowledge.

The Practice of Remembrance (Dhikr)

Fragrant wood-smoke
Leads the vigilant, listening world

Back to the Heart of the Fire.

Behind these knots of the Nafs are the true feelings, which are not to be confused with those so-called "positive" emotions, or habits of auto-stimulation or auto-sedation, that one is habitually using to distract oneself from emotional pain. These surface emotions are still part of the *Nafs al-ammara*; they are nothing but our way of avoiding the encounter with our psycho-physical knots, and are also a direct expression of these knots. Behind these knots of habitual self-avoidance are the true feelings themselves, the ones we may have spent a lifetime trying to stay unconscious of by distracting ourselves, creating false identities (which involve us with false situations in order to maintain and validate themselves) and generally polishing up our character-armor—notably *fear, hurt, anger* and *sadness*. No matter: feed them all to the *Dhikr.* Posit them not as shameful vices or terrible illnesses or impenetrable barriers to God, but as elements of spiritual fervor, of longing for union with the Beloved. There is no greater proof of love than to be willing to pass through the hell of your own soul in order to come closer to Allah—and only *Mahabbah*, the love of Allah, makes this passage possible. [NOTE: Depression, mania and panic are not feelings, but psycho-physical strategies for avoiding feelings. In depression we hide from them in a kind of auto-sedation; in mania we fly over the top of them; in panic we fight and/or flee them.]

On the level of the Nafs, *fear* is the denial that all things must return to Allah because they are without self-identity, and He the only Reality. On the level of the Heart, it is Vigilance in allowing no sense of self-existence to intrude upon the Presence of God. The fear of the Nafs is transmuted into the Vigilance of the Heart by means of Awe in the Presence of Allah.

On the level of the Nafs, *hurt* is the disappointment of expectations, the feeling of being teased, seduced or rejected by the person or situation we hoped to be united with. On the level of the Heart it is devotion to God as Beloved, whatever His actions may be, in the realization that, though He can never belong to us no matter what we do, we already belong to Him; it is to place ourselves in God's hands, "like a corpse in the hands of a Washer of the Dead." The hurt feelings of the Nafs, based on frustrated expectations, are transmuted into the Heart's submission to God's Acts by the practice of accepting, in humility, all events *as* God's Acts, and thus ultimately recognizing them all as the veils and manifestations of Mercy: If God's Mercy has precedence over His Wrath [Bukhari], then His Wrath is necessarily a servant of His Mercy. Because God is the Sovereign Good, every way He moves us, every way he turns our Heart, is good for us; the experience of Divine Wrath is based on our resistance, not His intent.

Anger on the level of the Nafs is the false arrogation to oneself of absolute power over circumstances, which is continually being frustrated, since we are not God; on the level of the Heart, it is God's righteous anger against this very arrogance, His overpowering demonstration that omnipotence is His alone. The anger of the Nafs is transmuted into the Heart's righteousness through swift obedience to God's command either to perform the specific action that confronts us, or else to renounce it completely.

Sadness on the level of the Nafs is the feeling that one is lost in an empty world, and that there is nothing beyond this world; on the level of the Heart it is the ability to repose deeply in Being. The sadness of the Nafs is transmuted into the Heart's repose by means of nostalgia for the Infinite, the longing for a distant Paradise, which culminates in the witnessing of the infinite generosity and abundance of God as present in this moment.

These four primal emotions are alchemized by God's grace consciously received and cooperated with, a transmutation that occurs on the border between God's real action and the apparent action of the Nafs—in this case most likely the *Nafs-i mulhama,* the "inspired Nafs", which some authorities place between the Accusing Nafs and the Nafs-at-Peace on the scale of spiritual development.

It is important to understand that fear, hurt, anger and sadness are not only subjective reactions but also objective realities; they represent forces operating on the psychic plane, beyond their momentary appearance in this or that individual—forces that are themselves reflections of metaphysical principles located on the

Spiritual plane. The ultimate metaphysical roots of fear, hurt, anger and sadness are to be found on the level of the most fundamental Divine Attributes; those who have a clear vision of these Attributes, as well as a vision of the nature of the Nafs in light of them, will be able to deal with these primal emotions from a standpoint of a transcendental objectivity. Allah is both Absolute and Infinite, both Transcendent (or Incomparable, *Tanzih*) and Immanent (or Comparable to created things, *Tashbih*). Therefore we can say that the four primal emotions are the four fundamental Divine Attributes as experienced through the veils of the Nafs. The ultimate root of *fear* is Allah as the Transcendent Absolute (*He neither begets not is begotten, and there is nothing to which He can be compared* [Q. 112:3–4]); of *hurt*, Allah as the Immanent Infinite (*Wherever you turn, there is the face of Allah* [Q. 2:115]); of *anger*, Allah as the Immanent Absolute (*We are nearer to him than his jugular vein* [Q. 50:16]); and of *sadness*, Allah as the Transcendent Infinite (*We have built the heaven with might, and We it is Who make the vast extent* [51:47]; *Everything is perishing except His Face* [Q. 28:88]). Before the Transcendent Absolute, manifest existence has no "rights"; it is as nothing; it is already annihilated. In the presence of the Immanent Infinite, all expectations are frustrated; closure cannot be made; to either possess or reject the loved object is impossible, since That One is simultaneously beyond one's grasp and at the root of one's desire. Before the Immanent Absolute, one's self-will is broken; God's Will alone prevails, because only what He Wills has the power to be. In the presence of the Transcendent Infinite, everything that can be desired lies beyond, and draws us beyond, all that can be seen or known in the realm of formal existence. The practice, then, is to recognize *fear* as the presence of the truth that only God exists, and submit to being annihilated; to recognize *hurt* as the presence of the truth that God exceeds and violates all one's expectations, thus allowing oneself to be passively moved in accordance with His Will, like a corpse in the hands of a Washer of the Dead; to recognize *anger* as God's command to us to cut the throat of self-will, instantly, and stand in wait for the dawning of His Will, equally ready to actively cooperate with it, or to renounce action entirely if that be His wish; and to recognize *sadness* as a call from God to let what is dying in us die completely, and to rest, undying, in the depths of the Divine Nature, renouncing all longing for future solace and accepting instead the influx of present Mercy, in the realization that, while *all is perishing except His Face,* nonetheless *Wherever you turn, there is the face of God.*

Due to these correspondences with the metaphysical order, any feelings which go to feed Remembrance instead of distracting one from it may be progressively transmuted into, or unveiled as, objective realities which transcend the subjective psyche—the reflections, in the feeling-substance of the soul, of the Names or Attributes of God.

"Negative" emotions are the faces of *Mahabbah*, the Love of Allah, as veiled by the Nafs; as we begin to realize this, they are transmuted into avenues leading to Love's realization. Conscious *anger* is the defense of Love against all that would violate it, especially in one's own soul. Conscious sadness—*dard* ("pain" in the Persian Sufi usage)—is the longing for the (apparently) absent Beloved. Conscious *hurt* is the ability to welcome the "unfairness" of the Beloved, all the plotting, the teasing, and the slaps. And conscious *fear* is the clear recognition, and full acceptance, that end of True Love is Death. According to the *hadith*, "Allah is Beautiful, and loves Beauty" [Muslim]. His nature is Beauty, and whatever is beautiful is intrinsically lovable; this is why the Sufis most often call Him "the Beloved" and not "the Lover." Yet, in the words of the *hadith*, Allah Himself *loves* Beauty; this Love is His eternal act of Self-witnessing. And in the identical way, God loves man. In the Qur'an [Q. 20:39–40, Arberry's translation] God says to Moses, *And I loaded on thee love from me, and to be formed in My sight.* Moses, here, stands for the Human Form, *al-Insan al-Kamil,* which is formed and created, by means of Love, as God's eternal act of witnessing His own Reality.

God loves man because God's rapture before His own Beauty is the essence of man; this rapture of Divine Self-regard is the first archetype and final end of all human emotion. Therefore, as human emotion is alchemized, "the obstacles become the Path." In the words of Mansur al-Hallaj, "The gnostic's ladder is his Nafs. His essence is the gateway to Union with God's Essence."

Metaphysically, the truth that "the obstacles are the Path" is based on the nature of God as both transcendent and immanent. Given that God is transcendent and unknowable, He is realized only by *Fana'*—by the letting go of the perishing, contingent self and the world it perceives, till nothing but Allah remains. This is the *Ma'rifah* of Allah. Yet the other side of *Fana'* is *Baqa'*. The duality of subject-and-object, based on our false sense of self-existence, is annihilated in *Fana'*—but in *Baqa'*, it "returns"; it appears in the realm of form, though understood to be unreal in the realm of Essence. Consequently, where once it was a veil over Reality, it is now a manifestation of Reality. What were once the obstacles to the realization of the Divine are revealed as aspects of the Divine; this is the *Ma'rifah* of the Nafs. And since this revelation, because it is objectively true whether or not we ever experience it, is virtual from the very beginning, the obstacles can indeed become the Path.

Hard, painful emotions are a lot closer to *Mahabbah* than is the intoxication of the self-satisfied Nafs, still veiled from *Ma'rifah*. To face such feelings directly is to practice spiritual poverty, *fakr*, in its most concrete form. When intolerable feelings arise, and the power to avoid them is nowhere to be seen, then God is our only refuge. And one consequence of such spiritual poverty is that we will not make the mistake of thinking that we can fight the Nafs with our own self-will; not only is our willfulness too weak a weapon to overcome the enemy, it is in fact an aspect of that same enemy. Our responsibility is to be present to the Presence of God, and let That One take the field against the rebellious Nafs on His Own initiative, no matter how much suffering this might initially entail. This is one meaning of the Qur'anic verse, *You did not slay them, but God slew them; and when thou threwest, it was not thyself that threw, but God threw* [8:15], alluding to the moment at the battle of Badr when the prophet Muhammad (peace and blessings be upon him) threw a handful of pebbles at the enemy, after which the tide of battle turned in favor of the Muslims.

Mahabbah, Dard, and Dhikr

Just as there is opaque thought and translucent thought, so there is opaque feeling and translucent feeling. When one is occupied by opaque thought, the *Dhikr* bounces off the Heart like hailstones off a slab of rock. When one is filled with opaque feeling, the *Dhikr* sticks to the Heart like pebbles sprinkled into a field of mud. But when *Mahabbah* arrives, opaque thought is dissolved; at the same time the feelings become subtle and permeable, such that the *Dhikr* sinks fully into the Heart, and keeps going deeper and deeper. That's when the polarity between thought and feeling is dissolved; thinking and feeling are perfectly united in *knowing*, opening the door to *Ma'rifah*.

In the Persian language the word *dard* means "pain, sadness, torment", often used by Sufis to connote "longing, nostalgia" for the Beloved—the nostalgic longing for Allah as we knew Him in preeternity, for the way we were before we came into existence, before the moment when Allah asked us *Am I not your Lord?*, to which we all answered *Yea!* [Q. 7:172] One way of dealing with emotional pain and sadness is to recognize it not as the sadness of "me" but as the sadness of *existence*. Your pain is not unique to you; it's merely your portion of the pain of all things, lost and struggling in separation from Allah, and longing for Him. If you can experience your pain in this way it is transformed from self-pity into compassion; a Heart filled with this *dard*, this "sweet sorrow", provides the perfect matrix— subtle, permeable, resonant, translucent—for the deepening of the *Dhikr*. (True remorse and repentance may have a similar effect.)

One purpose of music in Sufism—in the form of the *sama'* or spiritual concert—is to unfold this sort of subtle feeling-matrix for the growth of the remembrance of Allah; another is to volatilize the inner consciousness, to transform it from fixed form into flowing rhythm, allowing for *siyaha* or spiritual "traveling"—the passage onward from state to state and station to station. (This is the inner meaning of the *Hajj*.) In the presence of the spiritual power of music and rhythm, moved this way and that by the waves of it, we become like corpses in the hands of a Washer of the Dead; tombstones on our heads (the allusion here is to the "turning" of the Mevlevi dervishes, whose tall hats represent tombstones), we rise up and dance.

The Practice of Remembrance (Dhikr)

Dhikr vs. Ego/Evil

Evil is relative non-existence, which is why any view of Reality proposed by evil is necessarily absurd.

Anything that believes it can exist in its own right outside of the will of Allah is in a state of total despair; it "exists" only as a negation. This despair goes beyond the mere act of jumping into a bottomless pit; it is more like a bottomless pit jumping into itself, forever. This terminal yet endless negation is the true nature and description of any *ego*. To speak as precisely as possible, the self-commanding-to-evil is not the ego, but the ego *is* the evil to which it commands—the evil of believing oneself to be God, either euphorically or depressively (both beliefs being deeply unconscious), and thus falling into the profoundest state of unreality it is possible to imagine.

Because the ego is a negation of Truth as well as of Being, it generates lies and illusions that approach what might be called the degree of "absolute falsehood"—approach it but never reach it, because such a state does not really exist to be reached. Among these lies are the following: that the ego is not really despair and self-destruction but courageous self-affirmation; not total helplessness but titanic power; not non-existence outside of Allah but virtual divinity in itself. The "glamour and magnificence of evil", the "heroic" stance of "rather rule in Hell than serve in Heaven", as Satan put it in Milton's *Paradise Lost*, are therefore nothing but a (near)-complete negation of Truth—which is the only view of reality possible to something that is equally a (near)-complete negation of Being.

The essence of Reality—Allah, in other words—is Love and Truth; consequently a negation of Reality will despise Love and hate Truth. You can't fight a negation because to fight it you must hate it, and it *is* hatred, intrinsically; consequently to fight it is to participate in it and capitulate to it. And you can't refute a negation either, because to refute it you must grant it the capacity to hold or be an articulate conception of Truth capable of being refuted, which is something it can never hold and never be, given that it is nothing in itself but the attempted, though entirely futile, refutation of all Truth. To fight it, to refute it, is to grant it reality, which is precisely what it wants you to do because it possesses no reality of its own.

What, then, is to be repented of? The sin here, the essential sin of

95

the ego which also creates the ego, is to let one's primal attention be hijacked by something that is not only toxic to contemplate but doesn't even exist in the first place. *Attention* is the root of our faithfulness to, and participation in, both Love and Truth—which are names for Reality (*Al-Haqq*)—which is another name for Allah. The abyss of evil which is the ego is infernally attractive precisely because it *sucks*; it is a void in Reality that demands that we grant it the reality it lacks by paying attention to it, and then proceeds to destroy any reality it may have stolen through this act of perverted attention, after which it goes on to use this destruction only to increase its demand.

How is this repentance to be accomplished? It is accomplished only by remembering Allah, in the recognition that this remembrance is a gift of Allah and happens only by the power of Allah. That's it; that's the whole work.

May Allah remember us, and so inspire us to remember Him.

Stages of *Dhikr*

The *hadith* "Pray to God as if you saw Him, because even if you don't see Him, He sees you," can be taken to refer to three distinct levels of *Dhikr*. To begin with, "I" am speaking God's Name, struggling to remain conscious of Him, or asking Him to reveal His Presence—to "me." The "God" I am dealing with on this level is what Ibn al-'Arabi called "the God created in belief." He is inseparable from my self-image; in a way He is a projection of it; contemplating Him on this level is the same thing as contemplating myself: this is the meaning of "*as if* you saw Him." Nonetheless, as Ibn al-'Arabi points out, God still accepts the prayers we make to our image of Him, even if that image is an illusion—because, in another sense, it really *is* Him. God, as the Essence of all forms, is indeed worshipped—though in a veiled and blameworthy way—through the worship paid to idols, even if the idol is our own self-image. Those who worship God in the form of their own self-images will experience Him as Wrath, but if they were to allow that Wrath to dominate them and hurl them beyond the level of personal and religious idolatry, it would be revealed as a face of Mercy.

At a later stage of the *Dhikr*, the one represented by "even if you don't see Him," we realize that our image of God is really only the projected shadow of our ego, and begin to encounter God as He is. At this point the words of Abu Bakr apply: "To know that God cannot be known is to know God." The limited, egotistical "knower" is bewildered, neutralized; the unknowability of God consumes all our attempts to know God in the fire of Knowledge itself; this is one aspect of or approach to *Fana'*, Annihilation. Here we are no longer invoking God's Name; rather, God is invoking His own Name within us. The Name at this station no longer refers to a separate Object as perceived by a separate subject; God and His Name are One. This is an aspect of the *Ma'rifah* of Allah.

At the final stage, the stage of "He sees you," the only Witness is God, and God witnesses nothing and no-one but Himself. At this station, what was once "you" is now nothing but the Name. You—as witnessed directly by God, not conjecturally by yourself—are God's Name, or one of His Names. This is the perfection of *Fana'* (Annihilation in God), which is inseparable from *Baqa'* (Subsistence in God), the final stage of realization. "He sees you" is, however, not only *Baqa'* as the ultimate station; it is also virtual, and effective, from the beginning, and thus functions as the hidden Lodestone of the Path. It is not something that *becomes* true, it is something that *is* true. Truths are not established in time; they are realized in Eternity.

Once we reach certainty as to the reality of Allah as the eternal Source of our existence, He becomes the sole Object of remembering. And when this remembrance-of-Allah is perfected, He becomes the sole Rememberer as well; the limited subjective selfhood that veiled the spiritual Heart from remembering God is first forgotten (in *Fana'*), and then transformed into the object of God's remembering (in *Baqa'*), an object which is fundamentally none other than God Himself. To catch a glimpse of the reality of God while forgetting yourself is to realize that you are seen more fully and more penetratingly by Him than you could ever see yourself: *Remember Me and I will remember you* [Q. 2:152]. And such Remembering in reality begins not with you, but with Him: *It is indeed We who have sent down the Remembrance* [Q. 15:9]. To remember God until God becomes the only Rememberer is to unveil the *Nafs al-mutma'inah* as the mirror of Allah, as seen through the Eye of the Heart. This is the *Ma'rifah* of the Nafs. In the words of Ibn al-'Arabi, from his *Futuhat al-Makiyya*:

> [T]he recipient sees nothing other than his own form in the mir-ror of the Reality. He does not see the Reality Itself, which is not possible, although he knows that he may see only his form in it. . . . If you have experienced this you have experienced as much as is possible for created being, so do not seek to weary yourself in any attempts to proceed higher than this, for there is nothing higher, nor is there beyond the point you have reached anything except the Pure, the Undetermined, the Unmanifested. In seeing your true self, He is your mirror and you are His mirror in which He sees His Names and their determinations, which are nothing other than Himself.

Dhikr begins as a search for God. Later it becomes the only way we can withstand the power of God's gifts. Next the rememberer is annihilated; only the Remembered remains. At the end, the Remembered becomes the Rememberer—as He always was.

◇

You are not performing the *Dhikr*; it is really your shaykh who is performing it for you, and within you.

But, in reality, it is not your shaykh who is performing *Dhikr*, only Allah is performing it: no one but That One can remember That One.

But Allah is not really performing *Dhikr* either; since He perfectly IS Himself, He need not remember Himself. Rather, He is gradually replacing your Remembrance of Him with His Presence within you.

◇

You can aspire (from a distance) to the *Ma'rifah* of Allah and also intend it—though not without a degree of self-deception—because you already have some notion of what Knowledge is, and even an inkling of what Knowledge of Allah might be, since every other form of knowledge is derived from it; and what can be conceived can also be intended.

You can aspire to *Fana'* but you cannot intend it, because it is impossible for you to have a notion of what Annihilation might be.

And you can neither intend nor aspire to *Ma'rifah* of the Nafs, because the one who would intend it or aspire to it must already have been annihilated in Allah for *Ma'rifah* of the Nafs to dawn. You can look toward Annihilation—though you cannot actually see it—but you cannot look toward what is beyond Annihilation.

So the question arises: why mention things that can neither be aspired to nor intended? We mention them so that you won't resist them, through misunderstanding and bewilderment, when they come knocking at your door.

◇

Easy does it. It is possible to perform the *Dhikr* as a way of imploring Allah to make His Presence known to you, as if you were to awake in the middle of the night and start begging for the sun to rise. And certainly He can manifest Himself at any time and in any way He chooses. But it is probably better to perform it purely as a recognition, as you would if it were the hour of dawn and you were simply acknowledging: "Ah—here comes the sun."

A Short Form of the Path
(One of Many Possible)

Dhikr, the remembrance of Allah, leads to *Sakinah*, Tranquility-of-Heart, by which the Nafs is held in check.

Sakinah makes it possible to intuit the constant Presence of Allah, thus leading to *Mahabbah* or Love of God, in the face of which the Nafs is set aside and largely forgotten. It is possible to forget her now because *Mahabbah* has the power to pacify and satisfy her, until she stops making demands.

Mahabbah leads to *Ma'rifah* of Allah, Knowledge of God, through which the Nafs is annihilated.

The Annihilation (*Fana'*) of the Nafs as subject—the Nafs identified as "me"—leads to the Subsistence (*Baqa'*) of the Nafs as object —as "him"—the witnessing Subject of which is God alone: this is *Ma'rifah* of the Nafs. And God witnesses only God.

99

From the opposite point of view, however, it is also possible to say that the unconscious first dawning of *Ma'rifah* is what produces *Mahabbah*, that the dawning of *Mahabbah* produces the *Sakinah*, that it is the *Sakinah* that pacifies the Nafs, and that the pacification of the Nafs is what allows for constancy in *Dhikr*. Ultimately it is not you who are practicing the remembrance, but Allah Himself.

These stations, however, cannot be reached by simply willing to walk from one to the other; this is part of the deception of maps. Allah brings us from Remembrance to Tranquility, from Tranquility to Love, from Love to Knowledge, and—by Annihilation—from Knowledge to Subsistence as the Object of His Knowledge (always remembering that He knows only Himself) through many vicissitudes, many alterations, many nights and days. As Maghrebi said, we walk the Path with God's feet—and each of His strides is longer than the distance from horizon to horizon. We do not possess the scope to measure them, much less the foresight to anticipate them. All we can do is observe the *adab* of the Day by day, and the *adab* of the Night by night.

Nonetheless, if Allah wills Aspiration for you, then you can Aspire—and if you do in fact Aspire, it is because He is willing that Aspiration for you in this very moment—so be Vigilant to know His Will.

In terms of the *Dhikr*, Aspiration begins as Constancy in the practice of the silent recitation of the Name of Allah. (This Constancy can even be aided by various tricks of memory, such as remembering to pronounce the Name whenever you open or close a door or pass through a doorway, in line with the verse *enter houses by their doors* [Q.2:189].)

When you notice yourself performing the *Dhikr*, then you can consciously anticipate the arrival of Spiritual Tranquility, the *Sakinah*.

When the *Sakinah* descends, when the clamor of the Nafs begins to be pacified, then you can consciously anticipate the arrival of the *Mahabbah*, the Love of Allah, the moment when Tranquility opens to Divine Beauty.

As the *Mahabbah* deepens the moment will come when you can ask for the *Ma'rifah* and consciously anticipate its arrival. This does not mean, however, that Knowledge ever surpasses Love or leaves it behind. All gifts come freely from Love, and no greed or craving, for Knowledge or for anything else, can survive in the face of it. *Mahabbah* itself opens into *Ma'rifah* because Love is Intimacy with the Truth; *Ma'rifah* is the most complete expression of *Mahabbah* because Knowledge is the highest form of Love.

◇

In the presence of the Name of Allah, the Nafs progressively abandons the illusion of her self-determination, the false notion that she does or ever could exist outside Him. When this illusion begins to dissolve, she renounces her willfulness and makes *sujud* (prostration) to Him. And when this notion dissolves completely and the Nafs is annihilated, then she *is* Him.

◇

(And that's not the secret of the Nafs either—
Not by a long shot.
The *Ma'rifah* of the Nafs is Black Knowledge;
It overturns the Scales.
I dreamt I saw a woman,
And between her and me was Hell:
Before Allah took him
My Master was a snake-charmer.)

101

Part II

THE SCIENCE OF SPIRITUAL STATES

A Paraphrase of William Blake

I question not the doctrines and practices of my religion
Any more than I would question a window concerning sight:
I look through them, not with them.

Preface to Part Two

Assuredly in the creation of the Heavens and of the Earth; and in the alternation of night and day; and in the ships which pass through the sea with what is useful to men; and in the rain which God sendeth down from Heaven, giving life by it to the Earth after its death . . . are signs for those who understand. [Q. 2:159/2:164]

He causeth the night to pass into the day, and He causeth the day to pass into the night: and He knoweth the very secrets of the bosom! [Q. 57:6/57:6]

Allah holds the Heart between his two fingers, and turns it however he will.

Hadith [Ibn Majah]

T HE UNIVERSE AND HUMAN LIFE are woven on the loom of alternation: day and night, winter and summer, inhalation and exhalation, birth and death. *And all things We have created by pairs, that haply ye may reflect.* [Q: 51:49] This alternation or periodic motion stretches from the wheeling of galaxies to the oscillation of atoms; light itself is a wave with peaks and troughs. Likewise the spiritual Heart within us moves through its own seasons, through which Allah draws it toward Him. But if we don't recognize the alterations of our spiritual life as an intrinsic aspect of it, but instead see them only as imperfections or distractions, then we will end by unconsciously resisting the action of Allah in our lives. The only way to finally transcend change is to embrace it.

The Sufis have always recognized the intrinsic nature of the alteration of spiritual states, and developed a science of their forms and meanings. According to one view of the matter out of many possible, the most important pairs of states—remembering that not all states are paired like this—are Gathering and Dispersion, Expansion and Contraction, Fluctuation and Stability, Intoxication and Sobriety, Intimacy and Awe, Presence and Absence, and Annihilation and Subsistence. One effect of these alternations in the spiritual life is to prevent us from identifying with a particular state, from (so-to-speak) *becoming* Awe, or Expansion, or Dispersion, or Absence. As alternations, these states are the action of God in our hearts; as *fixations* they are elements of the ego, the *Nafs al-ammara* or "Commanding Self." The Heart submitted to Allah accepts these fluctuations as the results of His action, letting them come and go as they will, but the rebellious soul is always trying to hold on to one state and run away from another. In the words of Ibn Abbad of Ronda, "The fool is one who strives to procure at each instant some result that Allah has not willed." A further effect of this fluctuation of spiritual states is to prevent us from attempting to see or understand Allah through only one or a few of our "favorite" states, falsely identifying Him with a particular qualification of our own consciousness and forgetting that *He neither begets nor is begotten, and there is nothing to which He might be compared* [Q. 112:3–4]. Here we can see how Allah's *Tashbih*, His Immanence, His Comparability to all things—even a gnat, according to the Qur'an [Q. 2:26]—is inseparable from His *Tanzih*, His Transcendent Incomparability, which is why Ibn al-'Arabi can speak of Allah's freedom from the limitation of form as pervading all forms:

> My heart can take on any form:
> A meadow for gazelles,
> A cloister for monks,
> The *temenos* of the idols,
> The Kaaba for the circling pilgrim,
> The tables of the Torah,
> The leaves of the Qur'an.
> My creed is Love;
> Wherever its caravan turns along the way,
> That is my belief and my faith.

We need to understand that the distinctions between these *ahwal* are not hard and fast; they can be viewed from many different perspectives. Absence can be considered as the most intense form of Intoxication; the perfection of Stability, that of Sobriety, that of Gathering and that of Presence can be treated as virtually identical, etc. Nor is the order in which these fourteen *ahwal* or *maqamat* are presented necessarily the only valid one, though almost all accounts end with the stations of Annihilation and Subsistence. Sufi metaphysics and psychology have a great inner consistency, but they should never be seen as a closed system; to do so would be to arbitrarily, and faithlessly, limit the modes in which Allah is able to manifest Himself to the human soul. In the words of the Qur'an, *Every day doth some new work employ Him* [Q. 55:29/55:29]—and "day" in this context can be taken as referring to the *waqt*, the present moment of spiritual time. Spiritual time is not reducible to clock time, nor is the spiritual moment simply the empty space between memory and anticipation—though this space, if we truly empty it, may make room for the true *waqt* to dawn. Rather, it is *a particular instance of Eternity* intended by a specific Act of Allah (Allah *Al-Samad*, the Eternal) and manifesting one of His specific Names or Qualities, unique and never-to-be-repeated. Allah in his Name *Al-Wahid*, the Unique, cannot and will not repeat Himself; to do so would be to show Himself limited by what He creates—which is impossible, seeing that He is *Malik al-Mulk*, the King of Absolute Sovereignty. Each moment is unique because each is an act of *Al-Wahid* and an instance of His Presence.

All alterations in states or succession of stations can be seen, from one point of view, as aspects of the state, or station, of *Talwin*, Fluctuation. In terms of the Nafs, Fluctuation is a blameworthy instability and flightiness that destroys all Vigilance and prevents us from contemplating Divine realities—from reposing in, and letting ourselves be qualified by, the Names of Allah. It is an equal mixture of fear and complacency, of constant panicky flight and constant dreamy sedation. The drug that sedates us, the withdrawal from which produces fear and anxiety, is *al-Dunya*, This World, which in reality is nothing but the projection of the unconscious Nafs, into, and as, the realm of conditional existence. Stability, on the other hand, is one of the main goals of spiritual development; without *Tamkin*, Stability of Heart, there can be no steady awareness of the Presence of Allah, and consequently no Knowledge of Allah, no *Ma'rifah*.

On the other hand, from the point of view of the Heart, Fluctuation is the way we walk the spiritual Path. It is the steps we take, first with the right foot, then with the left. In the words of the *hadith*, "Allah holds the Heart between his two fingers, and turns it however he will." Seen in this way, Fluctuation is what prevents us from petrifying in a single station that allows no further progress; without Fluctuation, all stations would eventually be transformed into fixations, idols—into aspects of the negative side of Stability, Stability according to the Nafs. Fluctuation seems to be poles apart from positive Stability, Stability of Heart, and from one perspective this is true. But if we know how to relate to it correctly—"like a corpse in the hands of a Washer of the Dead"—Fluctuation is the only power that can *establish* Stability of Heart. Non-resistance to alteration is the one thing that can reveal the single Source, the single immutable Doer behind every change. The Heart continues to revolve, but now it knows and sees exactly what it is orbiting—the *Qutb* or Pole of the turning Heart, which is *al-Ruh*, the Spirit.

So the practice is: to totally submit to, and therefore fully witness (or we could just as well say "fully witness, and therefore totally submit to"), each change in psychic state, seeking nothing and excluding nothing, seeing all these changes as the direct manifestation of the Will of Allah. Instead of seeking "spiritual" states and fleeing from "unspiritual" ones, we recognize all states as Acts of Allah, as either merciful gifts or purifying chastisements. It is precisely this that constitutes the unveiling of the Spiritual Heart. "Allah holds the Heart between his two fingers, and He turns it as He will." As we have seen above, the Arabic word for "heart" is Qalb, and derives from the root QLB or QBL, which embraces a complex of meanings including "to turn, to turn around, to overturn, to turn back, to return." Submission to changing psychic states as Acts of God posits Allah as an Absolute Reality transcending psychic states. This understanding is an *insight*, not a belief—an insight that is available only to those who have first fulfilled all the duties God has laid upon them through the shari'ah; in order to meet Khidr, first you have to be Moses [cf. Q. 18:60–82]. If man's extremity is God's opportunity, then the end of man's will is the beginning of God's Will—and no-one can come to the end of human will except by the *willing* submission to God's commands. Before the vision dawns of all states as

Acts of God (and it will normally dawn in a gradual way) we are required to deal with psychic states *as if* they were the products of secondary causes: the state of the world, past experiences, present circumstances, individual psychology and physiology, the actions of other people, angelic and demonic influences, etc. But we must also make ourselves ready to receive the insight that they are ultimately the sovereign acts of the First Cause alone.

The ability to submit to psychic states as Acts of Allah succeeds, embraces and perfects the ability to submit to outer events as Acts of Allah, which normally comes first. Submission to changing psychic states as Allah's present action transforms those states from veils into unveilings. It posits Allah as the sole Witness of those states, according to the prophetic *hadith* "pray to Allah as if you saw Him, because even if you don't see Him, He sees you." To submit to changing psychic states as Acts of Allah is to know that Allah sees me—and *to know myself as known is to know the Knower*. To know myself as witnessed by Allah is to unveil the Absolute Witness; to submit to changing psychic states as Acts of Allah is to attribute the power of creation only to Him, not to myself or to the Dunya. It is to witness Allah in His present act of creating both me and the world around me. If I know myself, witnessed by Allah, as presently created and maintained by His direct action and attention, then all my "subjective" states become objectified. I have transferred the act of witnessing from the site of the illusory ego to the site of the Allah as *Al-Shahid*, the Absolute Witness; this is one of the many meanings of the *hadith* "he who knows himself knows his Lord."

The Function and the Danger of Spiritual States

Before we go any further it is necessary to point out that there is a danger in talking about the *ahwal*—the danger of substituting shadow for substance, imagination for reality. When traveling a spiritual Path that speaks of, and seems to be based upon, "higher states of consciousness", it is nearly impossible for us (at least to begin with) not to imagine what these states, or stations, might be like. The result of this nearly unconscious imagination is that we tend to generate for ourselves various self-created spiritual "ideals" that we then try to turn from fantasy into reality. And when our attempts to produce this great transformation fail, as they inevitably will, the resulting frustration can lead to any number of negative results, including misguided excursions into various psychic states that present themselves as spiritual, a descent into ruthless self-will in an attempt to crush our lower nature and "take heaven by storm", or a stunned exhaustion that opens us to spiritual despair. The cure for this malady is to accept, with resignation, trust and vigilance, every state we experience as coming directly from Allah, until we have learned how to forget the states and remember Him. Yet only a valid shaykh can really administer this cure; to the degree that he places us in the real Presence of Allah, the fantasy versions of spiritual states find no foothold, and ultimately dissolve.

Spiritual states alternate because the Heart turns. Allah turns the Heart toward a different Divine Name in every *waqt*, every moment of spiritual time, so as to untie the knots of the Nafs, one by one. *He* turns the Heart; we do not. Our job is not to seek different states, but to concentrate our attention upon Allah as *Al-Ahad*, the One. States supervene because the Nafs has many crystallizations and identifications—many idols. As the Qur'an says, *These are mere names: you and your fathers named them thus: God hath not sent down any warranty in their regard. A mere conceit and their own impulses do they follow* [Q. 53:23/53:23]. It is Allah's Unity that produces the many spiritual states we experience because, in order to draw the Heart toward It, His Unity must address our multiplicity, in every particular, so as to neutralize it and synthesize it: only unity-of-Heart can witness Unity Itself. Allah appears to be alternately Present and Absent, Merciful and Wrathful, Deceptive and Explicit; these changes, however, do not belong to Him, but to the Heart disturbed by the turbulence of the Nafs. The Nafs is flighty, fickle and unable to keep her promises, but Allah is constant. The alternating spiritual states He sends are for the purpose of "burning out" various aspects of our self-identification, the names we have given things without warrant from Allah, so as to retrieve the treasures of Divine Wisdom the Nafs has stolen from Him (or *thinks* it has stolen) and hidden away in its dark cave. The Nafs is only fickle, however, because our knowledge of her is partial; that's what presents her to us as the *Nafs al-ammara bi'l su'* or "self commanding to evil" (the unconscious ego, the passions), and the *Nafs al-law-wamah* or "Accusing Self" (the troubled, but impotent, conscience). The Nafs incites us to evil as if to prove that we are blind to her many aspects; the substance of her accusation is that we do not fully understand her. Yet all the temptations and accusations she sends are only for the purpose of hiding herself from us, as if she were ashamed of her condition. She tries to place us under her power and dominance because she is ashamed of having lost her pre-eternal station as the One Soul of All, of having been robbed of her divine status through our identification with her—even though this identification had to happen if we were ever to allow ourselves to be created by Allah as apparently separate beings in this world. When a young man informed the great woman Sufi Rabi'ah al-'Adawiyyah that he had never committed a sin, her answer was: "Alas, my son, thine existence is a sin wherewith no other sin may be compared."

Virtues

As we have already seen, the acquisition of the virtues in Sufism is sometimes described as being "qualified with the Names of Allah." These qualifications, however, are not *possessions*, seeing that it is impossible for a human being to possess attributes that are proper to Allah alone; consequently it is better, for example, to meditate upon Allah as *Al-Jabbar*, the Compeller, than upon ourselves as obedient, upon Allah as *Al-Mu'min*, the Faithful and Trustworthy, than on ourselves as capable of trust. Rather, at every point where a part of our ego—our habitual self-definition—is deconstructed, a particular Divine virtue takes its place; whatever is annihilated in its self-nature becomes an open door, allowing a ray of the Spirit to shine through. Vices are all elements of self-identity; the reason they are so difficult to overcome is because we think they are "us"—and they certainly do their best to convince us that without them we would not exist, or at least not be able to function. When our vices desert us, we no longer feel like our old familiar selves, especially since the virtues that replace them are elements of a Presence that we can in no way identify with or name with our name. When this Presence is established in the Heart, our actions no longer belong to us; the virtue or power that works through us is something we can't take credit for; it is the power of Another. When we imagine our familiar selves acquiring unfamiliar powers, we make those imagined powers part of our self-identity, effectively blocking their development. This is why it is best to contemplate the Names of Allah not as gifts we hope to receive but as eternal attributes of the Deity.

Virtues as Stations

A virtue established in the Heart is the same thing as a station, a *maqam*. Virtues are announced as states; when the repetition of a particular state is no longer necessary because it has dissolved the vice, or aspect of the ego, that was blocking the virtue out of which it grew, that virtue becomes established as a station. Below we will be analyzing the sort of states that appear as alternating pairs. These, however, in no way exhaust the states of the Heart, which are effectively innumerable; from one point of view, each *waqt* or moment of spiritual time is formed around a particular state, unique and never-to-be-repeated. Some of the more universally-recognized of the spiritual states include Repentance, Abstinence, Renunciation, Wariness, Vigilance, Discernment, Humility, Sincerity, Constancy, Gratitude, Patience, Trust in God, Aspiration, Veracity, Zeal, Courage, Mercy, Altruism, Constancy in Love, Generosity, Compassion, Shame, Submission, Reverence, Contentment, Serenity, Spiritual Poverty, Detachment, Discretion, Fear of God, Hope, Trustworthiness, Courtesy, Justice, Manliness, Dignity . . . and many more could be added. Ansari, in his famous *Sad Maydan* (*One-Hundred Fields of Battle*), enumerates a hundred different stations based on as many virtues. In the West we tend to see such virtues strictly in terms of morality—that is, as little more than arbitrary rules to be followed. It is much harder for us, apparently, to understand them also as states of mystical consciousness, as *ways of knowing*. This may be due to the fact that the culture of western Christianity—possibly following St. Augustine—has tended to separate the will from the intellect, and consequently to see a particular vice more as a will to transgress than as the result of a specific error or delusion or darkening of consciousness (modern anti-traditional Islam certainly shares this shortcoming), whereas in reality—as the theologians of Eastern Orthodox Christianity maintain—it is always both. Fear of God, for example, is based on the present knowledge that Allah is the only One who can claim Being intrinsically, that if I make this claim while in His Presence I am in the position of a thief who has just been apprehended, and whose stolen Being is about to be forcibly and shockingly re-possessed by its Owner. Likewise Altruism grows out of the knowledge that Allah is the Most Generous of the Generous, that

> He does not hoard the Being that is His by right,
> but endlessly gives of Himself as the sun gives light.

And Aspiration founds itself on the knowledge that "if I approach Allah walking He approaches me running" [Bukhari], that the Goal of the Path, which seems infinitely distant, is actually present in this moment, and that my intent and impulse to seek Allah is actually a reflection of His eternal seeking of me—which is, in Reality, an eternal finding. And Dignity is the direct result of the realization that "Heaven and earth cannot contain Him, but the Heart of His believing slave can contain Him."

Four Examples of Spiritual Stations Recognized by the Sufis

Shame (Haya')

Shame as a spiritual state is the Heart's recognition of a deficiency or an excess in our relationship with Allah—in other words, our discernment of the existence of an idol and of ourselves as willingly worshipping that idol. The false shame of the Nafs involves us in what we are ashamed of and perpetuates it; the true shame of the Heart immediately corrects this imbalance and disappears along with it—which is to say that the *hal* of Shame comes from beyond the Accusing Self and frees us from that Self.

Shame at its most intense appears at the apogee of Expansion or Dispersion. When Allah's Command that we expand into all the wonders of His Beauty and Generosity is exhausted, the moment comes when we begin to identify with this Expansion so as to hold on to it and prevent it from leaving—impossible though this may be. At this point Allah may send us Shame in order to break that identification. Likewise at the high point of Dispersion, we may suddenly feel that we are burdened with a million idols, each one of which, no matter how limited and partial it may be, we have foolishly identified with Allah Himself; this is when Shame may intervene to break these idols of multiplicity, to turn us and empower us to make *sujud* to the One.

Shame is the conviction that we have violated Courtesy, *adab*, and also the quickest way of redressing this violation. It stretches all the way from the gross Shame we feel in the case of an obvious transgression to the subtle Shame—no less fierce for all its subtlety—for presuming to assert our separate existence in the presence of the Absolute.

Repentance (*Tawbah*)

Real Repentance is *infused Shame*. Unless Allah is present to the Heart, we do not possess the power to be truly ashamed of our sins, whether they be gross moral transgressions or the subtler states of *ghaflah* or "sins of attention" from which all gross transgressions emerge. We may sincerely wish to repent, and do our best to listen to our rational faculty, *al-'aql*, as it attempts to guide our actions by reminding us, on the level of the conscious understanding of the shari'ah, of what is right and wrong. But the rational faculty has no power to produce true Shame, which does not only strengthen the will to combat a sin, but begins to burn out in us the very attractiveness of the sin itself. The fruit of Shame is Disgust, and the fruit of Disgust is Purity and Sobriety. And when real Shame comes it will most likely make us ashamed of many things that we never saw anything wrong with before, many little imbalances and discourtesies. If Shame did not possess the power to set right on its own authority the things it makes us ashamed of, we might descend into obsessive scrupulosity; this is what happens when Repentance without true Shame turns us over to the Accusing Nafs. But complete Shame does possess that power. The perfection of Shame is to be ashamed not of this or that act, but of our very claim to separate existence, and to renounce this claim forever.

Preface to Part Two

Courtesy (Adab)

Adab is the Arabic word for "etiquette"; its most literal definition is probably "table manners" —or, rather, the manners appropriate for eating a group meal from a mat laid on a carpeted floor. For Muslims, the encyclopedia of *adab* is the *sunnah* of the Prophet.

The Sufis raise *adab* to the level of a transcendent virtue by including in its definition the notion of courteous behavior in the presence of Allah; some have even maintained that "Sufism is all *adab*." In terms of the Noble Qur'an, the essence of *adab* before Allah is found in Q.53:16–17, in the account of the *miraj* or ascent-through-the-worlds of the Prophet Muhammad, peace and blessings be upon him: *When that which enshrouds did enshroud the Lote Tree, the eye turned not aside, nor yet was overbold.* The *Lote Tree* is the *farthest limit* of what man can know of God, in the presence of which the human knower is annihilated; when it is veiled once again, the knower comes back into (apparent) existence. This is the specific point where *adab* with Allah begins, and becomes necessary. We are prohibited from prying after mystical secrets, from presuming upon Allah's generosity (though to refuse His gifts, and to refuse to ask for more after He has specifically invited us to do so, is equally discourteous); we are also cautioned against becoming distracted in His Presence in the belief that He has already sent us the "message", already dealt with us—because in reality He never stops dealing with us. In these two verses we have the root of *adab*, as well as the essence of Sobriety in its highest degree, which is the station of Presence.

Spiritual Poverty (Faqr)

Sufis are also called *fuqara*, the plural of *faqir*, which means "poor man"; the essence of Spiritual Poverty is *poverty of identification*. You may be rich, but you do not say "I am rich"; if you're poor, you do not think "I am poor." It's the same with being healthy, ill, famous, unknown, intelligent, not so intelligent, emotionally rich, emotionally simple, highly sexed, relatively impotent, with many friends, with few friends; none of these things are used to construct an identity for yourself. You recognize that you, in yourself, are nothing; you are nothing but the one God sees you to be, and God sees only Himself.

You identify with things, persons and situations, and with your own psychic states, because identification is a drug—a stimulant, yes, but more fundamentally a narcotic, a source of oblivion. Identification builds the illusion that you have created yourself and have ultimate responsibility for your life and destiny; you unconsciously believe that if you can keep on inventing yourself by identifying with this or that thing, person, situation or state of consciousness you will never die, that you will always be able to defend yourself against unwanted feelings and shocking events since you are the one in control. You fear that if you stop maintaining your identity through identification then everything will fall into chaos, totally unexpected things might happen—*you might even see God.*

True Spiritual Poverty begins when you start to notice those moments when the mind reaches for identification, and you spontaneously say "no." What was once an easy blend, so easy that it never rose into consciousness, is now experienced (let us say) like a splash of muddy water on your car's windshield: something that isn't you, that need not be a part of your life, that is maybe slightly irritating, and that consequently is easy to let go of, to wash away. Many of these moments will be relatively trivial, moments like "I always liked that song, I used to sing it all the time" or "remember that stupid thing I said to that girl years ago, I'm so stupid" or "imagine how I would feel if I did or became this or that" or "here I am perfectly in character, on the stage of my life, walking down the street", etc., etc. The mind reaches for these things, touches the hot stove and immediately pulls back; no need to add these pieces of random litter to your bag of identifications; better to just forget them. When the virtue of Spiritual Poverty is perfected, the bag is empty.

At a higher station of Spiritual Poverty (which won't necessarily always come later in time), you can feel God deconstructing you, releasing whole cities and countries and continents of past identification, all the things that always meant "me" to you; if at the moment of death your whole life passes before your eyes, the same is certainly true of dying before you die. The closer you come to Intimacy with Allah, ravished by His Beauty, the more powerful the waves of Awe become, due to the unveilings of His Majesty. The shock and awe of these unveilings simply ruin you, blast down your

116

walls, dynamite your foundations. As Allah says in the *hadith qudsi*: "Who seeks Me, finds Me; who finds Me, knows Me; who knows Me, loves Me; who loves Me, I love him; whomever I love, I kill; whomever I kill, I Myself am his blood price" [*hadith qudsi* quoted by the Sufis].

The Day and Night of the Heart; the Night and Day of the *Nafs*

Each of the alternating pairs of spiritual states presented below is alluded to in specific *ayat* of the Qur'an. Each is the expression, on the human plane, of a specific metaphysical principle. And each may be viewed either according to its true form as it appears on the level of the Heart, or in its distorted form as it appears on the level of the Nafs. These paired states represent, from the point of view of the Heart, two opposite approaches, or invitations, to the Presence of Allah; from the point of view of the Nafs, they represent two different ways of trying to avoid that Presence. The Nafs wants to turn Expansion into inflation, Contraction into despair, Intoxication into heedlessness, Sobriety into coldness, Intimacy into complacency, Awe into panic, Dispersion into dissipation, Gathering into self-involvement, Fluctuation into chaos, Stability into petrification, Absence into oblivion, Presence into possessiveness, etc. Likewise the Heart hopes to find and possess Allah through the various states He sends. These states are not really paths to Him, however, but rather His ways of mortifying in us both our desire to flee Him and our desire to possess Him. This is how He breaks down in us the barriers His Presence, and opens the way to our full submission to that Presence.

Each of the *ahwal* unveils one or more names of Allah, which on the human level are virtues, or the seeds of virtues. When these virtues are established in the Heart, the state in question has become a station. From one point of view we can say that a station is a state that has become permanent; from another, that when the station is established, the state that initiated it disappears.

Every spiritual state can and should be dealt with by only one method: *Taslim*, Submission. And since Submission is the end of all self-assertion and self-definition, the goal of every spiritual state is *Fana'*, Annihilation. In the early stages of the Path we may have a relatively fixed idea of what Submission is. We may identify it with resignation, humility, passivity, or something similar. But what Submission really is, is obedience to God's command. He may command us to act with zeal and vigor, to stand firm with patience and courage, to lose consciousness of our surroundings and ourselves, to pay constant and vigilant attention to our surroundings and ourselves . . . passive resignation is not the only face of Submission to God. Furthermore, to believe that obedience to God's Command can be limited to passivity is in fact to *demand that God command us* to be strictly passive—most likely to pander to our own slothfulness; it is to attempt to conform God's commands to our own assumptions and desires, and this is the furthest thing from true submission.

Submission to Allah through the shari'ah requires responsibility and constancy. Submission to Allah as present in His immediate Command requires discernment, courage, and swiftness in obedience. Submission to Allah via His direct Touch demands the death of "me." The correct response to any spiritual state is Submission, but the one act of *Taslim* appears differently in relation to different states; this is why such states must be defined and differentiated. This work can never be complete, however, since the variety of spiritual states is effectively infinite; *Every day doth some new work employ Him* [Q. 55:29/55:29]. One reason for defining the changing states of the Heart is precisely to give us a sense of this infinity, and consequently prevent our view of the spiritual life from being reduced to a schematic system. If you think you always know exactly where you are on the map of your own progress, you are sunk in self-regard, and have forgotten God.

From one point of view, when the traveler passes beyond the clashing rocks of the paired spiritual states, each pair is synthesized as a single station (though any state, paired or not, can become a station in and of itself). This, however, may be an excessively schematic way of looking at the matter, so it would probably be best for the reader to allow this section of the book to "work" on him or her without turning the form in which it is expressed into a fixed idea, seeing that the changing spiritual states will eventually overturn all fixed ideas, and dissolve them. The patterns into which the *ahwal* are arranged in the following sections probably have more to do with the process of exposition than with the actual manifestation of the *ahwal* themselves. It is nonetheless true that whenever an opposition is transcended or synthesized within the Heart, the result is a deepening of spiritual peace. Consequently each station that is based on a synthesis of two paired spiritual states can be seen as an element of the *Sakinah*, the Divine Tranquility, which carries us into to the Presence of Allah with ever increasing constancy and depth. This is how the *Sakinah* opens us to the degree of *Mahabbah* or Divine Love, the kind of Love that lies beyond passion and possessiveness—and beyond willful self-sacrifice as well—ultimately opening us to the *Ma'rifah* of Allah, the Divine Knowledge that this Divine Love progressively warms, moistens and cultivates, till it bursts into full flower. Knowledge does not take us *beyond* Love, however; Knowledge itself is the perfection of Love.

States and Stations from the Standpoint of *Adab*

The Sufi doctrine of states and stations as outlined above may seem complex and arcane to some, and in many ways this is an accurate description: it is a science filled with mysteries that can never be made explicit, only alluded to, or indicated solely by the quality of our silence. Yet I believe that this science can be de-mystified to a degree, allowing us to get a feeling for the *ahwal* and the *maqamat* as natural and integral aspects of any spiritual life that is lived with the appropriate depth and sincerity.

The force of our sense of God's reality—if, that is, we actually believe in Him—may stretch all the way from a vague, abstract notion that such a Being or Principle must somehow exist, to a shockingly clear and acute sense of His real Presence, right here and right now. Imagine that you suddenly find yourself sitting across a banquet table from a distinguished and perhaps quite famous person whom you have always admired and hoped to meet, though you never thought you would actually get the opportunity. But now here he is, face to face with you, perhaps four feet away. How would you react? Unless you were a very mature and self-possessed individual, you would likely go into a *state*: acute shyness, bewilderment, giddy excitement, a sense of gratitude, a feeling of inflated status, fear . . . the list could be extended. Initially at least, only a crass indifference to the worth and presence of the distinguished guest sitting across from you could prevent such reactions from occurring—which is sufficient evidence that the state you would then find yourself experiencing, even though it might indicate a certain immaturity, would also be entirely appropriate. And if a meeting with an admired and important human being is capable of producing such effects, imagine the possible repercussions of a meeting with God—a sense that the Supreme Being is not only actually present with you here and now, but is completely aware of you, conscious of all your reactions to Him both visible and hidden, and awaiting—if not silently commanding—your response. If the idea or experience of spiritual states is something obscure and foreign to us, hard to account for or understand, it may be because we have had little or no concrete experience of the Presence of Allah. We may have faith in Him, a degree of trust in Him, a sincere desire to serve Him; nonetheless we rarely feel the power of His immediate Presence.

In the case of the distinguished person at the banquet table, your reactions would likely be both avenues of relationship with him and barriers to that relationship. Your shyness would be a barrier, but also an opportunity for him to start a conversation and put you at your ease. If he was a decent sort, your excitement at meeting him might cause him to open up to you, but also distract you from paying close attention to him and to what he was saying. A sense of stunned bewilderment would make relationship difficult, but could also have a positive effect by cautioning you against showing off or playing the know-it-all; the same could be said for shyness. If he saw that you were grateful to be near him his feelings might be touched, whereas if he got the sense that you were priding yourself on meeting him he might be put off. And if he sensed fear in you he could either withdraw into himself, or perhaps try to break through your fear by a direct overture, even at the risk of appearing a bit shocking. But in all these cases, a deeper and more mature interaction with the admired person would require that you move beyond your own reactions to him, positive or negative, enjoyable or painful, and learn how to relate to him directly.

It is much the same with those responses to the felt sense of God's Presence known as spiritual states. Insofar as they represent the direct action of Allah's Spirit on the Heart, they indicate closeness and intimacy with Him; insofar as they manifest as subjective reactions, they are elements of distance and alienation. This is why every *hal* represents a lesson to be learned on a concrete, existential level, both in terms of what is to be embraced and what is to be rejected; when that lesson is learned, the *hal* is transformed into a *maqam*. A state of shyness and Shame may result in the establishment of a station of Repentance and Trust in God's forgiveness, by which the initial state is transcended and its spiritual potential realized as a permanent acquisition. Likewise a state of giddy excitement may give way to a station of quiet inner warmth and joy; a state of Bewilderment to a station of Stability and Vigilance; a state of gratitude to station of heartfelt Piety; a state of Fear to a station of Wariness and circumspection. And a state of ego-inflation in God's Presence will necessarily invoke an element of Wrath—which, if the recipient is willing to endure it and not run away, may result in a well-founded station of Humility and self-effacement. As each of these stations is realized, the state that first announced it comes to an end; step by step we develop the ability to remain in the naked Presence of Allah without being imbalanced or distracted by our reactions to Him. Our *adab* is deepened, balanced and perfected.

In the court of *Malik al-Mulk*, the King of Absolute Sovereignty, in the Presence of both great possible reward and great potential punishment, we learn that to fawn, or to show off, or to cringe, or to play the fool, or to become sullen, or to loudly protest, or to daydream, or to withdraw into ourselves, or to make demands, or to interrupt, or to act in a seductive manner, or to hatch plots, or to refuse to respond when called upon are all violations of the *adab* proper to that Presence. But to the degree that our various conscious schemes and half-conscious reactions are mortified and laid to rest, and our practice of *adab* consequently developed and strengthened, we will ultimately find ourselves in the King's simple Presence—*just as if we had a right to be there.* Since we were willing to fulfill our duties as His subjects, we are rewarded by being raised to the status of His companions. We must never take this status for granted, however; to the degree that our ego-identity appropriates our position as the King's confidant—in other words, to the degree that we *identify with our station*—that station is transformed into an idol. Consequently we will be led—misguided, some would say—by the King's apparent approval of us to presume upon His good nature, with the result that various arrogant or foolish breaches of *adab* may again make their appearance. And if we don't catch ourselves in time, repent, repair our *adab* and regain our self-respect, the King's sudden Wrath will certainly bring us to our senses in the most shocking manner. It may ultimately become apparent that only complete self-effacement—only Annihilation—will have the power to prevent such breaches of courtesy from occurring in the future. Thus the immunity to spiritual states exhibited by the one in a station of Stability or Sobriety or Subsistence does not indicate a condition of indifference or blindness to the Beauty and Majesty of Allah, as it does in the case of the immature or worldly individual totally lacking in *adab*, but is rather a sign of the perfection of *adab*, which entails the realization that—in the words of Rabi'ah al-'Adawiyyah—"Thine existence is a sin"—a breach of spiritual courtesy—"wherewith no other sin may be compared."

4

Gathering (*Jam'*) and Dispersion (*Tafriqah*)

Verily, at the oncoming of night are devout impressions strongest, and
*   words are most collected,*
But in the daytime thou hast continual employ. [Q. 73:6–7/73:6–7]

◇

D ISPERSION IS THE SCATTERING of one's attention and
energy through an identification with many objects, either
internal or external. Gathering is a breaking of these multi-
ple identifications, and the withdrawal of the energy-of-attention
that had been bound by them, toward God, and by God.

The states of Gathering and Dispersion happen on the axis of
Batin and *Zahir*, Inner and Outer: *He is the First and the Last, and*
the Outward and the Inward; and He is Knower of all things [Q. 57:3].
The alternation of Gathering and Dispersion teaches us that, if we
know the *adab* of Inner and Outer, Allah can be found both in the
Night of the *Batin* and the Day of the *Zahir*, that *wherever you turn,*
there is the face of Allah.

The *Zahir*, the Outer, posits an inner Source, the *Batin*, of which
it is the manifestation. The *Batin*, the Inner, posits an outer manifestation, the *Zahir*, of which it is the Source. If it were not for the
Outer, the Inner would be inaccessible; if it were not for the Inner,
the Outer would wither away. *I will show them My signs on the hori-*
zons and in their own souls until they are satisfied that this is the
Truth. Is it not enough for you, that I am Witness over all things? [Q.
41:53] To fulfill our outer duties, of religion or of life, helps us locate
the inner Center, the Heart; to plumb the Heart puts us in touch
with the Divine Energies that underlie all manifestation, proving to

us that all that needs to be manifested, in our own lives or in the life of the world, lies hidden in the Will of Allah, and will inevitably make its appearance in His own time. Our only duty—either through active obedience or through passive renunciation—is to get out of His Way.

Meeting our responsibilities to the outer world "fills in all the holes" in that world so our attention is no longer drawn in and dominated by it—and when Allah fully occupies the *Zahir*, the *Batin* opens. In the words of some verses attributed by Jorge Luis Borges to Fariduddin Attar (which I have been unable to find in Attar himself),

> The Zahir is the shadow of the Rose
> And the rending of the veil.

These lines may in fact have been composed by Borges as a paraphrase or imitation of Sufi doctrine; nonetheless they are perfect in themselves: The Outer is merely the shadow of the Inner, the Secret Rose—yet when the presence of Allah, which we first recognize in the *Batin*, becomes powerful enough to also encompass the *Zahir*, then the veil is rent definitively. As 'Ali ibn Abi Talib reminds us, "Don't ask about who the speaker was; ask about what was said" [from the *Nehjul-Balagha* of Sayyid Razi].

He is the ... Outward (Al-Zahir) and the Inward (Al-Batin) [Q. 57:3]. The Nafs loves to chaotically mix *Batin* and *Zahir* until it becomes impossible for us to meet the legitimate demands of either. The Greater Jihad becomes politicized through magical thinking and the Lesser Jihad becomes psychologized through ego-identification; this is one of the methods used by the Nafs in setting itself up as a rival to Allah. An example of the politicization of the Greater Jihad is the belief that in struggling against one's lower self one is somehow magically affecting the outer world, consequently one need not faithfully fulfill one's legitimate responsibilities to that world. An example of the psychologization of the Lesser Jihad is the belief that the struggle against outer conditions is all that's needed in order to set one's soul in order; this another kind of magical thinking. But when the Heart awakens, then the *zahir* returns to the *Zahir* and the *batin* to the *Batin*, leaving the Nafs with no way to enforce its illegitimate claims on either. Obedience to God's command in one's work in the outer world does not veil the form of His command as addressed directly to the Heart, nor do the unveilings of God in the *Batin* veil His signs in the *Zahir*. *I will show them My signs on the horizons and in their own souls. . . .*

> And the believers should not all go out to fight. Of every troop of them, a party only should go forth, that they (who are left behind) may gain sound knowledge in religion, and that they may warn their folk when they return to them, so that they may beware. [Q. 9:122]

The *batini tafsir* of this verse is as follows: Don't let your battle against the *Nafs al-ammara*, the Commanding Self, consume all your spiritual attention; while you are struggling in the Greater Jihad against the Commanding Self by means of the *Nafs al-lawwamah*, the Accusing Self, remain attentive to the presence of Allah; don't make the mistake of thinking that you can put this attentiveness off until after you "win." Victory in the Greater Jihad establishes the *Nafs al-mutma'inah*, the Self-at-Peace, by which attentiveness to Allah becomes constant. But this victory and this peace will never be won unless it is already present in the midst of the battle; this is the inner meaning of the *hadith* "Paradise is beneath the shadow of the swords" [Bukhari]. And you must never forget, in the midst of struggle, that victory is not yours, but belongs to Allah exclusively.

A turn from Gathering toward Dispersion indicates the surfacing, by the power of Gathering itself, of some buried attachment to *al-Dunya*, which Allah will command you to either sacrifice or enact. To attempt to sacrifice it when Allah commands that it be enacted, or to attempt to enact it when Allah commands that it be sacrificed, are both temptations of the Nafs. Sometimes sacrifice is the straightest path toward the dissolution of a particular attachment; sometimes enactment is the straightest path. Allah alone knows which path is straightest—so listen well.

In the verse *All is perishing except His Face, all is perishing* refers to Dispersion, and *His Face* to Gathering.

The Relationship of Gathering and Dispersion
to Expansion and Contraction

According to the Bayazid al-Bistami, when the Nafs contracts the Heart expands, and when the Nafs expands the Heart contracts.

When the Heart is in a state of Dispersion, a turn toward Gathering Contracts the Nafs; when the Heart is in a state of Gathering, a turn toward Dispersion Expands the Nafs. When Contraction comes, the Heart uses it to serve Gathering, while the Nafs immediately seeks Dispersion so as to overcome its sense of constriction.

When Expansion comes, the Nafs uses it—just as it used Contraction—to seek Dispersion; it takes Expansion as an excuse to get involved with, identify with, interfere with everything under the sun, since the state of Expansion hides the pain of Dispersion and consequently gives the Nafs free rein to do its damage. Surah 94 of the Holy Qur'an warns against the tendency to succumb to the Nafs in the state of Expansion through laziness and dissipation:

> Have We not caused thy bosom to dilate,
> And eased thee of the burden
> Which weighed down thy back;
> And exalted thy fame?
> But lo! with hardship goeth ease,
> Lo! with hardship goeth ease;
> So when thou art relieved, still toil
> And strive to please thy Lord.

The Heart, on the other hand, uses Expansion (just as it uses Contraction) to serve Gathering, since Expansion reveals the Spirit in all things, including the Nafs, and the more Expansion reveals, the more the recollection and synthesis of the various elements of one's soul and one's life becomes possible.

Expansion results in *Wherever you turn, there is the face of Allah*—and when all the many things you have identified with in Dispersion have become signs of Allah, faces of Allah, and finally the single Face of Allah, then Dispersion has turned and become Gathering.

Gathering and Dispersion in Relation to *Fana'*

It might seem that Dispersion—*total* Dispersion—could be a way to *Fana'*: Annihilation through letting yourself be blown to smithereerns. But total Dispersion is not possible. And just because the traces of you are widely separated and out of relation to one another, this does not mean that they are annihilated—only that they are far from the Presence of Allah, which alone makes such Annihilation possible. For the ego to be lost in identification is not the same thing as for the ego to be annihilated. *Fana'* can only happen from a state of Gathering, not from a state of Dispersion. The perfect unification of the self, from one point of view, is itself *Fana'*; for the self to be unified, all self-referential habits, all forms of partial self-witnessing, must end. The only Witness to the self in the state of *Jam'* is the Absolute Witness, *Al-Shahid*—and to be perfectly Witnessed by Allah is to be annihilated in that Witnessing, and to Subsist before the face of the Witness as an aspect of His Knowledge of Himself.

The *Nafs* in Gathering and Dispersion

When the Nafs attacks, it will present itself either as a specific inner psychological conflict or as a negative influence coming from the world; it does this in order to hide itself. All disturbances in one's relationship with God—which also manifest as disturbances in any aspect of one's interaction with people, situations, emotions and ideas—have their origin in the Nafs. This is not to say that negative influences from people, situations, specific psychological complexes and demonic entities (the *kafir* Jinn) do not exist; clearly they do. But these things can only affect us through the Nafs, and can only be definitively dealt with by pacifying the Nafs, a process which cannot be completed until the Nafs is witnessed as a whole, not just in terms of this or that limited manifestation. Before this station is reached—before Unity of Being is realized in the state of Gathering—we exist in a world Dispersion, of many separate entities, beings and influences, each of which must be dealt with as if it were autonomous and self-determined, just as we must think of ourselves as autonomous and self-determined before we realize that the only Performer of any action is Allah. And when all we can see are limited influences and situations, it is our responsibility before Allah to deal with them as such. We can't *pretend* that "only God is the Doer" on the basis of belief; we must directly *see* this on the basis of Knowledge.

Love in Dispersion and Gathering

Love in the state of Dispersion is in most cases involved with identification; love in the state of Gathering is free of this entanglement. We have given our love to many things—at least they appear to be many. We love many people in both our present and our past; we love places we know but may never see again; we love the beauties of nature, the triumphs and achievements of art, the grandeur of beautiful human character; we love great truths and ideas; we love the profound and moving legends of the past; we love our visions of the celestial realms; we may even have loved (usually on a temporary basis) this or that social ideal. But none of these loves, sincere as they may be or have been, can ever be fully realized. If we were to pray for their realization and Allah were to grant our petition, we would be shattered into a million pieces. Space and time cannot contain Him, but the concentrated and recollected Heart can contain Him. The impossibility of giving the fullness of love to all the things we despairingly wish we could make objects of our affection can turn the Heart cold—until it learns how to turn to Allah—until Allah Himself turns it towards His district, where all loves are realized in a single Moment and a single Presence. Certain saints speak of having no room in their hearts for any love but the love of Allah, as if turning cold to all human affection and all fondness and care for Allah's creation were what was meant. But that's not what they're talking about. The wonders of the universe, and the beauty of our human beloved, cannot be loved in and for themselves, try as we might; the Love within us is too big for them, too powerful to be contained within such frail vessels. All Love is from Allah, returns to Allah, and *is* Allah. This Love would be the most jealous love of all if Allah were to see other than Himself, if He were to discern the existence of rivals. The universe would immediately be annihilated, could never have come into existence in the first place, if He were capable of seeing it like that. But Allah sees no rivals, though He knows that we ourselves see them, in our self-deception, and is consequently ruthless with such non-existent idols. Only when we love Allah exclusively because we *see* only Him, in the state of Gathering, do we love all the things we have given our love to in the state of Dispersion—perfectly, and for the first time.

GATHERING

(And remember) when Allah said: O Jesus! Lo! I am gathering thee and causing thee to ascend unto Me, and am cleansing thee of those who disbelieve.... [Q. 3:55]

There is not an animal in the earth, nor a flying creature flying on two wings, but they are peoples like unto you. We have neglected nothing in the Book (of Our decrees). Then unto their Lord they will be gathered. [Q. 6:38]

He it is Who gathereth you at night and knoweth that which ye commit by day. Then He raiseth you again to life therein, that the term appointed (for you) may be accomplished. And afterward unto Him is your return. Then He will proclaim unto you what ye used to do. [Q. 6:60]

I swear by the sunset redness,
And by the night and its gatherings.... [Q. 84:16–17/84:16–17]

◇

The state of Gathering is what's traditionally known in the Christian West as "recollection"; nowadays we refer to it as "centering" or the process of overcoming "scatteredness." In Gathering, Allah withdraws His Presence from the many and unveils Himself as the One. Our awareness has been scattered through identification with many things, persons and situations in the outer world, and many thoughts feelings and impulses in the inner one. Our identification with these objects has turned them into idols; the state of Gathering is sent by Allah in order to overturn these idols. When, after his conquest of Mecca, the Prophet Muhammad (peace and blessings be upon him) cast the idols out of the Kaaba, this was a reflection in the

Zahir of a state of Gathering in the *Batin*: in the inner human dimension, the idols are ego-identifications and the Kaaba is the Heart.

Metaphysical Principle

The state of Gathering is a reflection, in the human Heart, of *Tawhid*, the Transcendent Unity of Being, the Unity of God. Allah is not composed of parts. He loses nothing by creating the universe, and when all things return to Him, He gains nothing. Though Allah embraces all possibilities, both in terms of cosmic manifestation and His own intrinsic nature, He does not embrace them as a multiplicity, but as a seamless Unity.

According to the Heart

The state of Gathering carries with it the power of moral purity, the ability to resist temptation, to ignore the voices of the Nafs and the World. In the early stages, Gathering synthesizes the psyche by ordering thought, unifying feeling and stabilizing will, and brings thought, feeling and will into harmony with one another. In the later stages it unveils the Unity of God, at which point the various human faculties can no longer be differentiated, since to love God is simultaneously to know Him, to know Him is equally to love Him, and to know and love Him is immediately to choose Him. In the Presence of God, Who is the Only Reality, all the other "alternatives" have disappeared.

The perfection of the station of Gathering is the station of Presence.

According to the *Nafs*

The state of Gathering according to the Nafs results in intellectual pride, insensitivity to the uniqueness of other souls, and identification of everything with the Nafs; you renounce the worship of many things only to replace it with worship of yourself. You see yourself, not Allah, as the principle of Unity; you labor under the delusion that both the multiplicity of the outer world and that of the inner psyche can be unified if both worlds would only agree to prostrate to *you*—to the ego. In other words, Gathering according to the Nafs is what western psychology calls "narcissism." However, for obvious reasons, the attempt to found unification of the psyche upon the ego, the very principle of division, is doomed to failure; without this inevitable failure, you would be totally without hope.

Virtues to be Gained in the Station of Gathering

Vigilance; Renunciation of *Shirk*; Renunciation of the Dunya.

Mode of *Taslim* (submission to God)

Taslim in the state of Gathering entails letting Allah break all your identifications, one-by-one. In Gathering you are called to release whatever you might want to own so as to build an identity for yourself: things, persons, situations, thoughts, feelings, intentions, even images of God. The practice is to let go of any idea of yourself, none of which has any substance or reality, in order to become who you already are in the sight of Allah.

In Relationship

Gathering in relationship allows you to be mindful of other people without an excessive effort to pay attention to them or obsessively communicate with them.

DISPERSION

Allah coineth a similitude: A man in relation to whom are several part-owners, quarrelling, and a man belonging wholly to one man. Are the two equal in similitude? Praise be to Allah! But most of them know not. [Q. 39:29]

◇

Dispersion causes conflict between one's thoughts, one's feelings and one's will, and the fragmentation of thought, feeling and will in themselves. Contradiction in the realm of thought divides the will and thus paralyzes it, because it has no idea *what* to will. And this paralyzed effort and mental chaos also produce, and are to a degree produced by, ambiguity and contradiction in the realm of feeling. Feelings that are obscure, ambiguous or flighty can never reach the depth necessary to unify the will and unite it with its object, nor do they retain the power to reveal the full import and range of implications of mental knowledge, thus transforming it into true wisdom. Only *Mahabbah* has to power to accomplish this.

Nonetheless, Dispersion is a true *hal* and *maqam* sent by Allah. Its spiritual function is to dissolve a state of Gathering that has become stagnant and petrified through the action of the Nafs, and thus can no longer really be called Gathering. Concentration on Allah to the exclusion of all else is real Gathering, but to scorn and despise all that does not live up to your presumably exalted standards is not Gathering at all, since to judge something is to be involved with it. To the degree that the Nafs has set itself up as a false Unity and so filled you with self-righteousness and haughty disdain, Dispersion opens the way to real Unity. (The craft of the holy clown, who skillfully uses humor and chaos to violate assumptions and break down social hypocrisy, is one manifestation the state of Dispersion.) The ability to be interested in many things is, on certain occasions, a gift of the Divine Mercy and Generosity; catholicity of taste and breadth of sympathy are real virtues. And the ultimate fruit of Dispersion is the ability to see the Divine Uniqueness in all that is unique—that is, in every separate being and each separate moment—to be given the ability to witness the Names of Allah as the inner principles of all created things, until *wherever you turn, there is the Face of God*. This is the point at which Dispersion, having fully dissolved a state of false Gathering, gives way to true Gathering.

Dispersion in the Lesser Jihad

We may see final victory, insha'Allah, in the Greater Jihad on the field of the Inner, but we will likely never see such victory on the field of the Lesser Jihad to establish peace, justice and true religion in the Outer world of society and history, except in the most limited and temporary of terms—unless Allah wills otherwise. Islamic eschatology declares that a restoration of peace and justice must take place before the coming of the Hour, when the Mahdi arises and Jesus the Messiah returns to slay the Antichrist, but whether this is to be manifest in the Outer or take place only in the Inner, is known only to Allah. Nonetheless, before the final Event, we are faced with the inevitable limitations of the human power to enact Good and proclaim Truth within *al-Dunya*, coupled with the fact that Allah acts within His own time and for His own purposes. Furthermore, whatever strictly limited power Allah may grant us to do good works in the Outer World can only be based on our victories—or rather *God's victories over us*—in the Inner World; a call to perform a work in the Outer is only a valid expression of the Will of Allah, and can only remain in touch with and submitted to that Will, if it also supports our work in the Inner, if it is in fact something now required of us if we are to take the next concrete step on the spiritual Path. An attraction to the Lesser Jihad in a given instance may be no more than a temptation emanating from the *Nafs al-ammara bi'l su'*, the "Self Commanding to Evil", to pervert or abandon the Greater Jihad. But it may also be a grace given us by Allah to help us heal and purify an Innerness that has degenerated into self-involvement and stagnation under the influence of that same "Commanding Self." Unfulfilled duties in the Outer act to block our progress in the Inner, but a faithful completion of such active duties—as well as a conscious renunciation of action when circumstances have revealed that further advance along a particular line has become impossible to us, or at least impossible without incurring spiritual damage and opening to spiritual darkness—is sometimes the very thing that, by the power of Allah, can turn our hearts more deeply toward the Inner, free of the clutter of conflicting impulses and stagnant self-will. Certainly any militant action in the world makes the one performing it vulnerable to the sin of pride, but such action may also be seen as a battle *against* pride, in both one's enemy and oneself. If the Lesser Jihad to humble the pride of the oppressor is not accompanied by an inner, Greater Jihad to humble the pride of the *fata* or *javanmard* himself, the one upon whom has been laid the duty of heroic spiritual action in the world, then *al-Dunya* has conquered him before he begins—not to mention the fact that all militant action in either the Inner or the Outer Jihad is inseparable from the experience of abasement and defeat: no warrior can encounter only victories. [NOTE: *Fata* and *javanmard* are the Arabic and Persian synonyms for the English word *knight*; all three words mean "young man", with the connotation of "young hero."] In terms of the Inner Jihad, this abasement, if the *fata* is capable of fully accepting it as God's will, is precisely the sign of victory—of God's victory over *him*, which is the only triumph he seeks. And in terms of the Outer Jihad, the *élan* of struggle both inflames and chastens the will, since it pushes the *fata* on to the point where action is no longer possible, and defeat inevitable. While he is acting within the Will of Allah, he is victorious; as soon as he departs from that Will, either because his submission to Allah wavers or because he has transgressed the limits of the action which Allah has ordained, he is defeated; in terms of the Greater Jihad, this defeat, if accepted in the right spirit, is his best chance for victory. By the same token, the victories he sees in the Outer are in no way his, but precisely the victories of Allah: *It was not you who threw when you threw, but Allah threw* [Q. 8:17]. It is necessary for the *fata* to gain the power to discern the objective limits of the effective outer manifestation of this Truth in any given instance, the boundary of the Command of Allah, beyond which lies nothing but the outer darkness; and this is not always easy, because action produces its own momentum. Such momentum often feels like power, but it is really nothing but the blind will of the situation, which is inseparable from self-will of the person entangled with it, seeing that *al-Dunya* and *al-Nafs al-ammara bi'l su* are two sides of the same coin. The one blinded by action has fallen into self-will through unconscious identification with the outer situation he confronts, and consequently has lost his ability to discern the Will of Allah. Action in submission to that Will is aware of its own inherent boundaries; action outside that Will is not. May Allah grant us the unerring light to tell the one from the other.

> I was sleeping safe in my scabbard—
> Then God drew me like a sword.
> I awoke to war: to victory and defeat.
> The clean design woven in air by this
>   flashing of blades

Gathering (Jam') *and Dispersion* (Tafriqah)

Was drawn from the lettering
Of the Mother of the Book,
Written down before first breath
    was drawn on earth,
Or the earthen floor laid to receive
The prints of beasts and men.
The pounding of feet in battle
Writes the pre-eternal script of the stars
On the Guarded Tablet,
And all these forms of bodies
Transfigured in their moment of struggle
Have long since gone to their rest
In Garden or Fire.
It was not you who threw when you threw,
But God threw;
And the outcome, and the agon,
And all the exquisite uncertainty—
To human eyes—of the hour of contest—
He enacted, and *He* knew.

Although the Lesser Jihad must end in Dispersion when the momentum of Allah's Command is exhausted, its pursuit may also invoke the state of Gathering and teach the station of it; unless the warrior possesses the skill to remain collected within himself under all circumstances, he will meet with certain defeat.

Metaphysical Principle

The state of Dispersion is a reflection, in the human Heart, of the Divine Infinity, of Allah in His Name *Al-Wasi*, the Vast. The vastness of the earthly ocean is finally bound by shores, as the Dispersion of the Heart is bound by the state of Gathering—but the vastness of Allah has no shore.

According to the Heart

The state of Dispersion according to the Heart is the power of symbolic vision, the ability to see all things, persons and situations in the outer world, as well as all thoughts, feelings and intentions in the inner one, as Acts of Allah and signs of His Presence. *And in your creation, and all the beasts that He scattereth in the earth, are portents for a folk whose faith is sure.* [Q. 45:4]

According to the *Nafs*

Dispersion according to the Nafs produces identification with the Dunya, heedlessness and the fracturing of attention, and the loss of spiritual intuition through the veiling of the Eye of the Heart. The result is vulnerability to temptations of all kinds and dissipation in the pursuit of passion. (The sort of destructive humor that pokes fun at innocence, honesty and simplicity is one manifestation of the Nafs' idea of Dispersion.)

And the weak shall say to the mighty ones, "Nay, but there was a plot by night and by day, when you bad us believe not in God, and gave Him peers." [Q. 34:32/34:32] "The weak" in this verse are those under the power of the Commanding Nafs; the "mighty ones" make up the Commanding Nafs itself. In the state of Dispersion produced by the Nafs, each separate thing, person, situation or event is seen as not as the reflection of a Name of Allah, appearing in time as an Act of Allah, but as an autonomous, self-defined, self-determined being, as if it were a god in its own right. Such dispersion is the quintessence of *literalism*; it makes all things, persons, situations and events appear separate and unrelated to each other and renders them opaque to the Light of the Spirit. We no longer see them as signs of Allah, merely as the outer shells of themselves as perceived and defined by the five senses, dry husks with nothing inside them.

When the Heart is occupied by the Nafs, whose other face is *al-Dunya* or This World, the self is dispersed and divided. The Nafs-as-ego claims that only obedience to its endless demands can bring unity to your consciousness, your feelings and your intent, that such obedience has the power to make you the great hero of your own integrity. This is a lie. The Nafs cannot provide unity because it itself is the principle of inner division, of the fragmentation of consciousness, feelings, and life itself. *And We shall turn unto the work they did and make it scattered motes.* [Q. 25:23] The self can only be unified when the Heart is ruled by Allah as *Al-Ahad*, the One.

Virtues to be Gained in the Station of Dispersion

Generosity; Altruism; breadth of sympathy; the ability to see the Names and Signs of God in all manifest forms.

Mode of *Taslim*

Taslim in the state of Dispersion is to let go of the memory of what you consider to be the higher spiritual states you once enjoyed, and submit to Allah's will for you *now*, in the understanding that submission to His present action on your soul is the one thing required of you, and therefore the highest thing you can do. It is not to resist or complain against Allah's will when He chooses to veil Himself, in the understanding—which may not initially be available—that His Veil is also His Manifestation.

In Relationship

Dispersion in relationship allows you to see the good in everyone, the reflection of *Al-Wahid*, the Unique, no matter what their differences and idiosyncrasies might be, thus purifying you of all kinds of snobbery and bigotry and social prejudice.

The Synthesis of Gathering and Dispersion

What transcends Gathering and Dispersion? The station of the realization of *Wahadiyyah*, the Synthetic Unity of Allah. Allah is One, but that Oneness embraces and synthesizes every possibility. He allows every possible thing to be exactly what it is through participation in His Uniqueness, without the slightest hint of division or confusion or conflict.

In terms of the Spiritual Path, the final limit of Dispersion is precisely the end of the world in its inner or *batini* aspect—an approach to "infinite entropy" where the cosmic creative impulse, in

terms of a particular place and time, is entirely spent. But this dissolution can only be witnessed—and thus only actually occur—when
a turn is made from Dispersion to Gathering. Only when the Divine
Creative Word turns and begins to flows back into the Silence from
which it came can the world of outer manifestation, now deprived
of its principle of consciousness and vitality, finally die. The surahs
of the Holy Qur'an which have to do with the approach of the Hour,
particularly the shorter ones near the end of the Book, when interpreted in their esoteric aspect relate to this turn. The verse *A day
wherein mankind will be as thickly-scattered moths* [Q. 101:4] is a
description of the state of the human soul at the ultimate limit of
Dispersion: volatile, flighty and without stable substance. *When the
wild beasts are herded together* [Q. 81:5] refers to the Gathering
together of the facets and qualities of the Nafs that have been Dispersed through identification, the unification and pacification of
the soul by the power of the Ruh, the Spirit. And these verses, from
"The Sundering"—

> *When the heaven is split asunder,*
> *And attentive to her Lord in fear,*
> *When the earth is spread out*
> *And hath cast out all that was in her, and is empty,*
> *And attentive to her Lord in fear!*
> *Thou, verily, O man, art working toward thy Lord a*
> *work which thou shalt meet (in His presence). . . .* [Q. 84:1–6]

—these picture a state when our highest conception of spiritual
Reality is dissolved by the full presence of that Reality, and when all
the impulses and impressions and affections hidden in the soul, in
the Nafs, are divulged, released, and returned to their Center and
Source in Allah. And the effect of this Gathering is to unveil the
Secret of Allah, the Guarded Tablet upon which He has written the
names of all things—all the rocks, all the stars, all the animals, all
the angels—the *single soul* within Him out of which all things are
made: which is, precisely, the Human Form, no longer conceived of
as "me", but known entirely as *He*. This is the true Gathering.

The turn from Dispersion to Gathering happens when the limit
of Allah's Command to act in the world is reached. It is to directly

witness the truth that *all is perishing* (Dispersion) *except His Face* (Gathering). It is to let go of what is dying, to let it die, to turn toward *Al-Hayy* the Living, to understand that we never did possess Life and never will possess it, but rather that Life possesses us—to know that Allah is not only the Giver of Life, but Life itself. What dies is the mass of our identifications, made up of every occasion, big or small, when we said, of something in the Dunya, "I am that", so as to posit ourselves as entities capable of owning some object outside ourselves and making it part of our identity because we somehow exist in our own right and therefore can claim absolute ownership of a thing—identification being the most absolute form of ownership. But in reality we own nothing—least of all ourselves. The only Owner is Allah, and He is *Owner of the Day of Judgement* [Q. 1:4]. The Day of Judgement is the Hour when we will be separated from everything we have identified with (in Dispersion), and united with all we understand as belonging to Allah and no-one else, because there *is* no-one else (in Gathering). Every time the shell of an identification is broken, the kernel of a Divine Name is tasted. The identifications are Dispersed; the Names are Gathered.

In the earlier stages of the Path, Dispersion (a turn toward the *Zahir*) veils the *Batin*, and Gathering (a turn towards the *Batin*) veils the *Zahir*. In the intermediate stages, a turn toward the *Batin* veils the *Zahir* but a turn toward the *Zahir* does not veil the *Batin*. In the final stages, neither does the *Zahir* veil the *Batin* nor the *Batin* veil the *Zahir*; Gathering and Dispersion have become one.

5

Expansion (*Bast*) and Contraction (*Qabd*)

And whomsoever it is Allah's will to guide, He expandeth his bosom unto the Surrender, and whomsoever it is His Will to send astray, He maketh his bosom close and narrow as if he were engaged in sheer ascent. Thus Allah layeth ignominy upon those who believe not. [Q. 6:125]

Who is it that will lend unto Allah a goodly loan, so that He may give it increase manifold? Allah straiteneth and enlargeth. Unto Him ye will return. [Q. 2:245]

And to the three also (did He turn in mercy) who were left behind, when the earth, vast as it is, was straitened for them, and their own souls were straitened for them till they bethought them that there is no refuge from Allah save toward Him. Then turned He unto them in mercy that they (too) might turn (repentant unto Him). Lo! Allah! He is the Relenting, the Merciful. [Q. 9:118]

Lo! thy Lord enlargeth the provision for whom He will, and straiteneth (it for whom He will). Lo, He was ever Knower, Seer of His slaves. [Q. 17:30]

Allah maketh the provision wide for whom He will of His bondmen, and straiteneth it for whom (He will). Lo! Allah is Aware of all things. [Q. 29:62]

See they not that Allah enlargeth the provision for whom He will, and straiteneth (it for whom He will). Lo! herein indeed are portents for folk who believe. [Q. 30:37]

That which Allah openeth unto mankind of mercy none can withhold it; and that which He witholdeth none can release thereafter. He is the Mighty, the Wise. [Q. 35:2]

Expansion (Bast) *and Contraction* (Qabd)

Know they not that Allah enlargeth providence for whom He will, and straiteneth it (for whom He will). Lo! herein verily are portents for people who believe. [Q. 39:52]

His are the keys of the heavens and the earth. He enlargeth providence for whom He will and straiteneth (it for whom He will). Lo! He is Knower of all things. [Q. 42:12]

◇

While we are identified with the Nafs, Expansion and Contraction are related to what modern psychology has identified as the "bipolar disorder", which may be severe enough to be recognized as a pathology, or mild enough to allow us to virtually ignore it. On this level, Expansion and Contraction have to do with psychophysical temperament, not with the direct action of God. But to the degree that we have become identified with the Heart because the Eye of the Heart has begun to open, Expansion and Contraction become alterations in our ability to witness Divine realities. After we have passed this milestone—given that the Nafs is a veil over the Face of Allah—when the Heart contracts the Nafs expands, and when the Heart expands the Nafs contracts.

Expansion, though it may seem infinite, is never total since it is related to Contraction as its polar opposite; and so Expansion, which reveals so much, also tends to hide the deeper poisons of the Nafs, which are only revealed in the state of Contraction. Expansion serves the "unveiling" and "visionary disclosure" of spiritual realities; Contraction serves repentance and purification. If the Nafs expands while the Heart contracts, and vise versa, then we can add that the expansion of the Nafs exposes all the wiles and delusions and impulses and agendas concealed within it, thus informing the contracted Heart as to exactly what it needs to repent of.

Contraction is produced by a turn toward the Dunya, Expansion by a turn toward Allah. In terms of the first part of the Shahada, *La ilaha* is the source of Contraction and *illa Allah* of Expansion. The Dunya is Allah's creation apparently devoid of His Presence—*La ilaha*, "there is no god"—but when the Heart has turned entirely

141

away from the Dunya and toward Allah, then *wherever you turn, there is the face of God.*

Expansion, because it brings impurities to the surface, may later result in Contraction; likewise a Contraction that is beginning to give way to Expansion will allow these impurities to be released. When and if Contraction develops an ego (because we identify with it), that ego is purged by Expansion; when and if Expansion develops and ego (because we identify with it), that ego is purged by Contraction. To submit to Contraction is to repent of transgressions, and to begin to repent of self-existence; it is thus a step toward the station of Annihilation.

EXPANSION

He selecteth for His mercy whom He will. Allah is of Infinite Bounty. [Q. 3:74]

Jubilant (are they) because of that which Allah hath bestowed upon them of His bounty, rejoicing for the sake of those who have not joined them but are left behind: That there shall no fear come upon them, neither shall they grieve. [Q. 3:170]

So they returned with grace and favour from Allah, and no harm touched them. They followed the good pleasure of Allah, and Allah is of Infinite Bounty. [Q. 3:174]

And announce unto the believers the good tidings that they will have great bounty from Allah. [Q. 33:47]

Say: In the bounty of Allah and in His mercy: therein let them rejoice. It is better than what they hoard. [Q. 10:58]

Have We not caused thy bosom to dilate,
And eased thee of the burden
Which weighed down thy back;
And exalted thy fame?
But lo! with hardship goeth ease,
Lo! with hardship goeth ease;
So when thou art relieved, still toil
And strive to please thy Lord. [Q. 94:1–8]

Expansion (Bast) and Contraction (Qabd)

◇

Expansion is an opening of the Heart by means of a joy that arrives by direct "infusion" from Allah, entirely unrelated to any effort or lack of effort on our part.

Metaphysical Principle

Expansion is a reflection, in the human Heart, of the truth that Reality, and therefore all existing things that proceed from It, is intrinsically good. The root of Allah in His Names *Al-Basit*, the Expander, and *Al-Karim*, the Generous, is Allah in His Name *Al-Rahman*, the Infinitely Merciful. It is through His Mercy that Allah creates and expands the universe, conferring the gift of real existence upon every non-existent form hidden within His Essence. Since Allah is *Al-Ahad*, the One, the Only Being, there is nothing in the realm of manifest existence that doesn't lie within Him as an eternal potential. But by the same token, precisely because He is the Only Being—Eternal (*Al-Samad*), Self-Subsistent (*Al-Qayyum*), and without inner divisions—these potentials have no independent existence other than His. Allah as *Al-Ahad* is intrinsically without limits since there is nothing outside Him, consequently His Necessary Being endlessly overflows into the realms of Possible Being, giving them Life in His Name *Al-Hayy* and Reality in His Name *Al-Haqq*.

The Heart qualified by the Name *Al-Rahman* expands until every potential within it is fully realized.

According to the Heart

When an influx from the Spirit expands the Heart, the intellect, the feelings and the will expand along with it; simultaneously the Nafs shrinks away until it appears to have been annihilated. In the state of Expansion the intellect witnesses only Divine Realities, the feelings are suffused with Love of Allah and become capable of loving all things in Allah, and the will finds it easy to will what Allah wills, and experiences whatever it wills as Allah's Will. Expansion purifies the Heart of whatever elements of negative egotism might have grown up while the Heart was in the state of Contraction: despair, sadness, sullenness, lethargy, cowardice, self-hatred, etc.

143

Day and Night on the Sufi Path

The following quatrains of Jalaluddin Rumi were written from the state of Expansion:

In the fragrance of the meadow-flowers I inhale Your sweetness;
In tulip and jasmine I make out the hues of Your face.
And when flowers are gone, no matter: I need only open my lips,
Pronounce your Name, and hear it.

Town and valley are filled with your delight,
O Delight of earth and sky!
No one complains of you but Sorrow himself;
You have granted all men freedom
from the tyranny of his rule.

Because of you all hardships have become easy;
Rose, garden and cypress are drunk on your kindness.
The rose herself is drunk; even the thorn is sleepy with wine—
Then hand us a cup, so we may become like them.

The whole of the ocean rolls with the fervor of Your love;
Every cloud that rises scatters its pearls at Your feet,
Out of its love for You the lightning strikes the earth;
Out of its love for You the smoke rises up the sky.

If you are the Ocean, I am Your fish;
If you are the Desert, I am Your gazelle.
I am the servant of Your breath: blow it into me!
I am Your flute, Your flute, Your flute!

You have filled the entire earth with honey and with candy;
What roses and laurels your mouth has revealed!
"O Lover! O Sincere one! O Wise one!" He shouted;
These are the names my Beloved has given me!

When I take up the flute, I play only for You;
When I take up the Path, I make sure to pass by Your lane;
You've shown me such kindness and generosity
I can never take back my heart from You, in this world or the next.

[My transcreated versions, based on Ibrahim Gamard and A.G. Rawan Farhadi, *The Quatrains of Rumi: Ruba'iyat-é Jalaluddin Muhammad Balkhi-Rumi*, Sufi-Dari Books, 2008].

Expansion (Bast) *and Contraction* (Qabd)

Expansion of the Heart is the sweetest gift of Allah; and as we can see from Rumi, Intoxication may also be a form of Expansion, just as Expansion itself may be intoxicating. Expansion differs from Intoxication proper, however, by virtue of the fact that not only the feelings, but all the faculties of the soul—feeling, intelligence and will—are expanded as the Heart expands. It becomes possible to know with a portion of God's Knowing, to love with a particle of His Loving, and to will with a trace of the power of His own Willing.

Wherever you turn, there is the face of Allah is expressive of the state of Expansion. Everything in both the world and the soul becomes a sign of His Nature and His Presence. All secrets seem revealed, all sorrows drowned in gladness, all tasks so easy as to appear inevitable, if not already accomplished. The very events of the world seem to mirror, to correspond with, to lend their eager aid to, the motions of the Heart. In the state of Expansion it's hard not to believe that the end of the Path, the station of Subsistence in God, has been reached.

But it hasn't. In Expansion the Nafs has shrunk away to almost nothing, nearly disappeared, but it isn't really dead. It will come to life again. When it seems like all secrets are known, and then the thought "*I* know all secrets" occurs, even for a split second—when you see that God's intent is your intent, but then turn it around, even for a split second, by being foolish enough to maintain that *your* intent could determine *God's* intent—then the Nafs is reborn. And unless you catch the exact moment when it begins to stir, and sacrifice self-will and attachment-to-knowledge *immediately* by saying "there is no Might nor Power save in Allah, and Allah knows best"—saying it, and really meaning it—then the Nafs may eat up your entire state of Expansion and grow bigger and fiercer than ever before, while the Heart shrinks away till it is only the trace or the virtuality or the memory of a Heart. [NOTE: Ibn al-'Arabi maintains that "the determined determines the Determiner", and the Sufis recognize the station of the shaykh whose word is law, to whom Allah grants all petitions, doing this so swiftly and completely that the shaykh need only issue a command for it to be accomplished. But such a one certainly does not command Allah; it's simply that he has no intent of his own apart from Allah's intent.

Likewise "the determined determines the Determiner" not by any reversal of the intrinsic order of things, as if the effect could determine the Cause, but because Allah wills all determined things to be what they are, and issues His commands to them based only on what He knows them to be, commanding fish to swim because they are fish, and birds to fly because they are birds.]

According to the *Nafs*

And if Allah were to enlarge the provision for His slaves they would surely rebel in the earth, but He sendeth down by measure as He willeth. Lo! He is Informed, a Seer of His bondmen. [Q. 42:27]

Then, when they forgot that whereof they had been reminded, We opened unto them the gates of all things till, even as they were rejoicing in that which they were given, We seized them unawares, and lo! they were dumbfounded. [Q. 6:44]

Expansion according to the Nafs is ego-inflation; it results in titanic pride, either a Promethean rebellion against God or an actual identification with Him. At the very least, one in the state of false Expansion will believe that all is permitted to him, that Allah will never punish him because he enjoys the eternal favor of the Deity. This may result in an ironic, self-imposed punishment, a punishment produced by the arrogance of false Expansion itself—namely a willingness to embrace endless Dispersion in the mistaken belief that one's resources are infinite. The spendthrift of the Spirit will certainly know poverty—not the poverty of willing humility, but that of Divinely-imposed humiliation. If we find ourselves in this state, we can only pray that we have enough of our original store of potential *Taslim* left to transform Allah's abasement of us into willing submission to His decree.

Virtues to be Gained in the Station of Expansion

Visionary Disclosure; unveiling of spiritual realities in Contemplative Vision (*Shuhud*); Zeal; Aspiration; Generosity; Altruism; Mercy; Gratitude.

Expansion (Bast) *and Contraction* (Qabd)

Mode of *Taslim*

In the state of Expansion, the practice of *Taslim* is to be willing to receive more than you ever thought possible: more power of action, more power of insight, more power of mercy and compassion—and even more than that, and still more, and more, even, after that—to give up all resistances, based on weakness of faith or a desire to protect your shrunken (but familiar) self-concept, to the overwhelming Generosity of Allah. *Taslim*-in-Expansion requires that you renounce the fear that this great Generosity might end— and also the fear that it might *never* end.

In Relationship

Expansion in relationship gives you a vision of the mass of humanity as a single brotherhood and sisterhood, and of yourself as one of them—as one of *us*.

CONTRACTION

(Alms are) for the poor who are straitened for the cause of Allah, who cannot travel in the land. The unthinking man accounteth them wealthy because of their restraint. Thou shalt know them by their mark: They do not beg of men with importunity. And whatsoever good thing ye spend, lo! Allah knoweth it. [Q. 2:273]

◇

Contraction is a sense of sadness and constriction of Heart that is sent, like Expansion, via a direct infusion from Allah, in order to discipline the traveler, a constriction that it is impossible for him to banish no matter what he does, until Allah Himself lifts it.

Metaphysical Principle

The state of Contraction is a reflection, in the human Heart, of the Justice of God, according to whose judgment all self-identified beings are found wanting. By Contraction the Nafs is humbled, but the Heart is vindicated. Through Contraction one's possessiveness of God's gifts, a possessiveness that was hidden in the state of

Expansion, is unveiled; the spendthrift of the Spirit, glorying in his gold, is now revealed as a spiritual miser, so attached to the gifts he has received from Allah that they dwindle away to nothing in the grip of his avarice, greed and fear. *And let not those who hoard up that which Allah hath bestowed upon them of His bounty think that it is better for them. Nay, it is worse for them. That which they hoard will be their collar on the Day of Resurrection. Allah's is the heritage of the heavens and the earth, and Allah is Informed of what ye do.* [Q. 3:180] But to the degree that the Heart was humbly open to receive the bounty of Allah in the state of Expansion, it is now willing, in equal humility, to let these gifts return to their Owner, *Rabb al-Alamin*, in the state of Contraction.

The root of Allah in His Names *Al-Qabid* (He who Contracts), *Al-Mudhill* (He who Humbles) and *Al-Khafid* (He who Abases) is Allah in His Names *Al-Mutakabbir* (the Proud), *Al-Malik* (the King) and various similar Names. If Allah by His Mercy allows all things to participate in His Reality, by the same token He excludes from this participation, by His Wrath and His Justice, all that claims to possess existence in its own right. Yet since "My Mercy has precedence over My Wrath", His Wrath ultimately serves His Mercy. By the very fact that He is the Only Being, he ruthlessly excludes from that Being, which is the Real, all that would veil it with the veils of unreality, thus freeing created beings from the prison of that unreality and returning all things to Himself.

Contraction is something we usually either struggle to get out of, or submit to with a kind of despairing resignation; we rarely see it as a spiritual opportunity. When western civilization was Christian it was understood that God would send us "crosses to bear", and that these trials were important events in our spiritual lives. Now, however, we simply take them as evidence that something is wrong with us, and if we can't determine exactly what this "something wrong" might be, we will tend to explain them as the result of someone persecuting us, or as the cruel effects of blind fate, or maybe as a simple imbalance in our brain chemistry. There certainly is such a thing as a "vegetative" depression whose causes are largely physical, but the spiritual state of Contraction, though it may or may not be accompanied by depression, is something different.

Expansion (Bast) *and Contraction* (Qabd)

Contraction is a sign that we, or something in us, is avoiding the direct confrontation with Allah; consequently it might be taken as an indication that something is wrong with our inner life, but it is certainly not a "wrong" in itself. Any passion we have not repented of, any transgression we have not made amends for, will eventually produce a state of Contraction. This may lead us to feel that Allah is punishing us for our shortcomings, but this may not be the most useful way of viewing the matter. A state of Contraction sent by Allah, painful though it may be, is a mercy to us, an opportunity to purify our inner being and allow it to be imprinted with certain Names of God, which will result in the permanent realization of particular virtues. Ibn Ata'allah maintained that one is much less likely to violate *adab* with Allah in the state of Contraction than in that of Expansion. The potential for Contraction will remain until we attain Annihilation in God; the sense of our own self-existence is in itself a form of Contraction, and the root of all the others. As Rabi'ah al-'Adawiyyah said to a young man who claimed that he had never sinned, "Alas, my son, thine existence is a sin wherewith no other sin may be compared."

According to the Heart

The Heart experiences Contraction as a release of limitations, allowing it to locate the central Kernel of itself that is beyond both Contraction and Expansion—*al-Ruh*. The Heart knows that Humility is all unveiling, that nothing can be Contracted but resistance to God, and that this resistance, which is the immediate agent of Contraction, is released by Contraction itself. The Heart in the state of Contraction is grateful that Allah cares enough to purify it, and takes this purification, no matter how rigorous, as a sign that Allah will never abandon it.

According to the *Nafs*

Allah hath given you victory on many fields and on the day of Huneyn, when ye exulted in your multitude—but it availed you naught, and the earth, vast as it is, was straitened for you; then ye turned back in flight. . . . [Q. 9:25]

149

The Nafs takes Contraction as an opportunity to shirk responsibility by pleading helplessness, to avoid compassion by claiming a lack of the energy and resources to help or regard others, to reject submission by maintaining that it is impossible to willingly submit to a God tyrannical enough to send a state of Contraction. *But whenever He trieth him by straitening his means of life, he saith: My Lord despiseth me* [Q. 89:16]. In Contraction the Nafs struggles against the Will of Allah, seeks Dispersion in the passions as an avenue of relief, and ultimately sinks into spiritual despair. If the Nafs despairs, however, we can take this as an opportunity (insha'Allah) to despair *of* the Nafs instead, and let Allah fully enter the Heart.

Contraction as Experienced by the Body

As we have already seen, it is a central principle of Sufi psychology that "when the Heart expands the Nafs contracts." And as long as the body remains identified with the Nafs and controlled by it, the contraction of the Nafs contracts the body as well. When the great physical heaviness of the state of Contraction descends upon us, the "natural" reaction is to fight it, to try to expand or limber up somehow, to do our best to create some kind of physical or emotional or imaginative space so that we can breathe again. This, however, is only the Nafs fighting to maintain its illusory self-existence. When the crushing weight of God's Presence descends upon us, the correct *adab* is not to fight Him, not to struggle to get free from His grasp, but rather to submit to the state of Contraction he has sent while simultaneously turning our attention to the fact that for every ounce of contractive pressure exerted on the Nafs, an equal amount of expansive energy has entered the Heart. If we can concretely sense this "Expansion in the fist of Contraction" and follow it, we are then in the process of freeing our body from the grip of the Nafs and placing it under the rule of the Spirit.

And at the moment when the Nafs as the illusion of self-determination and self-creation is actually dying (so-to-speak), as a last resort it may try to convince us that the *body* is dying; this will be experienced as a deep physical faintness and shock, sometimes accompanied by a whole range of alarming symptoms. These, insha'Allah, will be temporary. The cure here is to remember, believe, and realize the *hadith qudsi*: "And when I love him (My servant), I become his ears with which he listens, and his eyes with which he sees, and his hands with which he strikes, and his feet with which he walks, [to which the Sufis sometimes add] until I am him" [Bukhari]. And we also need to remember, in relation to this process, that we can never really become Allah, whereas Allah *has always been us*; we are merely his creatures and His signs, while He is our Essence. All becoming is an illusion of the Nafs; it can never be a part of the true nature of God. Nonetheless the dispelling of the veils of the Nafs is experienced as a process of Allah "becoming", as it were, the limbs and organs of the one being filled with His Presence, this being a transition from illusion to Reality, from what has *never* been so to what has *always* been so.

Allah is *Al-Hayy*, Life—so breathe Him in.

Virtues to be Gained in the Station of Contraction

Fear of God; Humility; Repentance; Patience, Compassion for others' suffering (via *Al-Rahim*); Spiritual Poverty; Abstinence; Renunciation; Detachment; Sincerity; Trust-in-God; Submission, Self-effacement, Vigilance, Discretion, and many more.

Mode of *Taslim*

Taslim in the state of Contraction to stop fighting for space and air and submit to being crushed in the fist of Power. Submission in Contraction is the willingness to be humbled and abased by Allah, to have every one of His gifts taken away from you, not simply in helpless compliance but in active gratitude, in the faith that He is giving you exactly what you need by this abasement, that the reason He is stripping you of all His gifts is because you have turned them into idols through possessiveness and identification, which means that He is not actually withdrawing His blessings from you but rather purifying you of His curse. In Expansion, gratitude simply interrupts the flow of God's bounty, and consequently has no place; only in Contraction can you be grateful in full Sincerity, since you have now reached the certainty that your gratitude is not for the gifts of Allah but for Allah Himself. In the state of Contraction He will squeeze every gift out of you, all but one—*obedience*. When He reduces you to "just do it", then all you can do is do it—shoulder the burden and follow His commands with no thought of reward in either this life or the next. This is the deepest *Taslim* of all.

In Relationship

Contraction in relationship purifies you of your possessive need to constantly associate with other people for support or gratification or entertainment or protection.

The Synthesis of Expansion and Contraction

What transcends Expansion and Contraction? The station of Place-lessness. The sense of having insufficient spiritual room and the suffering this causes, the longing for wider spiritual space and the glorying in it, have to do with a sense that you are placed somewhere on the ladder of spiritual development. But in reality you are nowhere—nowhere but in the Presence of Allah. When the ego is forgotten it can contract no further; when the Heart contains Allah it can expand no further. To experience Expansion and Contraction is to have yourself in view, to attempt to measure yourself by the standard of yourself. But when identification-with-self dissolves and only Allah is seen, Expansion and Contraction come to an end.

6

Fluctuation (*Talwin*)
and Stability (*Tamkin*)

*Who made the earth a resting-place for you, and placed roads for you
therein, that haply ye may find your way.* [Q. 43:10]

*So know (O Muhammad) that there is no God save Allah, and ask
forgiveness for thy sin and for believing men and believing women.
Allah knoweth (both) your place of turmoil and your place of rest.*
[Q. 47:19]

◇

I f it weren't for the Fluction of spiritual states, it would be
impossible to travel the Path; all would be fixed in the distance
from Allah they occupied at the moment of their birth. If it
weren't for the manifestation of the state of Stability, no virtues
could be gained, no *hal* could become a permanent *maqam*, no
human Heart could become qualified with the Names and
Attributes of Allah. So both Fluctuation and Stability are gifts of *Al-
Rahman*, the All-Merciful. Without Stability terrestrial life would be
chaos; without Fluctuation it would petrify. But since both Fluctuation and Stability pertain, life is truly alive; it is graced with form
without being imprisoned in it, blessed with motility without being
dissolved by it. Thus we can say that the archetype of both Fluctuation and Stability is *Al-Hayy*, Allah as Universal Life.

FLUCTUATION

*Unto Allah belong the East and the West, and whithersoever ye turn,
there is Allah's Countenance. Lo! Allah is All-Embracing, All-Know-
ing.* [Q. 2:115]

153

It is not righteousness that ye turn your faces to the East and the West; but righteous is he who believeth in Allah. . . . [Q. 2:177]

And had We willed, We verily could have fixed them in their place, making them powerless to go forward or turn back. [Q. 36:67]

And We set, between them and the towns which We had blessed, towns easy to be seen, and We made the stage between them easy, (saying): travel in them safely both by night and day. [Q. 34:18]

He knoweth that there are sick folk among you, while others travel in the land in search of Allah's bounty, and others (still) are fighting for the cause of Allah. . . . [Q. 73:20]

Fluctuation is the Divine impulse to realize possibilities in time, the outer expression of Allah in the mode of *Wahadiyya*, His synthetic Unity, in the embrace of which all facets of Possible Being, under the power of His Necessary Being, are fully actualized in Him. *Every day doth some new work employ Him* [55:29/55:29], but in his own Divine Nature he is subject to neither Day nor Night. It is by the principle of Fluctuation that Allah enlightens and purifies the Heart through the alternation of spiritual States. The *human* attempt to actualize possibilities in time is inherently unstable, even though it draws upon the *might* of Allah to transform what only *might* happen into something that actually does happen. This is due to the fact that the realization of one possibility can only find its occasion through the neglect or abandonment of many others. In addition, an actualized possibility can only remain in this state of fulfillment if our attention to it never wavers—something that time makes impossible. Consequently the temporal actualization of possibilities is necessarily limited in both comprehensiveness and duration. Yet when the Heart is purified of self-will and reactivity, Fluctuation becomes the very Will of Allah in both the Day and the Night, His direct action upon the human soul by which its submission and obedience are perfected, by which it becomes like a corpse in the hands of a Washer of the Dead.

Metaphysical Principle

The state of Fluctuation is a reflection, in the Human Heart, of the truth that Allah is not fixed in His Eternity, but eternally overflows into motion and rhythm. Waves are nothing but water—yet no ocean, simply by virtue of the fact that it is all water, is without waves. In other words, Fluctuation is a manifestation of Allah in the mode of Possible Being, or rather of That One in Whom all possibilities are actualized. The state of Fluctuation is an expression of God in His Names *Al-Hayy* (the Living), *Al-Zahir* (the Manifest), *Al-Mubdi* (the Beginner), *Al-Muqadim* (the Promoter), *Al-Mu'akhkhir* (the Postponer), *Al-Sabur* (the Patient), etc. As Allah says in the *hadith qudsi*, "Why do they complain to Me of the fluctuations of fortune brought about by Time? I *am* Time" [Bukhari; Muslim]. Allah is most certainly *Al-Samad*, the Eternal; He is in no way subject to Time. But this Divine Eternity not any kind of fixity or motionlessness or petrification; it is filled with motion because it is filled with Life. Because Allah is *Al-Hayy* (the Living) and *Al-Qadir* (the All-Powerful), He is totally free of any limitations imposed on His Self-expression. He is not bound by His intrinsic nature but rather liberated by it, eternally free to create what He wills to create, destroy what he wills to destroy, and change what He wills to change. This Divine freedom—which is resonant, radiant Eternity in the *Batin*, vibrating around its own immutable Center—appears in the *Zahir* as Time.

According to the Heart

The Heart in a state of Fluctuation experiences all existence as music. Everything is change, but nonetheless there is a rhythm and a tempo to it. Everything passes, but the *waqt*, the Present Moment, the mirror that is a perfect host first to this state and then to that, remains forever. The Heart in *Talwin* responds to each change and each moment with the *adab* that is proper to it. It is not prevented by pride or fear, or by any fixed idea or attitude of feeling, from prostrating to a King in one moment, giving alms to a beggar in another, fleeing from an enemy in another, coming to the defense of a friend in another, or regarding the beauty of a bride in still another. No matter what changes Allah decrees for it, it always remains itself; it is the Son of the Moment. And, as with the state of Dispersion, the mercurial function of holy humor—when the occa-

155

sion is appropriate—serves to break down our attachment to the fixed ideas and hypocritical self-images that prevent us from being responsive to the Will of Allah in the dimension of time. In the Sufi world, the comic figure of Mullah Nasruddin is a manifestation of this function.

The ultimate knowledge to be derived from the state of Fluctuation is the vision of "occasion"—the recognition that Allah recreates the whole universe, including us, in each separate instant, and consequently that secondary causes, while it is permissible to discern them and work with them for this or that particular purpose, are at the same time eternally dominated and swallowed up by Allah in His Name *Al-Mubdi*, the First Cause.

According to the *Nafs*

The Nafs experiences changes in its state not as rhythm but as chaos. Fluctuation according to the Nafs is a perpetual flight from responsibility and reality, resulting in unreliability, faithlessness, heedlessness, disloyalty and dishonesty. In order to enforce these conditions, the Nafs will sometimes produce in us an addiction to triviality, frivolity and the sort of demonic humor that works to destroy meaning.

Virtues to be Gained in the Station of Fluctuation

Flexibility; versatility in Submission to God's commands, unveilings, and the needs of various situations in the station of *Ibn al-Waqt*, the Son of the Moment; Aspiration; Courage; Patience; Valor; Shame; Annihilation in God's Acts.

Mode of *Taslim*

Taslim in the state of Fluctuation is to be willing to be like a corpse in the hands of a Washer of the Dead—to let Him turn you, this way and that, without resistance—to let Time pass, and bring what it will, and take away what it will, and break every handhold, and fill the cup of every beggar, and kill and capture every rebel, and put down every resistance, and make every king a pauper, and make every pauper a king, and bring down every mountain, and raise up every valley, and end the regime of pride and self-will, the illusion that one is or ever could be in control of events, absolutely, once and for all.

In Relationship

Fluctuation in relationship allows you to accept alterations in other people, to learn not to imprison them in your own conceptions. It teaches you to change with the changing moods and conditions of the one you are presently relating to without feeling manipulated, hurt or teased, but rather as if you were being informed or instructed.

STABILITY

Who hath appointed the earth a resting-place for you, and the sky a canopy; and causeth water to pour down from the sky, thereby producing fruits as food for you. And do not set up rivals to Allah when ye know (better). [Q. 2:22]

Allah ordained this only as a message of good cheer for you, and that thereby your hearts might be at rest. Victory cometh only from Allah, the Mighty, the Wise. [Q. 3:126]

Who have believed and whose hearts have rest in the remembrance of Allah. Verily in the remembrance of Allah do hearts find rest! [Q. 13:28]

Those who have earned the Garden on that day will be better in their home and happier in their place of noonday rest. . . . [Q. 25:24]

And of His signs is this: He created for you helpmeets from yourselves that ye might find rest in them, and He ordained between you love and mercy. Lo! herein indeed are portents for folk who reflect. [Q. 30:21]

And the sun runneth on unto a resting-place for him. That is the measuring of the Mighty, the Wise. [Q. 36:38]

And He hath subjected to you the night and the day; the sun and the moon and the stars too are subjected to you by His behest; verily, in this are signs for those who understand. [Q. 16:12/16:12]

◇

Stability is the realization of the Unity of God, and the peace, constancy and completion which flow from it.

Metaphysical Principle

The state of Stability is founded, in human terms, on the knowledge of what is always true—of Allah as Necessary Being in His Names *Al-Haqq*, the Truth, *Al-Samad*, the Eternal Source, and *Al-Salam*, the Flawless—and the complete conformation of the human being to the One who is beyond all change: "He was before He brought place and time into existence, and He is even now as He was." [*hadith* recounted by Ibn 'Abd al-Salam, al-Mulha fi I' tiqad Ahl al-Haqq, in his *Rasa'il al-Tawhid*].

According to the Heart

The station of Stability according to the Heart is the station of the *Qutb*, the Pole around which all things revolve—something one western poet (T.S. Eliot) called "the still point of the turning world;" the "turning" of the Mevlevi Dervishes symbolizes Stability in this sense. The Pole is *al-Ruh* manifest not as a rising and falling Wind, but as an eternal, vertical Ray of Divine Light, piercing *al-Qalb* and ordering all its motions, transforming them from unpredictable flashes of Lightning into a dance of constancy and rhythm. To the one in the station of Stability, spiritual development is no longer achieved through Fluctuation, through passing from one state to another as if the *ahwal* were bound and conditioned by time, but is experienced as a progressive deepening of his realization and embodiment of the eternal Center. Whoever has reached the station of Stability becomes a refuge and a point-of-reference for all who aspire to freedom from chaos; thus he may be called *al-Qutb*, the Pole (though the one known as the Pole of the Age is at a much higher station—remote, inaccessible, and yet present at the Center of every center), and pointed to as a reflection of Allah in His Name *Al-Hadi*, the Guide. He is one of those "mountains" that Allah has placed upon the earth to give it Stability and duration: *And He hath thrown firm mountains on the earth, lest it move with you; and rivers and paths for your guidance* [Q. 16:15/16:15].

Stability flowers in the station of Sobriety and is ultimately perfected in the station of Subsistence.

According to the *Nafs*

The state of Stability according to the Nafs is paralysis and petrification masquerading as spiritual attainment. The mind is filled with prejudices and fixed ideas presenting themselves as eternal principles, the feelings with an icy coldness pretending to be spiritual impassivity and detachment, and the will with an impenetrable, petrified intent claiming to be strength of character and loyalty to the Truth. The one possessed by false stability is incapable of creatively, strategically or compassionately responding to the real needs of people and situations, and is unmoved as well by the daily commands of Allah, since he see these commands as already having been issued, and himself as having already fulfilled every one of them. He does not accept that Allah has the power to do anything new, consequently he views the ongoing actions and signs of Allah *on the horizons* and *in [his] own soul* only as innovations, deviations from the established order of things. The one bound by Stability according to the Nafs sees time as a barren sandstorm that he wishes to avoid, and eternity as a block of stone or ice that he aspires to emulate.

Virtues to be Gained in the Station of Stability

Trustworthiness; Constancy in spiritual practice; Courtesy; Justice; Veracity; mastery over the vicissitudes of time in the station of *Abu al-Waqt*, the Father of the Moment.

Mode of *Taslim*

Taslim in the state of Stability is to resist the temptation to seek novelty but be willing instead to embrace regularity and monotony, in the understanding that the "single tone" that makes up this monotony is, precisely, the Name of Allah. If each heartbeat is different, the Heart is diseased; if each heartbeat is identical, the Heart is whole. In the *maqam* of Stability the *Dhikr* of Allah is fully established.

In Relationship

Stability in makes you reliable and trustworthy in every relationship.

The Synthesis of Fluctuation and Stability

What transcends Fluctuation and Stability? The station of the perfection of Stability, in which Fluctuation is given free rein because it no longer has the power to produce bewilderment, heedlessness or dissipation. A dancer without Stability will fall; a dancer who has achieved Stability can move freely and never lose his balance; he is at rest in the center of motion.

The Relationship of Fluctuation and Stability to Expansion and Contraction from the Standpoint of Alchemy

There is a special relationship between the states of Contraction and Expansion and those of Stability and Fluctuation that has been partly elucidated by the science of alchemy. Stability is related to Sulfur in its "fixing" aspect, Expansion to Sulfur in its "volatilizing" aspect, Contraction to Quicksilver in its "congealing" aspect, and Fluctuation to Quicksilver in its "dissolving" aspect. Stability is Dryness; Expansion is Heat; Contraction is Cold; Fluctuation is Humidity.

The marriage of Stability and Fluctuation, *Tamkin* and *Talwin*, is the establishment of a fixed, transcendent point of consciousness witnessing universal change; it is Allah beholding the play of His Names and Acts in the mirror of the universe through the Eye of the Heart: *Allah, who brings to light the secret things of heaven and earth* [Q. 27:25]. The union of Expansion and Contraction, *Bast* and *Qabd*, is Unity of Heart contemplating the infinite expanse of the Divine Nature. The Heart is Contracted away from the world and Expanded in God. This is known as "Expansion in the fist of Contraction"; it is another name for Gathering. "Heaven and earth cannot contain Me, but the Heart of my loving slave can contain Me." The union of Expansion and Contraction is the Heart's contemplation of God's Names and Attributes as they appear within the depths of the Divine Nature; it is related to the *Ma'rifah* of Allah; its direction is from man to God. The marriage of Stability and Fluctuation is God's contemplation of His universal manifestation, whose synthesis is the human form; it is related to *Ma'rifah* of the Nafs; its direction is from God to man.

7

Intoxication (*Sukr*)
and Sobriety (*Sahw*)

T HE STATES OF INTOXICATION (Drunkenness) and Sobriety
operate by and through the feelings. In Intoxication the will
and the intellect are absorbed into the affections; in Sobriety
the intellect, affections and will are distinct and in conscious relationship to one another: *this* is what is known; *this* is what is felt;
this is what is intended.

Drunkenness is the merging of subject and object so that the
experiencer is no longer distinguished from his or her experience;
Sobriety is a clear differentiation between experience and experiencer.

In Drunkenness the world as a separate reality disappears; in this
it is like Absence from the standpoint of the Heart. The difference is
that one may be drunk on God's manifestations, not necessarily, or
always, upon His naked Presence. (al-Junayd, on the other hand,
treats Drunkenness, Absence and Annihilation as virtually identical.)

In Sobriety the world is clearly there; it is like Presence from the
standpoint of the Heart. The difference is that in the state Presence
one is conscious of the world as the Presence of Allah without any
discernible polarity between world and self, while in the state of
Sobriety Allah is the One Who shows His signs in both self and
world because He is known as the ultimate Essence of both. (al-
Junayd, however, considers Sobriety to be the station that succeeds
Annihilation, thus making it virtually identical to Subsistence.)

Drunkenness from the standpoint of the Heart is the obliteration
of all claims to separate existence in the Presence of God. From the

standpoint of the Nafs it is a repression, a denial, a glossing-over of these claims even though they still exist, a way of shielding them within heedlessness and oblivion so as to prevent them from being exposed and dissolved. Sobriety from the standpoint of the Heart is *adab* in the presence of God: *When that which shroudeth did enshroud the Lote Tree, the eye turned not aside nor yet was overbold* [Q. 53:16–17]. It is a clear awareness of one's claim to separate existence so that it may be consciously renounced on the plane of essence, while still being maintained, so as to allow one to bear the full responsibility for it, on the plane of form. From the standpoint of the Nafs it is the acceptance of *al-Dunya* and the various practical matters relating to it as the whole of reality, the act of putting the world in the place of God.

INTOXICATION

And He it is Who sendeth the winds, glad tidings heralding His mercy, and We send down purifying water from the sky.... [Q. 25:48]

A similitude of the Garden which those who keep their duty (to Allah) are promised: Therein are rivers of water unpolluted, and rivers of milk whereof the flavour changeth not, and rivers of wine delicious to the drinkers, and rivers of clear-run honey.... [Q. 47:15]

A cup from a gushing spring is brought round for them,
White, delicious to the drinkers,
Wherein there is no headache nor are they made mad thereby. [Q. 37:45–47]

Their raiment will be fine green silk and gold embroidery. Bracelets of silver will they wear. Their Lord will slake their thirst with a pure drink. [Q. 76:21]

They are given to drink of a pure wine, sealed,
Whose seal is musk—for this let (all) those strive who strive for bliss—
And mixed with water of Tasnim,
A spring whence those brought near (to Allah) drink. [Q. 83:25–28]

In the state of Intoxication, the overwhelming rapture of Allah's Presence paralyzes both thought and will. Thought cannot encompass Him, nor can the will will anything unless He wills it first. The ability to fulfill one's duties, worldly or religious, is swept away, proving that even the most impeccable faithfulness to the shari'ah cannot command Allah's Mercy nor avert His Justice, and that when religion becomes defined and conditioned by the Dunya, and the pursuit of and identification with religion constitutes membership in the Dunya, the only ones who truly remain faithful to Allah are those who are drunk and ruined. Intoxication is the *malamati* way, the Path of Blame, the road to liberation from the false shame of the World, from the chains of hypocrisy, and from the prison of social pride.

Metaphysical Principle

The state of Intoxication is a reflection, in the human Heart, of the reality that God is Love; it is an expression of Allah in His Name *Al-Fattah*, the Opener, *Al-Karim*, the Generous, and *Al-Wadud*, the Loving-kind. Love is the source of insight, but Love in Intoxication transcends insight, and bewilders it. Love is the source of loyalty, but Love in Intoxication—the Rapturous Love known as *Ishq*—by the profusion of its Generosity, swallows up loyalty, providing it with no fixed object to which it might remain loyal. Intoxication is a Divine infusion that arrives from beyond human feeling—and since it transcends feeling, it has the power to suffuse feeling, to transform it from this or that emotion, directed to this or that object, into *pure* feeling, feeling which is its own object. Intoxication is Love without a Lover, Love in which there is nothing but the Beloved—a state in which Love for the Beloved is not directed *to* the Beloved, but *is* the Beloved.

Hafiz (in my transcreation drawn from three of his odes, and based on the translations of H. Wilberforce Clarke) says of the state of Intoxication:

Intoxication (Sukr) *and Sobriety* (Sahw)

If that Turk of Shiraz takes my heart,
I'll give Bokhara and Samarkand both for the mole on
    that cheek. . . .

What does the Beloved's beauty
Need with our own flawed beauty?
Loveliness Itself requires neither makeup, nor rouge,
Nor painted mole, nor pencilled eyebrow. . . .

Our Pir abandoned the mosque last night
And headed for the tavern instead!
Now what should his poor disciples do?
How can we face toward the Kaaba
When our Teacher can't face in any direction at all
Except toward the Winemaster?
I suppose we'll have to take up residence
In the Tavern of the Fire-worshipper;
That must have been our destiny
Since before the beginning of time.

Locked in that lock,
In the hangman's noose of that dark hair,
His heart is happy.
(The wise would lose their minds—
If wisdom only knew.)

According to the Heart

Spiritual Drunkenness or Intoxication dissolves the knots and crystallizations of the affections that are produced by the heedlessness
and fixed ideas of the impure intellect and the impulses and refusals
of the impure will. In the state of Drunkenness the affections are
overwhelmed with the rapture of Divine Love, and both the will
and the intellect submit to this Love. Through this submission to
rapturous Love the will moves beyond the station of raw will-
power—which cannot be maintained for any length of time—and
gains the power to *love what it intends,* and intend it more forcefully, thus producing constancy in both interpersonal relations and
spiritual practice. And the intellect, through its own submission to

this rapturous Love, gains the power to come into true intimacy with the Object of its knowledge, and so learns to *love what it knows*, and through this love to know It more deeply. But these powers only come into play after Sobriety has returned. In the state of Sobriety, the rapture of the affections is moderated and muted; the faculties of intellect, affections and will emerge again from their state of Drunken Union as three distinct powers. Drunkenness has dissolved the deficient, excessive and imbalanced connections between these faculties so that the proper, sober balance between them can be achieved and maintained. Consequently the use of music and poetry in Sufism is not some kind of sentimentality or spiritual self-indulgence (though it can certainly degenerate into these) but rather a *science of Intoxication* to be employed only at the appropriate time and for the appropriate purpose—a method for dissolving, by the power of Allah, the knots and crystallizations of the feeling-substance (its *egos*, its *idols*) so that the energy of liberated emotion can give substance and depth to the intellect to *know* Allah, and also feed and strengthen the will to *obey* Allah. The following ode of Hafiz—my version based on the translation of H. Wilberforce Clarke—expresses something of what music and lyric poetry, and the state of Intoxication they may help to catalyze in the context of a Divine "infusion", can be and do in a Sufi context, and also how the state of Intoxication is allied to that of Expansion:

> The morning of good fortune has come!
> Where is the bowl, beaten and burnished like the sun?
> Bring the cup quickly, for opportunity knocks.
>
> In this house without strife, the Cupbearer is my friend
> And subtle wisdom flows
> From the minstrel's lips.
> It is the season of youth, the hour of ease;
> From hand to hand, the cup goes round.
>
> This cup of gold was mixed with ruby elixir
> Only to expand the heart, to adorn it with the jewel
> Of beauty and of gladness.

Intoxication (Sukr) *and Sobriety* (Sahw)

The drunken ones are dancing, the Beloved and his
    minstrel are waving their arms
In time to the music;
The Saki has stolen sleep from every eye.

This house of safety, this secret cell, this hidden chamber
    of pleasure
Where best friends meet—
Whoever has found his way into our company
Has found the locked and guarded house
Where a hundred doors stand open.

Thinking to add even further grace to the essence of wine
The subtle breeze, Nature's coutourier
Placed rose-water in the leaf of the rose.

When I knew that the Full Moon [*the shaykh for whom the
    sama' was performed*]
Had paid with his soul for those pearls of Hafiz [*his lyrics*],
In that very moment, the sharp twang of the lute
Touched the ear of Zuhra!

Zuhra is the female singer performing one of Hafiz' poems before
the assembly. Hafiz is saying that a state of Expansion and Intoxication on the part of the shaykh, an exquisite riff on the *setar* (the Persian "percussive lute"), and a moment when the singing of Zuhra
truly surpassed both itself and her, happened in the same *waqt*, the
same instant of spiritual time, without one factor or the other being
the cause; the True Cause, Allah in His Names *Al-Mubdi'*, the Beginner, and *Al-Fattah*, the Opener, is beyond time entirely, and consequently can influence the whole field simultaneously: *I will show
them My signs on the horizons and in their own souls until they are
satisfied that this is the Truth. Is it not enough for you, that I am Witness over all things?* [Q. 41:53] And Hafiz was there to hear it. The
poem seems to suggest that "real" wine was being drunk, but this
never has been the norm in Sufi gatherings. *Tasawwuf* is based on
an inner understanding of the Qur'an which was never considered
to abrogate its outer prescriptions for comportment and behavior,
except in the case of various deviant groups. Sufis—especially Persian Sufis—have nonetheless often adopted the slanders directed

against them by their opponents (much as the "Quakers", the "Shakers" and the "Methodists" did in Britain and America) for use as spiritual allegories; that's why they would sometimes call themselves "drunkards", "rakes", "libertines" etc., hiding Allah's gift of Divine Love in the language of social shame. (This is known as the *malamati* way, the "path of blame.") It was the woman Sufi Rabi'ah al-'Adawiyyah, a well-known ascetic of early Islam, who apparently introduced the metaphor of wine into Sufi poetry to represent the Intoxication of Divine Love—and no-one would ever accuse Rabi'a, the soul of sobriety, of being a wine-drinker. As for the presence of a female singer at the gathering in question, suffice it to say that there have always been woman Sufis, and that the attempt at total exclusion of women from public life and social intercourse in Islam is a comparatively recent development. In the words of the Prophet Muhammad, peace and blessings be upon him, "Three things have been made delightful to me: women, perfume and prayer." If a female singer is concealed behind a screen her voice may still be heard, and it is recounted by Alkami on the authority of Ibn Majah, that on one occasion when the Prophet, peace and blessings be upon him, returned to Medina after a battle, a slave woman came to him and said, "O Messenger of Allah, I have made a pledge that, if Allah returns you safely we will play the tambourine (*daff*) and sing in your presence." The Prophet replied, "If you have made a pledge then you should fulfill it."

In a more inner sense, the Full Moon is the Heart and Zuhra the Nafs it sacrifices in payment for the *hal*, which arrives that moment when the soul's dying shout and the naked listening of the Heart are one, when the cry becomes an ear, and the ear a cry. In this Drunkenness the Heart forgets its name and is named by the name of the All-Merciful. Does it suspect this new naming, or does it remain oblivious? Only Intoxication knows the answer, but because it is drowned in the Divine Speech, it cannot tell that answer. Sobriety may recount the legend of Drunkenness, but when does Drunkenness remember Sobriety? Speech may tell the story of Silence, but Silence, when asked about Speech, has nothing to say.

A more complete and transcendent state of Intoxication than even that of Hafiz is expressed in this quatrain of Rumi:

Intoxication (Sukr) *and Sobriety* (Sahw)

Because of You I beheld the jar of Love, bubbling and fermenting;
Because of You I attained to my true substance—*wine!*
But no! *You* are the wine; I am only the water.
When we are blended together, You alone appear;
I am nowhere to be seen.

[My version, based on Ibrahim Gamard and A.G. Rawan Farhadi, *The Quatrains of Rumi: Ruba'iyat-é Jalaluddin Muhammad Balkhi-Rumi*, Sufi-Dari Books, 2008].

The "sober Sufis" have always considered states of spiritual Intoxication to be dangerous, and so they are; if the Nafs gets hold of the Spiritual Wine it can go on quite a bender, even without the help of the "real" wine fermented from the grape. But the "drunken Sufis" know of a secret at the center of Intoxication that the sober Sufis have never suspected; the name of that secret is ... *Sobriety.*

According to the *Nafs*

Intoxication according to the Nafs is discourtesy, recklessness, heedlessness, the rejection of Knowledge, the illusion of invulnerability through God's favor, pursuit of oblivion in flight from Reality—which is, precisely, flight from Allah.

Virtues to be Gained in the Station of Intoxication

Sincerity; Divine Eros (*Ishq*); Renunciation of the World; Humility; Trust in God.

In Relationship

Intoxication in relationship allows you to drink in the essence of another person's identity, layer after layer of it, seeing that one as a mirror of Divine Beauty.

Mode of *Taslim*

Taslim in the state of Intoxication is to renounce all attempts to decide for yourself what to do next—even in terms of trying to show Allah how much you love Him—but to place yourself instead, with absolute trust, in the hands of the One who knows how to guide you, protect you in the darkness, and lead you safely to your destination, in the hour before dawn.

SOBRIETY

Say (unto them, O Muhammad): I exhort you unto one thing only: that ye awake, for Allah's sake, by twos and singly, and then reflect: There is no madness in your comrade. He is naught else than a warner unto you in face of a terrific doom. [Q. 34:46]

And those who keep their pledges and their covenant,
And those who stand by their testimony
And those who are attentive at their worship.
These will dwell in Gardens, honoured. [Q. 70:32–35]

◇

Sobriety is the ongoing ability to clearly distinguish between subject and object—within the context of the Presence of Allah, and in the recognition that Allah is the Essence of both subject and object, which can be distinguished only in the realm of form, but not in the realm of Essence: *I will show them My signs*—simultaneously and without division—*on the horizons and in their own souls* [Q. 41:53] This, here, is "myself"; that, over there, is "other-than-myself." "Myself" does not project parts of itself into "other-than-myself" through self-assertion, nor are parts of "other-than-myself" incorporated into "myself" through unconscious possessiveness and identification. I know what is proper to me and what is proper to the other, and I never confuse them. I know my own rights and the limits to those rights; I know the rights of the other and their own proper limits; I respect both sets of rights and both sets of limits by virtue of a single discernment, a single intention, a single act, all taking place within a single moment—an eternal moment. Sobriety is the principle of *respect* in all its modes, consequently it is the root-source of *adab*, Courtesy. As one Sufi declared, "Sufism is all Courtesy." In the words of the Holy Qur'an [Q. 53:16–17], referring to a state experienced by the Prophet Muhammad, peace and blessings

170

be upon him, during his *miraj: When that which shroudeth did enshroud the Lote Tree, the eye turned not aside nor yet was overbold.* The *Lote Tree* represents the limit of what can be known of Allah, the root and branch of His total manifestation. When the overpowering vision of Allah as the synthesis of all His Most Beautiful Names was veiled from him, the Prophet's attention *turned not aside nor yet was overbold;* he was neither indifferent nor curious; he neither became distracted, nor did he seek to pry into the Mysteries. Here we see the root of all courtesy in the human relationship with God. When one is in the presence of one's Beloved, and She in a reticent mood, it is impolite to boldly stare, and equally impolite to let one's attention wander—or to sulk, or to fawn, or to make demands. The practice is simply to wait, in humility, in vigilance, in self-respect, upon Her good pleasure. Thus, in both the Divine and the human dimensions, respect for boundaries is the necessary precursor to final Union.

The discretion and observance of limits that characterize Sobriety also extend to the primary faculties of the psyche. Sobriety understands the place of thought and the limits of thought; the place of feeling and the limits of feeling; the place of will and the limits of will.

Sobriety has to do with the balance and moderation of the feelings. When the feelings remain within their proper bounds, they do not trespass upon the realm of the thinking mind, an error that gives rise to partial, interested, emotionally-motivated thought and thus destroys the root-principle of thought, which is objectivity. Likewise, sober and disciplined feeling will not trespass on the realm of the will, distorting conscious intention by transforming it into blind, passionate impulse. In the state of Sobriety, feeling serves thought by giving it depth and sympathy; it equally serves will by giving it power and constancy.

Metaphysical Principle

The state of Sobriety is the reflection in the human Heart of the principle that Allah has complete knowledge of all things, and that all things are precisely as He knows them to be, given that His

Knowledge of them is what constitutes their reality. And since all things are required to be as Allah knows them and can in no way depart from this Knowledge, Sobriety can also be defined as a reflection in the human Heart of Allah as Necessary Being. When the Prophet, peace and blessings be upon him, prayed "O Lord, show me things as they really are," he was praying that Allah increase him in Sobriety. Allah's Knowledge of things is comprehensive and universal; to the degree that we participate in this Knowledge, we are beyond the turbulence produced by partial knowledge, the knowledge of *possibilities*, no matter how profound and ultimately accurate such knowledge may be. Partial knowledge seeks to be whole, possibility to be actualized, and in so doing seeks its opposite; this results in polarity and contention. But complete Knowledge is sober and tranquil—at peace both in labor and at rest. Sobriety is a reflection of Allah in His Names *Al-Shahid*, the Universal Witness, *Al-'Alim*, the Omniscient, *Al-Basir*, the All-Seeing, *Al-Muhsi*, the Knower of Each Separate Thing, and—as a consequence of these—also of *Al-Salam*, the Peaceful, the Flawless. Omniscience understands that everything follows its own nature, that everything is in its proper place, that all interactions between things and beings are lawful—even if some of these beings are transgressors, seeing that Justice and Retribution are also lawful—and consequently that no event is anomalous, unexpected or inappropriate; therefore it is sober and at rest.

According to the Heart

Sobriety is a realization, on the level of the Heart, of the *Fitrah*, the Primordial Human Nature. To be Sober is, as it were, to stand as Adam before God, Adam before he was expelled from the Garden. It is to be in possession of all the human faculties, in their original purity and completeness, without stress or strain. It is the spontaneous and intrinsic ability to put everything in its proper place. It is to be in the presence of God's realized Will in all objects, all conditions and all moments.

Intoxication (Sukr) *and Sobriety* (Sahw)

According to the *Nafs*

Sobriety according to the Nafs is a dry, wooden heartlessness, lacking in even the first stirrings of sympathy and eaten up with intellectual and moral pride. If one's Sobriety is invaded, conquered and counterfeited by the *Nafs al-ammara*, the result is a petrified egotism, a condition of arrogance and possessiveness based on a "mine-and-thine" that is certainly *not* the recognition that Allah is the essence of both subject and object, both *the horizons* and *ourselves*, but simply the delusion that "mine" is real and valid, and "thine," insignificant and illusory. The irony here is that to claim Sobriety for oneself alone is to see all things outside one's self-concept as dissipated and degenerate, and consequently to live in a mad, chaotic, drunken world. Allah forbid that we ever become "sober" in this way!

Virtues to be Gained in the Station of Sobriety

Courtesy; Vigilance; Dignity; Wariness; Discretion; Constancy; Discernment; Justice; Solitude-in-Company.

Mode of *Taslim*

Taslim in the state of Sobriety is to submit to being precisely what you are as God created you. It is to assume all delegated responsibility as the *khalifah* of Allah while renouncing both the longing for spiritual consolation and the pride of being in the number of the Sober Ones, including various flattering comparisons between oneself and others, in the recognition that Sobriety is not the only form of heedfulness and obedience, that Allah has infinite resources beyond Sobriety that Sobriety need not enquire after. Thus *Taslim*-in-Sobriety is also the renunciation of curiosity.

Sobriety in Work

Work defined as self-assertion is performed on the basis of self-will and its elán; defined as drudgery, on the basis of oppression and fear; defined as willing submission and obedience, on the basis of *meaning*. The era when entrepreneurial Capitalism was dominant in the western nations produced an ideology that exalted competition and initiative; obsessive or self-willed action was seen as the only alternative to the slavish role of a pencil-pusher or a beast of burden. The sense of work as of value in itself because, as a form of obedience to God, it serves the salvation of the soul—such as it was understood in a traditional monastic or craft context—all but disappeared under the Capitalist ethos. Work was seen as good in itself but not as serving any value or meaning beyond itself, other than that of acquisition; under the "work ethic" it had become a mere idol, a projection of the collective ego. Communism retained the idea of a meaningful goal for work—the building of the worker's state with a view toward creating a classless society; the same was true of various forms of liberal social idealism. But these ideals, whether Liberal or Communist, were divorced from any transcendent *raison d'être*; consequently the notion of work as promoting the dignity of the human person was either emptied of any real meaning or else discarded altogether. Partly as a result of these historical developments, it has become difficult for us in the West to understand submission and obedience to transcendental values, and to those who represent them—both in and outside of the context of work—not only as self-sacrificial loyalty but equally as true freedom.

The Sufi works neither on the basis of inner self-will nor that of outer oppression and coercion (seeing that many who labor under coercion by oppressors would gladly transform themselves into oppressors themselves if they got the chance). He works on the basis of submission, obedience, and service to Allah—service that, ideally at least, is free of any sense of oppression because it is free of resistance. He dedicates to Allah every action that is required of him in the course of his daily life; his practice of *Dhikr* and other spiritual duties and exercises takes place in the same spirit. The Sufi serves neither the tyranny of an oppressive superior nor the tyranny of his own Nafs; he serves *necessity*, which is precisely the Will of Allah as manifest in conditions. This necessity may appear via the self-will and egotism of another, or the burden of an oppressive situation, as well as through the wise prescriptions of a true Master, but the *faqir* sees beyond all this to its real point of origin, which is Allah as Necessary Being. One modern Sufi observed that necessity, because of its relationship not to what might be or what we would wish to be but to what *must* be, carries its own grace along with it. Service to necessity requires humility, and such service represents humility in its finest form.

In Relationship

Sobriety in relationship teaches you to *respect* people in the literal sense of that word, which means "to look again"; it frees you from your momentary impressions of, or fixed ideas about, other people, thus allowing you to see them as they really are, and so treat them justly. This way of relating to other people is an expression of the virtue of Solitude-in-Company.

The Synthesis of Intoxication and Sobriety

What transcends Intoxication and Sobriety? The station of "sober without and drunk within", based on the understanding that Love and Knowledge are One.

Sobriety may be seen as a higher station than Intoxication, but not if it still exists as a polar opposite to Intoxication. Just as the uncomfortable "dryness" of the recovering alcoholic shows that alcohol still has a hold on him even if he is not indulging in it, so a dry spiritual Sobriety is not complete until it incorporates Drunkenness and raises it to a higher level, the *maqam* of "sober without and drunk within." A rapturous intoxication with God—like an intoxication with one's human beloved—is imperfect if it leads to thoughtless behavior, discourtesy and lack of discretion, while the ability to "hold one's liquor" (so to speak) indicates a greater maturity in one's relationship with God. A love of God that results in instability may burn out certain lower passions, replacing them with higher ones, but it cannot lead to Knowledge of God, to *Ma'rifah*. In the words of Hafiz (possibly incorrect because quoted from memory),

> You will not become drunk on the spiritual wine
> If you pour it down your shirt.

To be sober without and intoxicated within may be compared to "banking the coals" of a wood fire by covering them with ashes, thus allowing them to stay hot for a long time. If the Love of God is always being passionately expressed in word and action, it may become cheapened and jaded—but Love held silently in the depths of the Heart, protected from exposure to profane eyes, will last long, and deepen.

And Sobriety itself can be intoxicating. The Sobriety of the simple confrontation between the human witness and the ultimate Object—between "man as such and God as such"—when the open space between them is entirely free of the turbulence of thought and emotion, and there is nothing left of the human witness but this very act of witnessing, is the subtlest intoxication of all, like breaking a long and difficult fast with a sip of fragrant jasmine tea. Thus the highest form of Intoxication—which is also one of the mature fruits of Sobriety—is the quality of serenity. (One modern Sufi spoke of the act of embracing Islam as being like awakening from a troubled sleep to the clear tranquility of dawn.)

And in the highest station of Sobriety, the Witness is no longer the human subject, but Allah Himself. When we know ourselves as known by *Al-Shahid*, the Absolute Witness, and understand that we exist only by virtue of His Witnessing, then the intoxicated attempt to lose ourselves in the Beloved comes to an end, for the simple reason that we no longer have any self to lose. Now the Self is not me, but HE; this is one of the many meanings of the *hadith*, "he who knows himself knows his Lord." Thus the perfection of Intoxication and the perfection of Sobriety are essentially the same thing.

8

Intimacy (*Uns*) and Awe (*Haybat*)

They only are the (true) believers whose hearts feel fear when Allah is mentioned, and when His revelations are recited unto them they increase their faith, and who trust in their Lord. [Q. 8:2]

And they will not heed unless Allah willeth (it). He is the fount of fear. He is the fount of Mercy. [Q. 74:56]

But for him who feareth the standing before his Lord there are two gardens. [Q. 55:46]

Lo! those who fear their Lord in secret, theirs will be forgiveness and a great reward. [Q. 67:12]

Their reward is with their Lord: Gardens of Eden underneath which rivers flow, wherein they dwell for ever. Allah hath pleasure in them and they have pleasure in Him. This is (in store) for him who feareth his Lord. [Q. 98:8]

◇

There is a fear of Allah that comes from distance and transgression; it is a sign that faith in Him has not been entirely lost. There is an Intimacy with Allah by which this fear is swallowed up in the Divine Beauty. There is another fear and awe of Allah that comes from nearness and the foretaste of Annihilation; it is Beauty itself which delivers us to this fear. There is another Intimacy which follows Annihilation, and is named Subsistence in God; it is the Intimacy not of the relatedness of two terms, but of finished Unity in the One.

Intimacy (beyond the fires of Awe) is the herald of Presence; Presence (before the abyss of Annihilation) is the herald of Subsistence.

Intimacy from the standpoint of the Heart is the perfection of trust in God; to see God as beautiful is to lose all fear of Him, to love Him as the most Beautiful of the Beautiful. Intimacy from the standpoint of the Nafs is the violation of *adab*, the foolish habit of taking God for granted, leading to forgetfulness of one's obligations to Him and His reduction from *Al-Malik*, (the King), *Al-'Aziz* (the Eminent), *Al-Mutakabbir* (the Proud), *Al-Hakam* (the Arbitrator), *Al-Kabir* (the Great), *Al-'Ali* (the Most High), *Al-Jalil* (the Majestic), *Al-Majid* (the Magnificent), and *Al-Qadir* (the All-Powerful), to a childish playmate or an indulgent parent; this is how the Nafs works to degrade Intimacy to the level of mere vulgar familiarity.

Awe from the standpoint of the Heart is rapture in the face of God's Majesty, trembling on the brink of Annihilation. In the state of Awe, God is too tremendous a Reality to draw near to, and at the same time too powerful a Force to escape or hide from; in the face of the Divine Majesty, the sense of separate self-existence becomes unbearable, and begs to be released. Awe from the standpoint of the Nafs is the slanderous accusation that God is a cruel tyrant, a lie that results in a freezing or petrification of the affections, coupled with a headlong flight into despair and self-destruction. (Nonetheless, on the threshold of despair, a chance for repentance may mercifully be offered—*take it.*) The Nafs may also produce in you the blasphemous tendency to play the tyrant yourself, to appoint yourself the representative of God's Majesty in the foolish belief that you will then not be subject to his Wrath because you are the agent of it. There are plenty self-appointed servants of the Wrath of God, however, who will end up as close companions of that Wrath for all eternity—unless God relent. All Wrath is from Allah, but this certainly does not mean that all who are wrathful are true servants of Allah! According to Ibn al-'Arabi, to extend Mercy is simultaneously to receive it; likewise to extend Wrath, without God's express command, is to be equally subject to Wrath. God does not first punish or reward us in recompense for our actions, but by means of them.

The Nafs does its best to turn Awe into anger, and then offers us lust as a way of appeasing that anger, thus corrupting Awe and Intimacy at the same time. Awe may indicate that the one experiencing it is brought near to Allah while still in a state of transgression and idolatry; the traveler's closeness to the Majestic purges his Heart of its impurities, until *Al-Jalal* gives way to *Al-Jamal*, Awe to Intimacy. Conversely, Intimacy may be seen as Allah's seductiveness, his drawing of the traveler, by means of the unveiling of His Beauty, inexorably toward His Majesty, so that *Al-Jamal* gives way to *Al-Jalal*, conducting the *faqir* to a state of nearness that would have been impossible to him to approach or endure if Allah had unveiled His Majesty at the outset. But in any case, both Awe and Intimacy only arrive after God has become entirely real to the *faqir*—real and inescapable; thus the finished and established sense of the Presence of God may be seen as the synthesis of the Majesty of God and the Beauty of God. Awesome Majesty is a Beauty too great for us to encompass—and Beauty itself, however merciful, however welcoming, has its own awesomeness; it is the first sign of the swift arrival of death, the herald of Annihilation. But just as "My Mercy has precedence over My Wrath" [Bukhari], so, in the experience of His faithful servants, His Beauty has precedence over His Majesty. To the lover of Allah, the Majesty of Allah is no less beautiful than His Beauty, and the very Awe of Him the deepest Intimacy conceivable.

It was to demonstrate the Majesty of His Beauty that God made horses; it was to show forth the Beauty of His Majesty that God made lions.

INTIMACY

[Allah] was their Protecting Friend. In Allah let believers put their trust. [Q. 3:122]

Who is better in religion than he who surrendereth his purpose to Allah while doing good (to men) and followeth the tradition of Abraham, the upright? Allah (Himself) chose Abraham for friend. [Q. 4:125]

Say: Shall I choose for a Protecting Friend other than Allah, the Originator of the heavens and the earth, Who feedeth and is never fed? Say: I am ordered to be the first to surrender (unto Him). And be not thou (O Muhammad) of the idolaters. [Q. 6:14]

For them is the abode of peace with their Lord. He will be their Protecting Friend because of what they used to do. [Q. 6:127]

Thou sendest whom Thou wilt astray and guidest whom Thou wilt: Thou art our Protecting Friend, therefore forgive us and have mercy on us, Thou, the Best of all who show forgiveness. [Q. 7:155]

And if they turn away, then know that Allah is your Befriender—a Transcendent Patron, a Transcendent Helper! [Q. 8:40]

Say: Naught befalleth us save that which Allah hath decreed for us. He is our Protecting Friend. In Allah let believers put their trust! [Q. 9:51]

Lo! verily the friends of Allah are (those) on whom fear (cometh) not, nor do they grieve. [Q. 10:62]

And when the awe departed from Abraham, and the glad news reached him, he pleaded with Us on behalf of the folk of Lot. [Q. 11:74]

[Hold] fast to Allah. He is your Protecting Friend. A blessed Patron and a blessed Helper! [Q. 22:78]

But Allah, He (alone) is the Protecting Friend. He quickeneth the dead, and He is Able to do all things. [Q. 42:9]

And He it is Who sendeth down the saving rain after they have despaired, and spreadeth out His mercy. He is the Protecting Friend, the Praiseworthy. [Q. 42:28]

Allah is the friend of those who ward off (evil). [Q. 45:19]

◇

The state of Intimacy is produced by the witnessing of the Divine Beauty, and results in trust, tranquility, and confidence in submitting one's petitions to God.

Metaphysical Principle

Intimacy is a reflection, in the human Heart, of *Al-Jamal*, the Beauty of God; in the words of the *hadith*, "Allah is Beautiful, and loves Beauty" [Muslim]. When Beauty dominates, the most formidable Presence is welcoming, the most inaccessible Reality is near, the most bewildering Unveiling offers itself to our contemplation as familiar, easily accepted and gratefully cherished. Those Sufis who habitually refer to Allah as "the Friend, the Beloved" are dominated by Beauty and Mercy, by Allah in His Names *Al-Rahman* (the All-Good) *Al-Rahim* (the Compassionate), *Al-Latif* (the Subtle, the Benevolent), *Al-Karim* (the Generous), *Al-Wadud* (the Loving-kind) *Al-Ra'uf* (the All-Pitying), *Al-Majid* (the All-Glorious), *Al-Halim* (the Mild), *Al-Wali* (the Patron, the Friend), and *Al-Shakur* (the Grateful). This last name is a true mystery: because how can Allah, the Self-Existing (*Al-Qayyum*), the One Who has no need of anything, the One that the creation or destruction of the universe can neither enrich nor impoverish, possibly experience gratitude? Gratitude for what, gratitude to whom? That the One in need of nothing would be willing to condescend to a mere creature, even to the point of manifesting gratitude for such a non-entity's appreciation of That One's ravishing Beauty, is truly the height of Mercy and Generosity. Our own imperfect gratitude to another creature, or even to Allah, no matter how deep and sincere it may be, is conditioned upon our sense of need and our relief that a need has been fulfilled. Imagine, then, the perfection of Gratitude possessed by the *Al-Razzaq*, the All-Provider, the One totally beyond need, who fulfills the needs of all the worlds! That the Perfection of Beauty should be grateful to be seen and appreciated by the likes of us is truly beyond conception—unless the solution to the riddle lies in the fact that Allah eternally contemplates none other than Himself, and consequently is both the Witnessed and the Witness.

According to the Heart

Intimacy of the Heart is solitude without loneliness. You've lost every companion but gained the Companion, you've sent away every friend but found the Friend. What room is there in Intimacy for the discourtesy of loneliness? You have unloaded the dying past and purchased the eternal present, you have sold the world and bought Allah—and that is the superlative bargain.

The great exemplar of the station of Intimacy was the Prophet Abraham, known as *khalil-Allah*, the Friend of God. One definition of meditation (*muraqabah*), according to the Sufi conception of it, is that the meditator watches over and protects the Presence of

Day and Night on the Sufi Path

Allah in his Heart, and is simultaneously watched over and protected by that same Presence. Intimacy with the Beloved requires a degree of "hermetic" secrecy; the bower of the Heart, where best friends meet, must be sealed off from the prying eyes of both the World and the Nafs. In the following poem, Abraham says:

> If you were not my Secret,
> How could I ever have found you,
> Among the tents?
>
> If I were not your own Secret, jealously guarded,
> How could I ever have submitted
> To being called Your friend?
>
> When I knew myself alone,
> Exiled from the world,
> I discovered your secret Name
> Engraved on the Guarded Tablet.
>
> When I emerged from that solitude,
> To lose myself in tribes and armies,
> You felt my loss.
> You searched for me everywhere,
> Found me in my exile,
> And named me Your friend.
>
> At Your command I raised my right hand
> To slay my only son;
> I looked again, and he was Thou:
> I dropped the knife.
>
> When we sat together on a cushion of grass
> Inside the Walled Garden of the Mysteries,
> Eating from our own vine and fig tree
> And talking to our heart's content,
> The desert, shimmering white and yellow
> On the horizon beyond us
> Stood in need of the clear Arabic tongue.
>
> In love you led me
> Into the barren places of the earth.

Intimacy (Uns) *and Awe* (Haybat)

In anger you drove me, with slaps and bitter words
Toward the chamber of Night
Where you were waiting for me already,
Watching over my sleep,
The rising and falling of my breast,
Till the mazes of the stars and the night of time
Passed over, and the morning came.

God's command to Abraham that he sacrifice his only son was an example of Divine Jealousy in the state of Intimacy, where two is company but three's a crowd: only Two can truly become One. This is the station of intimate conversation between the soul and God, where all formalities are dispensed with and nothing is hidden.

According to the *Nafs*

False Intimacy is the great discourtesy of taking Allah for granted; one of its fruits is unfaithfulness in relationships based on lack of discretion. In the Intimacy of the Nafs, Allah is your imaginary friend, the puppet of your solitary fantasies of divine companionship and favor. Your image of Him is like a boon companion, your partner in dissipation, or like a doting father who is rich but nonetheless weak; consequently it pampers your self-indulgences, it forgives every transgression while requiring no repentance, in an attempt to convince you that lust and desire are your birthright and your playground. Like a false father it will always bail you out, until the day your are held without bail and hauled before the Judge; like a boon companion, when you are finally in the gutter it will desert you, in a shower of scornful laughter, and go seeking others to corrupt. The Intimacy of the Nafs is all narcissism; the face of Allah to which you gave your love and to whom you confided every secret turns out in the end to be nothing but your own face—the face of self-betrayal and shame. May Allah grant that this shame be fruitful for purification and repentance.

Virtues to be Gained in the Station of Intimacy

Love (*Mahabbah*); Tranquility and Serenity (*Sakinah*); Contentment; Constancy of Affection and Service; Visionary Insight in the role of a Spy of Hearts; appreciation of every uniqueness; Gratitude; Trust in God; Sincerity; Divine Eros (*Ishq*); Sincerity; Veracity; Loyalty.

Mode of *Taslim*

Taslim in the state of Intimacy is to quickly reject every rival within the soul who might divert the constant attention of the Heart from the Beloved—to say NO to all the thugs and whores who are continually trying to make the Heart unfaithful to Him through lust and anger, and to the many voices of the Dunya working their endless magic and seduction to make eternal death look attractive—because everything that lies outside the secret chamber of the Heart where Lover and Beloved meet is only death and corruption: *All is perishing except His Face.* Our own jealousy is selfish, petty and manipulative, but the jealousy of the Beloved is a Righteous Jealousy; it allows no outside partners to intrude in the seamless Union between Heart and Spirit. To submit to the dictates of this Jealousy is the perfection of *adab. Taslim* in Intimacy is to become free of all desire, to return it to the *Ishq* of Allah, the Divine Eros. All the desire and longing and tasting and fulfillment you thought were intrinsic to you because you identified with them have never been yours at all; they have always belonged only to Him, in Whom desire and its fulfillment have never been separated, even for a single instant.

In Relationship

Intimacy in relationship is true love and true friendship.

AWE

And do thou (O Muhammad) remember thy Lord within thyself humbly and with awe, below thy breath, at morn and evening. And be not thou of the neglectful. [Q. 7:205]

The thunder hymneth His praise and (so do) the angels for awe of Him. He launcheth the thunderbolts and smiteth with them whom He will while they dispute (in doubt) concerning Allah, and He is mighty in wrath. [Q. 13:13]

Intimacy (Uns) and Awe (Haybat)

Allah hath said: Choose not two gods. There is only One Allah. So of Me, Me only, be in awe. [Q. 16:51]

He knoweth what is before them and what is behind them, and they cannot intercede except for him whom He accepteth, and they quake for awe of Him. [Q. 21:28]

Those who fear their Lord in secret. . . . [Q. 21:49]

Lo! those who go in awe for fear of their Lord. [Q. 23:57]

Who feareth the Beneficent in secret and cometh with a contrite heart. [Q. 50:33]

> *When the heaven is split asunder*
> *And attentive to her Lord in fear,*
> *And when the earth is spread out*
> *And hath cast out all that was in her, and is empty*
> *And attentive to her Lord in fear!*
>   *Thou, verily, O man, art working toward thy Lord a work which thou wilt meet (in His presence).* [Q. 84:1–6]

◇

When the Nafs arrives at the banquet of Intimacy, the ordeal of Awe supervenes.

Awe is the shocking realization that the Fires of Jahannam are also the Fires of Allah, that the Presence of God is relentless, inescapable, and that the unrepentant Nafs can no way stand in the face of it. The Presence of Allah is awesome, tremendous, devastating. How can you face it—especially since you can't turn away from it? Maybe the shocks of life, the shocks of the Heart and the soul and the body, are really the shocks of God. Why does man make war? Maybe because war is the poor man's mysticism, because most of us are not close enough to Allah to feel His tremendousness in the *Batin* without first creating tremendous stress in the *Zahir*. In the words of Muhammad, "Paradise is beneath the shadow of the swords" [Bukhari]. But how can we withstand the tremendous Presence of Allah if we are not yet ripe for Annihilation? Only through Absence. Awe heralds Absence; Absence heralds Annihilation; Annihilation is the essence and gateway of Subsistence. *There is no refuge from God but in Him* [Q. 9:118] is a way of saying that there is no refuge from Awe except in Absence. And while you are Absent, all that's left you is being pounded—both out of shape and into it—on the anvil of Allah.

The first two verses of the surah *The Pilgrimage* [Q. 22:1–2] allude to the state of Awe:

> *O mankind! Fear your Lord. Lo! the earthquake of the Hour (of Doom) is a tremendous thing.*
> *On the day when ye behold it, every nursing mother will forget her nursling and every pregnant one will be delivered of her burden, and thou (Muhammad) wilt see mankind as drunken, yet they will not be drunken, but the Doom of Allah will be strong (upon them).*

These *ayat* describe the state of Awe in the face of the Majesty of God, which fulfills the command to "die before you are made to die." The "nurslings" are unfulfilled potentials that now must be abandoned; the "burden" delivered by a pregnant mother is a person's spiritual destiny in post-eternity that is now revealed. The intensity of emotion produced by the Divine Majesty can cause Awe to give way to Intoxication, in which both thought and will are annihilated.

Metaphysical Principle

Awe is a reflection, in the human Heart, of *Al-Jalal*, the Majesty of God, of Allah in His Names *Al-Jalil*, the Majestic, and *Al-Azim*, the Tremendous. In the Presence of Allah in the Majesty of his Absolute Transcendence, universally Immanent within all things, manifest existence has no rights and can make no claims—because only God is. All it can do is await, in fear and trembling, its own Annihilation. And it can't even cry to Allah for His Mercy to shield it from this Awe—because Awe itself *is* that Mercy.

According to the Heart

Awe according to the Heart is to be transfixed and motionless in witnessing the Victory of Allah, His triumph over all things, His abasement of all that would presume to stand against Him. The King has stormed the city of the Heart, breached its walls, broken its gate and subdued the Nafs with the sword of His Power. In the state of Awe, the terror of the Nafs and rapture of the Heart are identical: there is not the slightest shadow of separation between them.

> When You unveiled Your tremendous
>   Majesty
> And I knew there was no escape,
> I went and lay down on Your anvil
> Under the hammers of Your remembrance.
> What I had made of myself, You unmade
> With the blows of Your speech,
> The relentless pounding of Your moments
> That mark the course of time.
>
> When You unveiled the fires of Your
>   Absolute Justice
> Against which there is no appeal,
> I crept into the forge and lay down
> Under the bellows of Your remembrance.
> Your Face gave light
> Till I reached white heat.
>
> What refuge from the hammer, except on
>   the anvil?
> What refuge from the fire
> Except in the forge itself?
> What does it matter if I become a cup or
>   a blade, a stirrup or the head of an axe,
> If I bear the stamp of the Master?

According to the *Nafs*

Awe according to the Nafs is delight in the presence of anger considered to be your legitimate heritage and intrinsic power—a delight that, when you come to realize that to embrace anger is to become the victim of it, is transformed into a tremendous horror and despair before Allah falsely conceived of as a merciless tyrant, a torturer, King of the *Shayatin* and the Chief of them; its fruits are panic, cowardice and headlong flight into destruction. In the absence of Love, of *Mahabbah*, the Nafs is willing to endure even this so as to hold on to the sense of its own existence apart from God; instead of dying before it is made to die, it tries to kill itself, over and over again, precisely in order to take total possession of itself and so *avoid death*. In the words of Ali ibn Abi Talib, "Anger is a raging fire. Whoever can subdue his anger puts out the fire; whoever cannot gets burnt himself" [*Nehjul-Balagha* of Sayyid Razi]. And as for those who fail to put out this fire, "It is reported—but Allah knows best—that the Prophet Muhammad—may peace be upon him—said, 'He who commits suicide by throttling himself shall keep on throttling himself in the Hell Fire forever and he who commits suicide by stabbing himself shall keep on stabbing himself in the Hell-Fire forever ... [and] whoever commits suicide with a piece of iron [*or a bomb*] will be punished with the same piece of iron [*or bomb*] in the Hell Fire'" [Related in the *Sahih Bukhari* on the authority of Abu Huraira].

Virtues to be Gained in the Station of Awe

Reverence; Fear of God; Shame; Vigilance; Wariness; Submission; Manliness; Courage.

Mode of *Taslim*

Taslim in the state of Awe is simply not to flee the awesome Presence of Allah through pursuit of passion, distraction or oblivion, but to gaze in nakedness upon naked destruction, enduring blow after blow and continuing on until you know the ecstasy hidden inside pain and witness the Beauty hidden inside Majesty—witness it and are ravished by it, to the limit of endurance and beyond. This *Taslim* has the power to free you from all anger, to release whatever anger was in you so that it returns to the Wrath of God. All anger belongs to Allah, none belongs to you; whatever anger you thought of as yours was really His all along. By identifying with it you became subject to it and were forced to suffer the consequences of it; but now you are free from it. The Wrath of Allah, once you recognize its presence and understand its true nature, has the power to pull all the anger right out of you, returning it to the only One with both the right and the power to satisfy it.

In Relationship

Awe in relationship manifests as spontaneous reverence and veneration for saints and sages, for those great in achievement, for the ones whose characters are qualified with the Names of Allah, without a trace of either flattery or abasement, or any seeking of benefit, protection or advantage. It also includes an instinctive fear of trespassing upon the Secret of another, since this is an exclusive affair between that person and Allah.

The Synthesis of Intimacy and Awe

What transcends Intimacy and Awe? The station of True Love. Only Love can immerse itself in Intimacy with the Beloved and not soil this Intimacy with vulgar familiarity; only Love can suffer the Majesty of the Beloved and still know it as Beauty, and Truth, and Justice, and Mercy; only Love can be subject to both Awe and Intimacy, to both the pleasure and the displeasure of the Beloved, and see no difference whatever between them because it sees only That One, and has reached certainty as to the truth that whatever the That One sends is good.

9

Absence (*Ghaybat*)
and Presence (*Hudur*)

We have made the night and the day for two signs: the sign of the night do We obscure, but the sign of the day cause We to shine forth, that you may seek plenty from your Lord. [Q. 17:12/17:13]

◇

"ABSENCE" IN TRADITIONAL Sufi terminology usually refers to to the Absence of the Sufi's consciousness from the world, including his own body, and its Presence with Allah—an obliviousness to his surroundings due to a Divine "infusion"— while "Presence" proper indicates a Presence with Allah that does not entirely negate consciousness of the world, the body and other people. Thus "Presence" usually refers to a conscious sense of God's Reality, though it may also indicate "Presence" with *al-Dunya* and alienation from God, while "Absence" will often be used to indicate the outer appearance of someone who, inwardly, is in a state of Presence.

Here, however, we are employing these terms in a slightly different and more specific sense, where the alteration between Presence and Absence is the alteration between Allah's action on us through flooding our awareness with His Presence, and His action to change our state without our being aware of it, or such that we become aware of it only later, when the affects of His secret action on the Heart rise to consciousness, or are indicated by events. The action of God on the Heart outside or beyond the consciousness of the recipient will sometimes still dominate that consciousness; the Heart will be turned by God's decree toward something that it can neither see nor understand, and it will not be able to turn away until God releases it. If the Presence of Allah does not fill our consciousness, we cannot deliberately and knowingly obey His Will or conform ourselves to the truths He reveals to us; yet if It does not also affect us outside of and beyond our consciousness, then this conscious obedience may result only in an illusory knowledge that we believe we have acquired and now are free to possess, not a true *Ma'rifah* that in fact possesses us. There is no *Taslim* without conscious submission; yet if conscious submission were the only mode of response to Allah's actions upon the Heart, it would be as if we in our limited human nature could actually encompass Him. Allah enlightens our intellects, but He also operates on us without our knowledge—necessarily so, because He absolutely transcends us.

Absence and Presence have to do with the will. Absence is *infused Taslim*; the will is completely dominated by the Will of Allah, so much so that the Nafs cannot make even the shred of an independent motion in terms of either will, affection or intellect; consequently, though not yet annihilated, it disappears. Presence, on the other hand, is *intentional Taslim*. The will wills to submit to the Will of God immediately, consciously and totally, and the affections and the intellect fully participate in this intentionality. Presence without Absence is, or becomes, spiritual self-will, and is consequently dominated by the Nafs; Absence without Presence is, or becomes, helplessness, the lack of all conscious ability to intentionally submit to Allah. This is why Allah, in his education of the Nafs, wills that Absence and Presence should alternate. Absence destroys the root of self-will; Presence concentrates the intentionality of the will in submission. Together they demonstrate that, in the last analysis, no-one but Allah is willing anything—and Allah Wills nothing outside Himself because there *is* nothing: He Wills only what He Is.

The difference between Absence/Presence and Annihilation/Subsistence is that Absence and Presence alternate, while Annihilation and Subsistence (from one point of view) are simultaneous. Absence is the seed of Presence, as Presence is of Absence. In terms of Annihilation and Subsistence, however, the Annihilation of the partial, self-referential self ("me") *is* the Subsistence of the true self ("He") as a Name of God. Who we *think* we are has never existed; who God *knows* we are is unborn—undying—eternal. And God knows only Himself.

Absence

When the young men fled for refuge to the Cave and said: Our Lord!
Give us mercy from Thy presence, and shape for us right conduct in
*   our plight.*
Then We sealed up their hearing in the Cave for a number of years.
And afterward We raised them up that We might know which of the
*   two parties would best calculate the time that they had tarried. . . .*
A speaker from among them said: How long have ye tarried? They
*   said: We have tarried a day or some part of a day, (Others) said:*
*   Your Lord best knoweth what ye have tarried. . . .*[Q. 18:10–12; 19]
He neither begets nor is begotten, and there is nothing to which He
*   might be compared.* [Q. 112:3–4]

◇

The state of Absence—when we return from it—teaches us that
God knows more about us than we will ever know about ourselves,
that His action on the Heart is His business, not ours, and consequently that most of the changes He puts us through will always be
beyond our ability to gauge. Without Absence we might be tempted
to keep a mental journal of our spiritual progress, our passage from
station to station, instead of concentrating on the *hal* presently at
hand, and the task it represents in terms of obedience and submission and insight. Thus Absence, by temporarily obliterating our
conscious experience, works to erase our attachment to personal
history; the obsessive recall of this history is one of the major pillars
of the ego. To always be reviewing one's progress is to strengthen the
illusion that one can "lead" one's own spiritual life—whereas, in the
words of Maghrebi,

> No-one can journey to God on his own feet;
> To arrive at God's district, one must go with God's feet.

It is crucial to remember that our intrinsic need for God—even
when it is seemingly fulfilled—never really ends.

Metaphysical Principle

The state of Absence is the reflection, in the human Heart, of the
Transcendence of God—of *Tanzih*, Allah's incomparability. In His

Absence (Ghaybat) *and Presence* (Hudur)

Transcendence, is He inaccessible to creatures—not only that, but no created being who might conceivably try to access Him appears anywhere at all. To be with Him is to be Elsewhere—Absent from the world, Absent also from the self.

According to the Heart

The Heart experiences the state of Absence as a complete dominance of the Presence of Allah over any human intent to remain conscious of this Presence. In Absence, every attempt to place one's attention upon the Absolute is understood not only as a distraction but as an impossibility; consequently it is immediately dispelled—or perhaps it would be better to say that it never occurs to begin with.

According to the *Nafs*

Absence according to the Nafs is Absence from Allah, a flight from God into heedlessness and oblivion.

Virtues to be Gained in the Station of Absence

Trust in God; Submission.

Mode of *Taslim*

Taslim in the state of Absence is to resign yourself not to God's Will, but to the fact that you do not know God's Will—to fully accept whatever He is doing with you, without needing to understand what it is. One may sincerely intend to submit to Allah, and without this purity of intention nothing will be accomplished. But given that much of one's resistance to His Will is profoundly unconscious, only infused *Taslim* in the state of Absence is can bring these deeply-buried resistances to the surface, and release them.

In Relationship

Absence in relationship empties your Heart of the flatteries, insults, seductions and demands of other people—occupying you due to your identifications with them—as if you had never met them, as if they had never existed at all.

PRESENCE

Verily God is not ashamed to set forth as well the instance [Pickthall has *similitude*] *of a gnat as of any nobler object.* [Q. 2:24/2:26]

And then We should bestow upon them from Our presence an immense reward. [Q. 4:67]

And the king said: Bring him unto me that I may attach him to my person. And when he had talked with him he said: Lo! thou art to-day in our presence established and trusted. [Q. 12:54]

Unto Him belongeth whosoever is in the heavens and the earth. And those who dwell in His presence are not too proud to worship Him, nor do they weary.... [Q. 21:19]

Oh, but I call to witness the planets,
The stars which rise and set,
And the close of night,
And the breath of morning
That this is in truth the word of an honoured messenger,
Mighty, established in the presence of the Lord of the Throne.... [Q. 81:15–20]

[Allah is] Lord of the Worlds ... Owner of the Day of Judgment. [Q. 1:2; 4]

◇

In the state of Presence, everything is here, and everything is Allah, or a sign of Him; He is the essence and the totality of consciousness. You no longer need to "pay" attention, because attention is intrinsic. If separate objects, or the totality of the material world, were recognized and identified with Allah, this would be polytheism or pantheism—but since only Allah exists, and He is one with our consciousness of Him, these heresies do not apply. *Wherever you turn, there is the Face of Allah.*

Absence (Ghaybat) *and Presence* (Hudur)

Metaphysical Principle

The state of Presence is the reflection, in the human Heart, of the Immanence of God—of *Tashbih*, Allah's comparability to created things. All things are like Him and signs of Him because without Him they would not exist. He is with all things and within all things; He is also the Essence of all things. In themselves, all things are nothing; in Allah, all things are He.

According to the Heart

The state of Presence according to the Heart is to be suffused with the Reality of Allah to such a degree that the illusion of other-than-Allah can nowhere make its appearance; one's attention is fixed upon this Reality and is incapable of departing from It, since there is no other place to which it might depart. Wherever the fish swims it encounters the ocean and is immersed in it; wherever the Sufi turns, in the state of Presence, *there is the Face of Allah.*

The station of Presence is the Eternal Day.

According to the *Nafs*

The state of Presence according to the Nafs is to be sealed into a partial reality that one takes as total, thus blocking one's progress to higher stations. Everything you see is God, but everything you see is also you, so it's as if your consciousness itself were divine, as if you in your conscious self were virtually identical with Allah. Because all is immersed in your consciousness and nothing is perceived or posited as existing outside it, this is not experienced as pride or arrogance or self-assertion, since there is nothing outside of you against which your self might be asserted. But submission is also negated because nothing is felt to exist beyond your consciousness to which you might submit. Presence according to the Nafs is the origin of the heresy of pantheism; it results in a near-absolute complacency whose ultimate effects are disastrous. Pantheism presents itself as the vision of all things as Divine, but all it really is—a truth that will be inevitably revealed at the end of its trajectory—is a false deification of the Dunya, leading to immersion in the darkness of materialism and worldly concerns.

Virtues to be Gained in the Station of Presence

Dignity; constant effortless Vigilance; triumph over heedlessness; Annihilation in God's Attributes.

Mode of *Taslim*

Taslim in the state of Presence is the total willingness to be exactly where you are, the complete renunciation of any desire to be someplace else—because there *is* no "someplace else." It also entails rejecting the temptation to identify the All you are presently immersed in as "me."

In Relationship

Presence in relationship lets you be perfectly mindful of other people, allowing no projection or expression of yours to come between you and them, as if your attention to them in this moment were your whole reason for existing.

The Synthesis of Absence and Presence

What transcends Absence and Presence? The station of the synthesis of *Tanzih* and *Tashbih*, the knowledge that Allah is attached to nothing and separate from nothing, and consequently that it is impossible either to enter His Presence or to escape from it, thus putting both self-willed flight and self-willed aspiration to rest definitively.

10

Annihilation (*Fana'*) and Subsistence (*Baqa'*)

In the first part of the Shahadah, *La ilaha* refers to Annihilation, and *illa'Lla* to Subsistence.

And it is He who maketh alive and killeth, and of Him is the change of the night and of the day: Will you not understand? [Q. 23:82/23:80]

And He it is Who gave you life, then He will cause you to die, and then will give you life (again). Lo! man is verily an ingrate. [Q. 22:66]

Thou causest the night to pass into the day, and Thou causest the day to pass into the night. Thou bringest the living out of the dead, and Thou bringest the dead out of the living. . . . [Q. 3:26/3:27]

◇

THE GOAL OF THE SUFI PATH is Annihilation in God, *Fana'*, according to the command of the Prophet. "Die before you are made to die." *Baqa'*, Subsistence in God, may be considered to be higher, but while we are still "ourselves", self-identified and self-defined beings, we cannot aspire to Subsistence—which to us, in our initial condition of self-involvement, could only mean subsistence of the ego. We are called to seek Annihilation; if Allah wills to make us subsist in Him after that Annihilation, that's His work and His decision, not ours. We did not create ourselves in the first place, we merely submitted to be created, when Allah asked the permanent archetypes of all things within Him (the *ayan al-thabitah*) *Am I not your Lord?*, to which we all answered "*Yea!*" [Q. 7:172]. By the same token we cannot somehow "prepare ourselves" to sub-

197

sist after our Annihilation because, considered in ourselves apart
from God, Annihilation is our true nature, which may be why the
Arabic word for "absolute nothingness", *adm*, is close to the Hebrew
word for "human being", *adam*. Our Subsistence after Annihilation,
like our existence after being created, springs from Allah's intrinsic
generosity—and, since Allah is the Only Being, He has nothing to
give to His creation but a participation in that very Being. God as
al-Khaliq, the Creator, is motivated by God as *Al-Karim*, the Generous; likewise God as *Al-Karim* is a particular aspect of God as *Al-
Rahman*, the All-Merciful, a name which, according to the Qur'an,
is equivalent to "Allah" itself. *Say: Call upon God (Allah), or call
upon the God of Mercy (Al-Rahman), by whichsoever you will invoke
Him: He hath most excellent names.* [Q. 17:110/17:110]

Strangely enough, there is no essential contradiction between
Annihilation and self-actualization—but exactly how this is true is
hard to express in words, and also rather formidable to live with in
the realm beyond words. Self-actualization is not self-assertion; it is
simply being truthful with yourself about who you are, accepting
yourself as formed on the specific Names of God He invoked on the
day when told you *kun!*—"be!" [Q. 2:117]. You can't attain *Fana'* on
the basis of a false, made-up identity; first you have to be willing to
be who you really are as God created you. Only from a standpoint of
integrity and self-honesty can you find the door to Annihilation.
And integrity is never asserted, only accepted; likewise Annihilation
can only be accepted, it can never be actively sought. And since we
are intrinsically nothing apart from Allah, not only can we not effectively intend to subsist within Him after our Annihilation, we can't
intentionally annihilate ourselves either, since in order to intend to
annihilate yourself you have to *be* there. It is Allah who produces
Annihilation and Subsistence, which were our original state before
He created us, before He asked us *Am I not your Lord?* to which we
answered *Yea!* [Q. 7:172]. Annihilated and Subsisting within Him in
pre-eternity, we were nonetheless imperfect because we had not yet
been given the opportunity to surrender to Him, which is something
only existing beings can do. So the Annihilation-and-Subsistence of
those who have died before they die is greater than the Annihilation-
and-Subsistence of the permanent archetypes before they were cre-

ated, before they were drawn into existence by the *Nafas al-Rahman*, the "Breath of the Merciful." This is why Creation is equivalent to Mercy.

Annihilation and Subsistence according to the *Nafs*

The Nafs has the ability to counterfeit any spiritual state, to present mania as Expansion, depression as Contraction, ADHD as Dispersion, narcissism as Gathering, etc. It is even capable of counterfeiting the highest mystical states of Annihilation and Subsistence.

Existential psychologist R.D. Laing, in his books *The Divided Self* and *Self and Others*, presents three self-descriptions often found in schizophrenia that remind one of the statements of many mystics, namely: "I am dead"; "I am God"; "I am someone else"; users of psychedelic drugs sometimes describe their experiences in similar terms. Yet clearly the states of consciousness of the schizophrenic are very different from those of the mystic, particularly in terms of the effects produced by these states of consciousness upon the individual's life and the lives of those around him. The Prophet Muhammad, peace and blessings be upon him, said: "die before you are made to die", thus indicating the state of *Fana'*, which is experienced as a glorious liberation from the burden of self-existence, including total freedom from the fear of death. Yet this state is poles apart from the state of some schizophrenics, who also may sincerely say, experience and believe that "I am dead", but who feel this condition as an excruciating lack of substance, validity and integrity, the result being that they see themselves as zombies, machines, living corpses, or walking ghosts. The Sufi Mansur al-Hallaj once cried out in an ecstatic state *"Ana l'Haqq!"* or "I am the Truth!" (*Al-Haqq* being one of the Names of Allah), an indiscretion for which he was tried and executed. Likewise Muhammad said "He who knows himself knows his Lord"—yet no Sufi, and no true mystic of any other tradition, has ever asserted that *oneself* as Tom, Dick or Harry is, or ever could be, God; if this was al-Hallaj's meaning, then he was a certainly a heretic. It is nonetheless true that people with a literalistic mind-set cannot accept many of the statements of the mystics, simply because they don't understand them. They will see a *hadith qudsi* like "Heaven and earth cannot contain Me, but the heart of my believing slave can contain Me" as asserting *hulul*, incarnation-ism, as if for the heart to contain God is for the human being to *become* God. But why? When a glass is filled with milk, does it become milk? Those Sufis who, unlike most of al-Hallaj's contemporaries and successors in *Tasawwuf*, came to accept him over the centuries—accept him not as normative in Sufism but as a kind of imbalance in the *batini* direction necessary to compensate for a prevailing imbalance in the *zahiri* direction—maintain that when he said "*Ana l'Haqq*", it was not al-Hallaj who was speaking but Allah; at that moment, al-Hallaj was is a state of Absence. (And Allah alone knows the truth of the matter.) On the other hand, the schizophrenic who *literally* believes that he or she is God has in effect deified the ego, which is the worst conceivable form of delusion and idolatry, equivalent to the sin of Iblis [Q. 38:71–78] who on one level represents the ego or self-concept in the act of refusing to grant ontological precedence to the *Fitrah*, the true self as Allah created it, but instead claiming existence in its own right. This way of believing that "I am God" may lead the madman either to perform criminal acts because he has arrogated to himself the powers of life and death that belong legitimately only to Allah, or else to ask himself why, if he is indeed God, he is incapable of introducing order, harmony and beauty into the universe, or even into the universe of his own experience, and consequently to fall into a state of metaphysical despair based on the proposition that "God does indeed exist—but He is evil, woefully inadequate, or effectively insane."

As for "I am someone else", the schizophrenic experiences this in terms of an obsessive identification with a tiny part of his own psyche, from which vantage point he sees the bulk of the psycho-physical processes that go to make up his phenomenal self, most of his mind and virtually all of his body, as alien realities. "He", that tiny fragment, is the puppet-master, while everything else in his body and mind make up the puppets—puppets that are always breaking free of their strings so as to run off on their own, or else pulling on them so forcefully that *they* become the masters, and he (now) the helpless puppet. The mystic or *'arif*, however, understands that "*I*" *is another* because he knows that he only truly *is* as seen by Allah—and Allah mercifully allows him, from time to time and up to a certain point, to participate in this way of seeing. He is not the alien puppet of some unconscious psychic complex, but the fully obedient, and thus fully liberated, object of an Absolute Knowledge, of Allah as *Al-Shahid*, the Transcendent Witness. This is the second and complementary meaning of "he who knows himself knows his Lord", whose correlative theorem is "he who knows his Lord thereby knows himself"—he *knows himself as known*. The experience of the schizophrenic is an excruciating, twisted form of self-reference; that of the *'arif*, a total freedom from self-reference. The schizophrenic is alien to himself. The *'arif*, on the other hand, is known by Allah with an intimacy that surpasses and annihilates every degree of psychic reflexiveness. Reflexiveness only veils this Knowledge, but when it is dissolved, then Allah—in seeing, knowing and loving the *'arif*—sees, knows and loves only Himself.

ANNIHILATION

Allah hath chosen for you the (true) religion; therefore die not save as men who have surrendered (unto Him). [Q. 2:132]

O ye who believe! Observe your duty to Allah with right observance, and die not save as those who have surrendered (unto Him). [Q. 3:102]

No soul can ever die except by Allah's leave and at a term appointed. [Q. 3:145]

And what though ye be slain in Allah's way or die therein? Surely pardon from Allah and mercy are better than all that they amass.

What though ye be slain or die, when unto Allah ye are gathered? [Q. 3:157–158]

Our Lord! Vouchsafe unto us steadfastness and make us die as men who have surrendered (unto Thee). [Q. 7:126]

Creator of the heavens and the earth! Thou art my Protecting Guardian in the world and the Hereafter. Make me to die muslim (unto Thee), and join me to the righteous. [Q. 12:101]

Die before you are made to die.

~*Hadith*

◇

Annihilation is the loss of awareness of oneself as a separate entity due to the power of the embrace of the Infinite Reality of God.

The Sufis recognize at least three distinct stages of Annihilation (Ibn al-'Arabi enumerates seven); these three are: Annihilation from one's own acts in God's Acts; Annihilation from one's Attributes in God's Attributes; and Annihilation from one's essence in God's Essence.

To be annihilated in the Acts is to know that the only Doer is Allah—that *there is no Might or Power save in Allah*—and see that you are not *doing* anything.

To be annihilated in the Attributes is to know that all the qualities that go to make up your unique individuality are not your own qualities, but attributes of Allah—and see that you are not *like* anything.

To be annihilated in the Essence is to know that Being pertains to Allah alone, not to creatures—that the essences of things, including yourself, considered as apart from Allah, are nothing—and so see that you *are not* anything.

Annihilated in the Acts, you see your own actions, and those of other people too, not as actions but as *events.* You are not performing them, you are witnessing them, like clouds passing across the wide expanse of the sky. Your actions are objictified in the sight Allah in His Name *Al-Shahid*, the Absolute Witness.

Annihilated in the Names, you see all aspects of your character, your personality and your physical body not as pertaining to you, but as universal and eternal qualities subsisting in their own universe, like the stars in the sky. You do not identify with them, you simply observe them. Your qualities, too, are now objictified in the sight of Allah. [NOTE: The astrological analysis the human character can be a preliminary approach to this way of seeing: *And verily in the heaven we have set mansions of the stars, and We have beautified it for beholders.* [Q. 15:16] Astrology based on the false belief that the stars rather than the Will of Allah, or in addition to it, determine the course of events is *haram*; astrology as a way of meditating on the Attributes of Allah in both the universe and the human character, *on the horizons and within their own souls*, is *halal.*]

Annihilated in the Essence, you see not a trace of yourself anywhere; all is Allah, Allah, Allah. And Allah himself, gazing into the flawless mirror you have now become, sees only Allah, Allah, Allah.

Metaphysical Principle

The station of Annihilation is the expression in the human Heart, and in the Spirit, and in the totality of the *Fitrah*, of the truth that only God is. We might call *Fana'* the complete unfolding of the Transcendence of Allah—except that in Annihilation, there is nothing left for Him to transcend. He is Alone, and always has been, and always will be—devoid of partners—the Only Being—One without a second—*Al-Ahad—Al-Dhat.*

According to the Heart

Annihilation, from the standpoint of the Heart, is Annihilation *of* the Heart—the disappearance of the vessel by which all spiritual states sent by Allah are received, the organ through which they are experienced. The ultimate goal of every *hal*, by virtue of one's perfect submission to it, is *Fana'*; here that goal is finally attained—and is consequently Annihilated in its turn.

According to the *Nafs*

The state of Annihilation according to the Nafs is absolute unconsciousness, infinite heedlessness, total oblivion—something that can be more or less achieved by anyone if they drink enough alcohol, ingest a powerful sedative, or receive a sharp blow to the skull. Its most complete and characteristic expression is suicide. In reality, however, total oblivion is impossible to achieve, even in death, seeing that "Men are asleep, and when they die they awaken" [*hadith*, Ibrahim ibn 'Ali al-Husri]. *Death cometh unto him from every side while yet he cannot die* [14:16–17].The Nafs can only understand Annihilation as literal destruction; to continue to be, but no longer be "me", is inconceivable to it.

Virtues to be Gained in the Station of Annihilation

Absolute submission as 'abd Allah, the Slave of God—this being the seed of every other virtue.

Mode of *Taslim*

Taslim in the station of Annihilation is to give up trying to remember who you were.

In Relationship

Annihilation in relationship allows you to see all other people as intrinsically nothing, because only Allah is.

SUBSISTENCE

The second part of the *Shahadah* is the door to *Baqa'*, Subsistence in God: *Muhammadun Rasul Allah.*

And do not regard those who have been killed in the cause of Allah as dead, rather are they alive with their Lord [Q. 3:169].

◇

Subsistence is the experience of remaining in God after one's experience of oneself has been annihilated along with one's sense of Dispersion in the multiplicity of the Divine Names, leaving only Gathering and Concentration in the Name of Unity.

Metaphysical Principle

The station of Subsistence is a reflection, in the human Heart and all the universes, of the truth that Allah, All-Seeing and Omniscient, sees only Himself. What to us are the multitude of creatures, to Him are His many Names, each Name being precisely a Name of *Al-Dhat*, His Essence, and nothing else. There is nothing that is not a mirror to Him; He gazes eternally into all things, contemplating His own Face. Turned toward that face, the mirrors of His manifestation are mirrors indeed, revealing only Him; turned toward anything else they go dark, they cease to exist as mirrors, they fall back into the nothingness of "existence outside Allah"—an intrinsically false proposition and one that can never be established as a positive reality. Because Allah has Self-Knowledge—and understands this Self-Knowledge as in no way separate from His Essence—all forms, which are nothing in themselves, Subsist within Him, and *as* Him.

According to the Heart

The following *hadith qudsi* alludes to the station of Subsistence:

This *hadith* is related on the authority of Masruq (may Allah be pleased with him), who said: We asked 'Abdullah (Ibn Masud) about this verse: *And do not regard those who have been killed in the cause of Allah as dead, rather are they alive with their Lord, being provided for* [Q. 3:69]. He said: "We asked about that and the Prophet (peace and blessings of Allah be upon him) said: 'Their souls are inside green birds possessing lanterns suspended from the Throne, roaming freely in Paradise wherever they please, then taking shelter in those lanterns. So their Lord cast a glance at them and said: "Do you wish for anything?" They answered: "What should we wish for when we roam freely in Paradise wherever we please?" He asked them this question three times. When they were told that they would not be spared from being asked again, they said: "O Lord, we would like for You to put our souls back into our bodies so that we might fight for Your sake once again." And when He saw that they were not in need of anything they were let be.'"

Those lanterns in Paradise that are also bird cages (wonderful image!) are symbols of *Baqa'*. When the green birds return to them they enter Subsistence in Allah, and when they fly out of them again they have in no way left that Subsistence. The Lantern is the Eye of Allah. Through this Eye He sees the flying birds as manifestations of His own Essence, and when they return again to the Unseen, so as to be reunited with that Essence (though they never really left it), then, no longer seen, they become all Seeing. And since they have already fought in the Greater Jihad and died in the station of *Fana'*, they need not fight again.

The human form in Subsistence is no different from the human form in Existence. It is still composed of body, speech and mind, of thought, will and feeling, still subject to birth and death, still under obligation of submission and obedience. The only difference is, it is no longer "me." It subsists precisely as Allah knows it; it has become objectified before the face of *Al-Shahid*, the Absolute Witness. And because the form still designated by my name is no longer "me", it is no longer subject to states, nor is it in need of stations—even the state and station of Annihilation; there is no longer any self-referential subjectivity that could manifest state or station, nor any ego in need of being deconstructed by them. As *Al-Khaliq*, the Creator, Allah's work is perfect; when that work loses the last trace of the delusion that it is self-created, then this perfection is revealed. In Ibn al-'Arabi's words, the one in the so-called "station" of *Baqa'* "sees nothing other than his own form in the mirror of the Reality.... In seeing your true self, He is your mirror and you are His mirror in which He sees His Names and their determinations, which are nothing other than Himself."

Baqa' is *Ma'rifah* of the Nafs.

According to the *Nafs*

Subsistence according to the conceptions and dictates of the Nafs is the sin of the Pharaoh, the heresy falsely attributed to Mansur al-Hallaj—the unimaginable crime of self-deification.

Virtues to be Gained in the Station of Subsistence

The Dignity of the Primordial *Fitrah* who is the Evident Imam, al-Insan al-Kamil, the Khalif of Allah on earth, in Paradise, and in all the worlds—the single fruit of every seed.

Mode of *Taslim*

As *Taslim* was completed in the station of *Fana'*, and annihilated along with its subject, so now in the station of Subsistence, since it has reached perfection, it no longer exists as a separate practice. Alternatively, we could say—speaking figuratively—that *Taslim* in the station of Subsistence is to submit to being created, in the knowledge that one's creation does not negate one's Subsistence within Allah, nor does this Subsistence compromise one's intrinsic Annihilation one iota.

In Relationship

Subsistence in relationship allows you to see all other people as concrete instances of the Divine Presence.

The Synthesis of Annihilation and Subsistence

What transcends Annihilation and Subsistence? Allah alone, in Whom all things exist because He exists, in Whom not one thing exists because He Alone exists.

In *Fana'*, everything that is not capable of Subsistence is Annihilated. In *Baqa'*, the Annihilation of all subjectivity, ego and self-reference is established as the Annihilated One's true and eternal essence in the sight of Allah—which is to say that perfect Annihilation and perfect Subsistence are one and the same.

> Never. You never came into existence. You stayed wound in self-ken,
> lapped in Your own delight.
> Ships were sent out from Your harbor at midnight, but never found
> You.
> There was no breach in Your courtesy; no guest was turned back
> from Your door.
> Only I, of all your companions, was sent away empty. [*"I" is the
> Nafs imprisoned in self-identification.*]
> I adopted Your own method then. I shared your impassiveness. I
> was as annihilated in the heart of You
> As You had ever been.
> I heard your suitors singing and pleading in the alley behind Your
> balcony;
> I heard the heedless drunkards
> Pounding at Your door. [*This indicates that those in the states of
> Intoxication and Absence are still on the far side of the door of Anni-
> hilation/Subsistence.*]

[From Charles Upton, The *Wars of Love and Other Poems*; Sophia Perennis, 2011.]

Day and Night on the Sufi Path

The one who has realized his or her intrinsic and eternal Annihilation in the station of Subsistence has not simply become a featureless void. You are still yourself; you simply no longer identify with yourself. You are free of yourself forever.

AFTERWORD

The Shame of States;
the Shame of Talking

CERTAIN "SOBER" SUFIS, such as al-Junayd—as opposed to "drunken" Sufis like Abu Yazid al-Bistami—felt it rather unseemly to speak of the Path in terms of ecstatic states. In our time, however, when the human soul has become volatile and chaotic—*as thickly-scattered moths* [Q. 101:4]—it may be less inappropriate and increasingly useful, if not necessary, to speak about the *ahwal*, in order that the people of the postmodern era might avoid the dangers, and also reap the potential benefits, of the psychic instability that characterizes us. The postmodern soul is thoroughly *pixilated* ("pixie-led"), filled with inner conflicts and contradictions, obsessed and hounded by the Jinn. The initial requirement is to for us to be able to discern the difference between the psychic states produced by the Jinn, or our own psychological complexes, and the Spiritual states sent by Allah; ignorance of psychology and insensitivity to the psychic forces of the Jinn world are part of the veil that blinds the Heart. The second step is to learn how to endure and put to good use *all* the fluctuations in one's consciousness and spiritual condition, so that each state one encounters is seen as coming not *primarily* from psychic forces or beings but directly from Allah, in the understanding that no Jinn nor any psychological complex can operate unless He wills it. Viewed in this way, every change in one's mental or emotional state can be seen as teaching one a new lesson about Allah, and as a unique opportunity for submitting to Him. Those whose basic station is Sobriety or Stability may still be able to ignore fluctuations in consciousness and concentrate solely upon Allah as *Al-Shahid*, but in our time it is becoming increasingly likely that many of those who opt to relate to Allah in a strictly sober manner may end by exchanging true Sobriety and Stability for the kind of petrification-of-soul that first closes the Heart to the Spirit, and then leads to an explosion of imbalanced zeal or fanaticism, based both on the attempt to impose upon other people the fixed ideas that false Sobriety always becomes infested with, and also to escape the inherent constriction of these ideas through this or that violent effort. This is not the true Sobriety of the Heart, only the counterfeit sobriety of the Nafs.

However, the psychic volatility of our times also increases the dangers faced by anyone attempting to approach Allah through the states of Fluctuation and Intoxication. The collective human soul is now susceptible every sort of sentimentality, fascination, frenzy, seduction and excess; Sufism itself, in some cases, seems to have fallen from the Spiritual to the psychic level, to have opened itself ongoing intercourse with the Jinn, and consequently to have degenerated into little more than magic and countermagic—the very sort of "backwards superstition" that the modernists, the Iranian revolutionary regime, and the Wahhabi/Salafis want to forcibly expel from Islam. These "Sufi" circuses, however, have nothing whatever to do with the true Spiritual Intoxication, only with the false intoxication of the Nafs.

Thus to seek Allah through austerity, severity and dryness, and to seek Him through emotionalism, intoxication, visions and dreams, are equally dangerous—as well as being, in many ways, two sides of the same deviation, two different styles of egotistical self-involvement. And while a moderate indulgence in emotional intoxication may, under certain circumstances, legitimately compensate for an obsessive austerity and dryness (the reverse also being true), the danger is that in flight from an excessive addiction to intoxication one might embrace an excessive austerity, and that an excessive dryness of soul might make the excesses of intoxication all-too-attractive as an avenue of relief—not to mention the fact that no intoxication or sobriety that we *seek* for this or that purpose can be a true *hal* sent by Allah. At this point one must never forget one of the cardinal rules of the Sufis: *never seek spiritual states.* When the Qur'an commands us, *And among His signs are the night, and the day, and the sun, and the moon. Bend not in adoration to the sun or the moon, but bend in adoration before God who created them both, if you would serve Him* [Q. 41:37/41:37], it is telling us not to follow spiritual states, but to seek Him alone.

The simplicity of the *Maʿrifah* of the One God, the realization of Transcendent Unity of Being, cannot be built on the foundation of worldly or psychological complexity; the reason we talk about complexity of states and stations, map it and analyze it, is in order to synthesize it, to reduce it to simplicity. Through His innumerable Beautiful Names, Allah addresses Himself to the complexity of our lives, both inner and outer, so as to draw everything back to Himself.

There is always a certain shame in talking about spiritual states; it's like talking about yourself. The narcissist in love, or the narcissist pursuing knowledge, is more interested in his own reactions to the object of his love or knowledge than he is in that object itself—and so love and knowledge are reduced to pride and self-satisfaction, to lack of consideration, to discourtesy, exploitation and insult. The perfect Sufi, as we have seen, is beyond states and stations. And the traveling Sufi, even if he is short of perfection, nonetheless knows how to immediately see through the state he is experiencing to the One who has produced it, and to let the state itself, all the subjectivity and self-indulgence of it, drop away. When the postman brings us a letter from our Beloved, we don't make love to the letter, or the postman; we forget all else and remember only That One. States are merely reminders; when the Beloved takes up permanent residency in the Heart, they are no longer necessary.

APPENDIX I

The Dangers of the Strictly Intellectual Approach to the Spiritual Path

[NOTE: Sufis often use the English word "intellect" to translate the Arabic *'aql*, which most commonly refers to the rational mind. English speakers also, more often than not, use "intellect" in this sense. Here, however, we are employing this word to translate the Latin *intellectus*, which in Scholastic Philosophy denotes the faculty that knows truth not discursively or through logic (the Scholastic *ratio*), but with immediate intuitive certainty, just as the eye knows light; the Sufi name for this faculty is "the Eye of the Heart." *Intellectus* is the conscious aspect of the Spirit of God within the human soul—and what it knows, it also is.]

◇

A knowledge of metaphysics, for those who are called to such knowledge, is an important aspect of the Path; this book could not have been written without it. Yet it is not without its dangers. Those who have sought metaphysical insight through a study of the spiritual classics of the world will be familiar with the principle that the Transcendent/Immanent Intellect (*al-Ruh*, the Eye of the Heart, the Divine Spark within man) is higher than either the will or the affections. The will may will this or that, the affections love this or that, but the Divine Intellect is always fixed upon, and also a direct manifestation of, a single reality: the eternal Truth. Thoughts may be clear or clouded, beliefs may be true, partially true or entirely erroneous, but the Indwelling Divine Intellect is never compromised and never distorted; as its own Object, it is eternally one with Itself.

This principle, however, does not mean that an intuition of the

Transcendent/Immanent Divine Intellect is all that is needed for the successful completion of the spiritual Path. We may be host to direct intuitive perceptions derived from this Intellect, we may understand the truths it reveals on deeper and deeper levels, and still have a great mass of unredeemed and unregenerate psychic material polluting our souls: chaotic thoughts, erroneous beliefs, obscure, distorted and reactive feelings, concupiscent passions, along with every shade of faithless and volatile—or stubborn and rebellious—self-will. An intellectual grasp of the spiritual Path is of great value since it represents a revelation of the esoteric mysteries; yet this very exteriorization of inner realities may reduce our understanding of these realities to the conceptual level. And when the spiritual life becomes conceptual, when an appreciation of subtle doctrine takes precedence over both concrete action and pure contemplation, then action is paralyzed and contemplation darkened.

The spiritual intellectual is faced with a great temptation. When the psychic pollution the Sufis call the *Nafs al-ammara bi'l su'*, the "soul commanding to evil", presents itself, he or she is faced with two alternatives, one pleasant and the other distinctly unpleasant. The correct but unpleasant choice is to recognize the evil in one's soul and take steps against it, through healthy shame, sincere repentance, and the immediate invocation of Divine aid. The more pleasant course, the one that is infinitely easier for the intellectual, is to shirk the call of the Greater Jihad and simply rise up into the world of spiritual ideas, into an abstract and imaginal paradise untroubled by the turbulence of the passions. That turbulence still goes on, of course, beneath the surface—and all the more virulently now since it knows it has won a point and triumphs in it—but one no longer hears its demonic laughter since one is "above all that." And this is precisely as the *Nafs al-ammara* would have it. The Intellect when used in this way is like a weak and ineffectual King who issues edicts claiming a particular territory but lacks the will or the resources to invade, occupy, subdue and rule that territory; consequently it remains the haunt of rebels and bandits who laugh at his inflated pronouncements and continue on their merry way, robbing travelers and plotting to overthrow the Throne—the spiritual Heart.

Unless one's conscience is entirely dead, however—and the true conscience, we must remember, is an aspect of the Indwelling Divine Intellect itself—we will feel that there is something wrong somewhere with simply rising above the passions, since in order to do so we must (as it were) invoke the Intellect in order to drown out the very voice of that Intellect. So we begin to develop an ideology designed to justify those passions—an *intellectual* ideology, of course. And in this task the *Nafs al-ammara* becomes our greatest ally: an infernal genius, lightning-swift, irresistible, relentless, posing (what else?) as our willing slave—the true and original Jinni from the Lamp. Its ingenious but only half-heard dialectic may go something like this:

"If the Intellect is greater than the will and the affections, then it is their Ruler, am I correct? And, if so, can it not command and dominate will and affections? Why, then, cannot it simply command the affections to be pure, whatever they may feel, and the will to be pure, whatever it may choose? If Knowledge is King then it has all power; it is the Talisman that transforms all that it touches. Furthermore, given that the Knowledge gained by direct intellectual perception, since it is Unitive and transcends polarity, is higher than discursive knowledge—the 'knowledge of good and evil' upon which morality is based—and in view of the fact that such Knowledge is Knowledge of the Absolute and the Absolute has no opposite, morality no longer applies to the pneumatic, the batini, *the one in whom the Indwelling Divine Intellect, the Eye of the Heart, is open. Do you see any flaws in my argument?"*

Yes; the flaws are as follows: The power and pre-eminence of Knowledge lies in its discernment of what is; Knowledge cannot command that something be other than it is and still remain Knowledge. To claim that Knowledge could magically command the impure to be pure *without purifying it* is to falsely characterize Knowledge as a sort of blind, all-powerful will, and simultaneously to falsify the true relationship between Intellective Knowledge as known through the Eye of the Heart, the rational mind which properly turns to the Heart-Intellect for its first principles, and the obedient and submissive will which obeys the dictates of the rational mind. Knowledge purifies the will and the affections first by unveiling the *Fitrah* or primordial unfallen human nature, the *Insan al-Kamil* or Complete Man who remains virtual within the individual, no matter how far he or she may have fallen away from it; secondly, by discerning the distortions, fixations and imbalances of the will and the affections; thirdly, by guiding the rational mind so that it might in turn direct and pacify the will; fourthly, by acting directly upon the affections so as to purge and transmute them by planting the seed of Divine Love within them; and fifthly, by acting to conform the human psyche in its entirety to the Spirit by means of the spiritual states it sends and the resulting stations of the spiritual Path it establishes. The pernicious and deluded idea that Knowledge could posit the impure as pure without guiding us through even the first concrete step necessary to purify it has the ability to effectively short-circuit the entire spiritual life.

The next level of deception produced by the *Nafs al-ammara* is based on the fact that those who violate morality yet pretend to wisdom and sanctity must dissemble from time to time, which is why the "pneumatic" ideology of the Nafs is often further elaborated to justify lying. The justification might go something like this: "*Is it not true that the ontological hierarchy is a fundamental principle of metaphysics and cosmology? And does not each higher rung of this hierarchy possess both ontological priority and effective authority over all levels that lie below it—the Absolute over the First Intellect, the First Intellect over the realm of the Metaphysical Principles or Platonic Ideas, the Principial Realm over the Imaginal or Psychic Realm, the Psychic Realm over the Material Realm? And is not the realized Sage the effective manifestation in human form of the Principial Realm and the First Intellect, if not the Absolute Itself? Does it not therefore follow that the Sage holds priority and authority not only over the Psychic Realm, the world of beliefs and impressions, but also the Material Realm, the world of 'facts'? And if this is the case, is he not justified in denying any 'fact' that challenges his principial pre-eminence? The uninitiated may vulgarly characterize this denial of facts as 'lying', but since the Sage holds absolute precedence and authority over all mere facts, does his denial of an apparent fact not possess the power to actually make it false, to negate its very factualness, to effectively annihilate it—just as Allah annihilates, in His Justice, all that would presume to stand against Him? Do you see any flaws in my argument?*"

We have already pointed out that Knowledge cannot claim that something is other than it is and remain Knowledge. But another level of error makes it appearance here, one that bears a certain relationship to the heretical Gnosticism of the ancient world. The heretical sectarian Gnostics departed from the Primordial Tradition by accepting the Transcendence of God but denying His Immanence. God is Truth, but if Truth were to be exclusively Transcendent—rather that Immanent in all things *by virtue of this very Transcendence*—then metaphysical principles would indeed have the power to negate facts. But in reality, according to the principle of the Divine Immanence, facts cannot be negated by metaphysical principles because they universally *illustrate* these principles. Furthermore, if a person lacks the objectivity to correctly discern and deal with facts, he or she will certainly not possess the much greater degree of objectivity necessary to understand and apply metaphysical principles. In the words of Matthew 25:21, which can certainly be applied to the fruits of honesty and objectivity on the factual level, "(because) thou hast been faithful over a few things, I will make thee ruler over many things: enter thou into the joy of thy Lord."

Finally, if passion, concupiscence and lying are to be effectively justified, Love must of course be discredited, since the above transgressions are all violations of Love, and can never take root in any soul where Love is firmly established. It is at this point that the *Nafs al-ammara bi'l su'* produces its masterwork, the one that will open the world to the advent of *al-Dajjal*: "*In the purified and edified soul, does not the Intellect have precedence over the discursive mind, the discursive mind over the will, and the will over the affections? Does it not then follow that Knowledge has intrinsic ontological priority over Love, and that in any conflict between the claims of Love and those of Knowledge, Knowledge can, will and must hold the right of absolute victory? Nor does Knowledge, in its intrinsic and eternal triumph over Love, suffer any privation on that score, since it still holds in its possession the highest essence that Love foolishly pretended to while continuing to press its inflated claims—namely, Beauty! With Beauty in its grip—that magical Glass in which all metaphysical Truth can be serenely contemplated—what need has Knowledge of the turbidity and chaos of mere Love—Love which has been the downfall of many a reckless pretender to the station of Transcendent Knowledge? Do you see any flaws in my argument?"*

More all the time, actually. A Luciferian knowledge wedded to an infernal cold-heartedness, which it falsely portrays as spiritual impassiveness and detachment, will necessarily see Love as all impulsive willfulness or vulgar sentimentality; this is its perennial slander against the Sovereign Good. But only a profound ignorance, as corrupt as it is benighted, could ever view Love in this manner. If God is Love, as Jesus the Messiah taught—if Allah is *Al-Rahman*, the All-Merciful, and *Al-Wadud*, the Loving-kind—then even the slightest tendency to damn Love with faint praise demonstrates both a total departure from Tradition and a serious lack of insight into the nature of Absolute Reality Itself, and its relationship with the various levels of its own manifestation, both cosmically and *in divinis*. Love and Truth are two names for the same Reality—Whose other name is God. Love directly touches the affections but cannot be strictly identified with them because it is also infinitely beyond them. Love is intimacy with Truth, and can thus be seen as the father of Knowledge. Knowledge, without Love, always remains partly conceptual, and consequently imperfect. But Knowledge in union with Love has reached full existential realization, of which moral purity is one of the inevitable, later, and lesser effects, two others being clear conceptual thought and depth and clarity of the affections. When Knowledge and Love are united in the Heart, then for the first time it can be truly said that what one knows, one also is. And this is precisely why Love, since it is intrinsically one with Knowledge and also a name of the Absolute, cannot be "demoted" with impunity. Those who see Love as secondary to Knowledge and consequently slight the Sovereign Good will eventually be driven beyond their pose of false narcissistic detachment into concrete acts of cruelty, demonstrating for all who still have eyes to see how Love is jealous of His rivals—His only true rival being the *ego*—and ruthless, often in the most ironic terms, with anyone foolish enough to blaspheme His eternal sovereignty and power. And as for Beauty, its precise metaphysical function is to unite Truth and Love—to reveal the Truth as intrinsically lovely. Beauty *without* Love, however, is the quintessence of deception, the power of the Lie; speaking in mythological terms, such delusive beauty is made up of what Iblis was able to steal from the vision of Divine Love he knew in the Paradise of the First Intellect, before he disobeyed God and fell. And the attempt to contemplate Beauty as separate from Love—via the beauty of the human form, for example—as well as from sound traits of character such as justice, compassion, humility and courage, is to transform it from a manifestation of Divine Gentleness, Innocence and Mercy into one of Divine Wrath: there is nothing more wrathful than a cold beauty, like that of the cobra hypnotizing its victim, which doubtless attracts, but attracts only to destruction. And though lust may be fascinated by this sort of frigid beauty, the fascination of it appeals even more fundamentally to pride. The belief that one could separate Beauty from Love in the metaphysical domain—or beauty of form from viciousness of soul in the human one—and contemplate it in isolation while coming to no harm, is inseparable from the sort of pride which believes that, *through power alone* rather than through intelligence and virtue, it might extract the juice of life and discard the rind. Such are the moral and metaphysical dangers of aesthetic pride.

Classics of the spiritual Intellect have been composed for millennia; they are among the greatest gifts of Divine Mercy, the rarest treasures of human wisdom as touched by that Mercy. In more traditional times, however, they could do their work without invoking certain dangers we must contend with today. To begin with, they were not universally disseminated, which meant that they operated within the context of a traditional Path, a Path that always included some degree of competent spiritual direction. When such classics are studied today, however, it is often in the absence of such direction; consequently the beauty of profound spiritual Ideas can work directly upon our faculty of spiritual intuition without the necessary counterbalance of systematic and progressive moral, emotional and mental purification—the result being that the intuitions can soar unfettered into the world of transcendental Ideas, leaving the other faculties of the soul unaddressed, virtually abandoned, and in danger of sinking ever deeper into unconsciousness in the shadow of the great Consciousness the spiritual intuition is enamoured of and fascinated by. Speaking in Sufi terms, complete Intellection, *gnosis, Ma'rifah* of Allah, is the fruit of the pacification of the Nafs in the Greater Jihad. It is accomplished, with our cooperation and submission, by Allah himself, not by our own researches and speculations, and can be completed and perfected only through the medium of *Mahabbah*, Divine Love. Incomplete intellection, however, always retains a degree of self-will, and so is open to misuse.

The misuse of spiritual intuition has, let us say, three stages. The first is *incomplete intellection as entertainment.* In a time of universal ugliness and vulgarity, when demonic evil and sinister fascination are the standards of popular aesthetic, and continue to invade all aspects of human life, the spiritual classics and the momentary intellectual unveilings they may produce in us stand out as beacons of light in the darkness. In the vast wilderness of postmodern meaninglessness, they alone may give us any sense of meaning; consequently they are immensely attractive to those who are open to them. The danger is that they may come to be loved and sought for themselves alone, for their very attractiveness, not for the guidance and power they can provide to us for the actual traveling of the spiritual Path. Intellection sought and experienced as entertainment forgets to ask both "what is God's will for me in this unveiling?" and "what light does this unveiling throw upon my own deficiencies, moral, emotional and cognitive? How can all the faculties of my soul be better conformed to the truths I have just witnessed?" Instead, it simply feasts upon that Beauty that Plato called "the splendor of the True", and leaves entirely out of the picture any deficiencies or excesses that this Beauty might in fact have the power to reveal and put right.

The second is *incomplete intellection as flight.* This stage begins when the one open to real but imperfect intellection begins to use his or her spiritual-intuitive abilities to actively avoid those aspects of the soul that are disturbing precisely because they are crying out to be dealt with, re-balanced, and healed. The habit of running to the realm of elevated spiritual Ideas whenever a psychological or practical or interpersonal conflict raises its head subtly saps the will power and moral stamina of the one indulging in it, until this imbalanced, one-sided intellection begins to progressively rob the soul of its authenticity, its existential substance. And of course the best way to hide from the fact that this is taking place is to "rise above it" even further into the realm of spiritual Ideas.

The third is *incomplete intellection as self-justification*. Once the consequences of an imbalanced approach to spiritual development manifest themselves as various habitual vices, obsessions and delusions, the faculty of spiritual intuition, working in concert with the discursive mind, is called upon by the *Nafs al-ammara*, virtually enslaved by it, in an attempt to justify these irregularities, to posit them as legitimate aspects of the spiritual life. A vice will be seen as a symbolic dramatization of an "esoteric" reality, an obsession as a special God-given command or dispensation, etc. When this stage is reached the self-deception of the victim is extremely hard to overcome, seeing that the *Nafs al-ammara* in delusive "spiritual" guise has effectively replaced the presence of Allah in his or her Heart.

When the spiritual classics that have come down to us were first produced, they arrived through the medium of saints and sages. But now anyone can read them, and many have the ability, due to the unique conditions of our time, to understand them on a fairly sophisticated level, though without the inner spiritual purification that used to accompany and make possible such understanding. Consequently it is more likely all the time that one might encounter a spiritual teacher, either self-styled or apparently with legitimate traditional credentials, who is intellectually sophisticated but morally either indifferent or corrupt. He may bring a message which is true in many ways, intelligent, even profound, and still have failed to existentially realize his own message in many important ways. Thus his followers or would-be followers are put in the difficult position of having to call upon a degree of esoteric understanding and insight in order to evaluate him, and—if necessary—separate the true message from the inadequate or corrupt messenger.

When the corruption of a spiritual teacher who has brought a legitimate esoteric message becomes apparent, his followers separate into three groups. Those who cannot distinguish the message from the messenger are lacking in the *gnosis* necessary to understand that message on a deep enough level, as well as to discern any distortions that might have crept in; they have accepted it in part due to their devoted veneration for the messenger. These are the *zahiris*, the exoterics, who remain limited to the moral level. If they are sincere and courageous, they will reject both message and messenger, and in so doing remain faithful to the exoteric norms of the religion they follow.

Those who can separate the message from the messenger are the *batinis*, the esoterics. Because they have a degree of *gnosis* or *Ma'rifah*, they are capable of recognizing the Truth of the message—apart, that is, from any errors that might have crept in—based not on the supposed personal authority of the messenger, but on the authority of the Truth itself, and their discernment of that Truth. Like the *zahiris*, the *batinis* will reject the corrupt messenger, because esoteric knowledge never negates morality. But they will not reject the message itself because they have understood it, and have consequently become the slaves of it.

It is the false esoterics, the *awliyya' al-Shaytan*, who arrogate to themselves the right to accept both the corrupt messenger and the true message. They do this because they are *antinomians*—people who believe that esoteric knowledge negates morality and the shari'ah by virtue of transcending it. The true esoterics have certainly transcended morality, but at the same time they are careful to preserve it. The false esoterics, on the other hand, delight in the notion that a true message might come through a corrupt messenger, first because this seems to free them from all authority according to Aliester Crowley's maxim "let *do what thou wilt* be the whole of the law", and secondly because it appears to justify the claim that the simple ability to discern, articulate and transmit metaphysical Truth has the power to purify the one transmitting it, without submission to the Will of God or the norms He has laid down, without the development of compassion, without the education of the soul. This, however, is not the case.

Al-Dajjal, along with his fallen cherubim whose role it is to pervert the spiritual Intellect, wishes above all to unite a true message with a corrupt messenger. In doing so he accomplishes two things: first, to lend the corrupt messenger an aura of legitimacy and false authority based on his articulation of the Truth, and secondly to corrupt the Truth itself (insofar as this is possible, given that the Truth can never be corrupted in its essence because it is it is always true), thus perverting the will and the intelligence at the same time. This sort of radical subversion is made possible by the spiritual quality of the Latter Days, which allows for an intellectual sophistication of an apparently "spiritual" nature coupled with heartlessness in terms of the feelings, corruption in terms of the will, and a depletion of the very existential substance of the human form, all this accompanied by an extremely imbalanced psychic permeability and volatility, which has opened the souls of many to subversive suggestions by the *kafir* Jinn, the Powers of the Air. When the Qur'an predicts that the men of the end times will be *as thickly-scattered moths* [Q. 101:4], it is alluding to this precise set of conditions. The massed powers of the infernal regions are now moving to corrupt Knowledge by associating it with lovelessness and to poison Love by associating it with stupidity, all so as to separate Knowledge from Love, or rather spread the lie that such a separation is possible, in order to usher in the regime of Antichrist. Those, however, who have endured the *agon* of being forced to separate a true message from a corrupt messenger have been *inoculated* against the contagion of *al-Dajjal* through vaccination (so to speak) with a weakened strain of the same virus; this is the providential aspect of the transmission of a true doctrine through the medium of a false teacher. If they survive the rigors of this vaccination, they will have gained the power to discern the actions, agendas and lies of *al-Dajjal*, and to guide others toward the same discernment.

APPENDIX II

The Vulnerabilities and Duties
of "Civic Sufism"

J ALALUDDIN RUMI SAID: "There is not one Sufi in the world—
and if there were, he would be non-existent." If *Tasawwuf* in the
West is to retain its independence from *al-Dunya*, it will have to
sever ties with the national governments and globalist organizations
that are presently attempting to exercise control over it, groups
whose influence is deeper and more widespread than many suspect.
One goal of these forces is to groom Sufism as an alternative to
"fundamentalist" Wahhabi/Salafi Islam, an alternative that will
hopefully be more passive to control by the West and/or the Globalists than even the Wahhabi/Salafis, who have been used (from time
to time) as proxies of western imperialism ever since the British
supported the followers of Ibn Wahhab against the Ottoman
Empire. Certain Sufis may naively think that there is nothing wrong
with playing the role of "tolerant Good Muslims" according to the
model provided by the powers-that-be; after all, haven't they been
oppressed by these fundamentalist/Islamicists? And aren't they now
collecting powerful allies at last? Success! It is unfortunately the
case, however, that various Islamicist groups—as well as various
Sufis who identify with them—are also being supported by the West
and the Globalists. Certain self-styled Sufis in the United States have
even brought these extremes together by preaching religious tolerance to the Interfaith world while at the same time publicly sup-
porting the Takfiri death squads in Syria who continue to burn
churches and massacre Christians. The CIA all but founded al-
Qaeda through their support for the Afghan *mujahidin* against the
Soviet occupation, and the major "ally" of the U.S. in the Muslim

world, Saudi Arabia, is also the stronghold of the Wahhabis. Those western military or CIA forces presently fighting al-Qaeda, ISIS and the Taliban may know—or their leaders may know—that they can't "win." But they also know that they can create chaos and accelerate the dissolution of traditional dar al-Islam; perhaps that is their real goal. And such warfare may also be designed to pressure the Islamicists—or various mercenaries posing as Islamicists—to go over to the western/globalist camp, at least in the context of certain operations that could be considered "mutually beneficial" to both sides.

But why would the powers that be in some cases want to support both sides in the present conflicts? That question is easy to answer: because the powers that be *always* attempt to control both sides—as when various international Capitalist financiers bankrolled the Bolsheviks—so they can "play both sides against the middle", the middle in this case being traditional Sufism and traditional Islam; the creation of a "controlled opposition" is a venerable tactic in *realpolitic*. The West and the Globalists are dedicated to destabilizing and deconstructing dar al-Islam, both by military force and by cultural/spiritual infiltration. They want to destroy Islam as a religion because it is one of the main obstacles to their plans for a One World Government, or at least a one-world financial system possessing many of the powers of such a government, though largely on a clandestine basis; the traditional Islamic prohibition of *riba* or usury is a roadblock to the full development of this system. And they have realized that the best way to do this is to separate *Batin* and *Zahir* and set them at war. The more violent the Islamicist terrorists become, the more vulnerable the "tolerant" Sufis become to co-optation and control by those forces who oppose the Islamicists on one level, attempt to control them on another level, and are actually behind some of them on a third. The co-optation of *Tasawwuf*, the spiritual heart of Islam, by these forces leaves the remaining *Zahiri* Islam that much more vulnerable to radicalization; if hearts are veiled from true remembrance of Allah, all that people can see any more is *al-Dunya*, the world of politics and its "imperatives."

The matter is put succinctly in an article entitled "State-sponsored Sufism" by Ali Eteraz which appeared in June of 2009 on the website of the Council for Foreign Relations; the author, though he appears to disagree with the policy of the western powers to groom Sufism as the spearhead of anti-Islamicist "moderate" Islam, none-theless treats this policy as common knowledge. Here is the sum-mary of the article:

Why are U.S. think tanks pushing for state-sponsored Islam in Pakistan?

Once certain ideas go mainstream, it often takes a pretty big flop to disprove them. The United States was supposed to be hailed as the liberator of Iraq, just as it was going to be easy to turn Afghan-istan into a democracy. Well now, according to commentators from the 'SC to the *Economist* to the *Boston Globe*, Sufism, being defined as Islam's moderate or mystical side, is apparently just the thing we need to deal with violent Muslim extremists. Sufis are the best allies to the West, these authors say; support them, and coun-tries as diverse as Pakistan and Somalia could turn around.

The Sufi theory has a lot of variations, but at its core, it's pretty simple: Violent Muslim extremism, rather than having material and political bases, is caused by certain belligerent readings of Islam usually associated with Salafism, a movement that attempts to resurrect the Islam of the prophet Mohammed's time, and Wahhabism, a similarly conservative branch. If Muslims can be indoctrinated with another, softer, interpretation of Islam, then the militants, insurgents, and guerrilla fighters will melt away. http://www.cfr.org/publication/19959/fp.html

Some Sufis have not even suspected that they are vulnerable to such forces. Others are suspicious, but uncertain as to how they might find out more. Still others know quite well already. And Allah most certainly knows, and has known, from all eternity. He, in His Name *Al-'Adil*, will be the final Judge, and no human being or Jinn can avoid being brought before His Bench at the end of time, or simply at the end of his or her short life. If only we truly feared Allah! If we did, then the fear of *al-Dunya*, which is always hidden under some sort of glamour or blandishment or bribe, would have no power over us. And perhaps the worst danger, for those who opt to act in *as* Sufis in *al-Dunya*—especially if they fear the world more than they fear Allah—is that it may influence them to develop an *idea* of themselves, whereas the ideal of the true Sufi is to have no idea of him- or herself whatsoever.

Certain Sufis may feel that to refuse to take sides against the Islamicists, no matter who they must ally with to do so, is to lend them support: "The enemy of my enemy is my friend." However, the actual situation may be more on the order of "The enemy of my enemy is also the friend of my enemy, and therefore both my friend and my enemy at the same time." Some groups may be in a sufficiently desperate situation that they must accept any help that offers itself, no matter what strings may be attached, simply to survive. But any Sufi *tariqah* that can maintain true independence from political influence of any kind—which is still more or less possible in the west—should, in my opinion, not throw this opportunity away while it still exists.

In conclusion, I would advise:

1) Never accept funding or patronage from a group, foundation, or interfaith organization whose background you have not thoroughly researched—and even then be wary. Be especially wary of any group that approaches *you*.

2) Be extremely wary of the interfaith movement; it is one of the main vectors of secular, Globalist control over the world's religions. (For an exhaustive analysis of this from the Christian perspective see *False Dawn: The United Religions Initiative, Globalism and the Quest for a One-World Religion* by Lee Penn.) Local interfaith groups are often sincere, but in many cases they have never thought to question the motives and hidden agendas of the groups and foundations who support them. For example, one rather small Christian/Muslim dialogue organization whose meetings I have attended, and whose motives seem entirely admirable, has hosted speakers from the FBI, the State Department, the Federal Attorney's Office and Homeland Security. And if our central duty is to remember God, why do we need to spend a lot of our precious spiritual attention dialoguing with people from other religions? We certainly ought to familiarize ourselves with the basic tenets of the other faiths, but beyond that, why dialogue with them, as if this were somehow an unmitigated good? In specific instances, when difficult community relations are involved, or when a pressing need to dif-

fuse potential inter-religious violence presents itself, such dialogue
certainly has an important place. But if we are reasonably sure that
no-one from the other religions in our community plans to bomb
our mosques and khaniqas and zawiyas, just as we have no plans to
bomb their churches or synagogues, or even to speak disparagingly
of them either in public or behind their backs, then let us turn our
attention to Allah and how he is dealing with us in our own lives,
and forget useless dialogues that at best are necessary responses to
pressing situations; more often, simply a waste of time; and at
worst, a preparation of the groundwork for the syncretistic One
World Religion that the globalists ultimately wish to impose on all
of us, which will without a doubt be the religion of *al-Dajjal*.

3) Beware of the desire that "Sufism take its place on the public
stage." If individual Muslims feel called to participate in peace
efforts or interfaith dialogue, let them do so as Muslims, or simply
human beings, not as Sufis. Beware especially of public demonstra-
tions, particularly if they are organized by groups you don't know.
Don't militantly demonstrate for peace to the point where all peace
is driven from your life; rather, BE peace. Realize the *Nafs al-
mutma'inah*, the Self-at-peace. And be willing—not just willing, I
would say, but eager—to embrace anonymity, marginalization, irrelevance—irrelevance to anything but the eternal destiny of your
soul, and the souls of your brothers and sisters. It is through this that
you will serve Islam and humanity, more deeply than you can possibly know before the Day of Resurrection. According to the *hadith* of
the Prophet Muhammad, peace and blessings be upon him, "Islam
began in exile and will end in exile; blessed are those who are in
exile!" [Muslim] And if it so happens that Allah calls you to active
duty, detachment from the world is still important, seeing that you
might not even hear His call, or hear it only in a distorted manner, if
your own self-willed activism has banished silence from your Heart.

That said, I must allow for the possibility that certain Sufi
shaykhs may be called by Allah to play a role in the world *as Sufis*; a
shaykh who finds himself at the head of a large community has
responsibilities that more reclusive dervishes, un-involved with
worldly affairs, need not concern themselves with. Nonetheless, it
must never be forgotten that the renunciation of the world, on one

level or another, is a spiritual necessity—especially in view of the fact that many whose intentions are entirely idealistic and sincere have discovered, after attaching themselves to the rich and power- ful, that the power of the Dunya to change sincere idealists into the lackeys of kings is much greater than their own power to convert those kings into wise and just rulers.

In the words of the Noble Qur'an, *He is the First and the Last, and the Outward (al-Zahir) and the Inward (al-Batin); and He is Knower of all things* [Q. 57:3]. Some are servants of the *Zahir*, some of the *Batin*, and some occupy—or at least find themselves temporarily passing through—that fiery point where *Zahir* and *Batin* meet. In 2001, in my book *The System of Antichrist*, I called for a "united front ecumenism", an alliance of the traditional religions against the forces of secularism and corruption that threaten to pervert and destroy every one of them. Worldly, liberal ecumenism necessarily tempts the religions to gradually embrace the kind of doctrinal homogene- ity that destroys their providential uniqueness as revelations of Allah; it also acts to undermine their independence by increasingly placing them, in the name of "tolerance", under various kinds of sec- ular authority. In 2013, however, a concrete expression of united front ecumenism—which I never thought I would I would encoun- ter in this life—suddenly presented itself. It is based upon a book entitled *The Covenants of the Prophet Muhammad with the Chris- tians of the World* [Angelico/Sophia Perennis, 2013] by Ilyas 'abd al- 'Alim Islam (Dr. John Andrew Morrow). The author has re-discov- ered, in obscure monasteries and libraries and books long out of print, and in some cases newly translated into English, the covenants concluded by the Prophet Muhammad, peace and blessings be upon him, with various Christian communities of his time. They uni- formly command Muslims not to attack or rob peaceful Christian communities—in the words of the *achtiname* he granted to the Monastery of St. Catherine in the Sinai, "until the End of the World." Based on my role as one of the editors of that book, I conceived of a movement called the Covenants Initiative, which allows Muslims to subscribe to the proposition that these covenants of the Prophet are binding upon them today, and in so doing stand in solidarity with the Christians of the Middle East and elsewhere now suffering persecution and martyrdom at the hands of the Takfiri terrorists, in some cases with the apparent support of the United States or its allies. Some Muslims are breathing a sigh of relief in the knowledge that they now have a way to come out against the Takfiris and other anti-traditional Islamicists, without acting as lackeys to the West and while remaining entirely in line with the commands of our Prophet. The heart of the Covenants Initiative is the following declaration:

> We the undersigned hold ourselves bound by the spirit and the letter of the covenants of the Prophet Muhammad (peace and blessings be upon him) with the Christians of the world, in the understanding that these covenants, if accepted as genuine, have the force of law in the shari'ah today and that nothing in the shari'ah, as traditionally and correctly interpreted, has ever contradicted them. As fellow victims of the terror and godlessness, the spirit of militant secularism and false religiosity now abroad in the world, we understand your suffering as Christians through our suffering as Muslims, and gain greater insight into our own suffering through the contemplation of your suffering. May the Most Merciful of the Merciful regard the sufferings of the righteous and the innocent; may He strengthen us, in full submission to His will, to follow the spirit and the letter of the covenants of the Prophet Muhammad with the Christians of the world in all our dealings with them. In the name of Allah, Most Gracious, Most Merciful. Praise be to Allah, the Cherisher and Sustainer of the worlds.

Any Muslim may add his or her signature to the Covenants Initiative at:

www.covenantsoftheprophet.com

That the Covenants Initiative, like the Covenants of the Prophet themselves, is fundamentally in line with Qur'anic norms is demonstrated by the following *ayat*:

> *He hath revealed unto thee (Muhammad) the Scripture with truth, confirming that which was (revealed) before it, even as He revealed the Torah and the Gospel.*
> *Aforetime, for a guidance to mankind; and hath revealed the Criterion (of right and wrong). Lo! those who disbelieve the revelations of Allah, theirs will be a heavy doom.* [Q. 3:3–4]

*Say (O Muhammad): We believe in Allah and that which is revealed
unto us and that which was revealed unto Abraham and Ishmael and
Isaac and Jacob and the tribes, and that which was vouchsafed unto
Moses and Jesus and the prophets from their Lord. We make no dis-
tinction between any of them, and unto Him we have surrendered.*
[Q. 3:84]

Not every Muslim, however, is called to participate in a movement like this. Those who are firmly established as servants of *Al-
Batin* must resist the temptation to involve themselves with *al-
Dunya*, even for the most idealistic of purposes. *And the believers
should not all go out to fight. Of every troop of them, a party only
should go forth, that they (who are left behind) may gain sound knowledge in religion, and that they may warn their folk when they return to
them, so that they may beware* [Q. 9:122]. Nonetheless, given that
"there is no monasticism in Islam" [*hadith*, Majma'al Bayan; Ibn
Kathir], the possibility that principled action in the world might,
under certain circumstances, enhance rather than dilute the quality
of contemplative spirituality cannot be entirely discounted.

Furthermore, we must now face the uncomfortable truth that the
space where "principled non-involvement" remains possible seems
to be shrinking fast. In these days of ISIS, and other similar armies
of outlaws and mercenaries cynically pretending to religion, both
yet to appear and already in evidence, every Muslim who does not
speak out against the atrocities being committed in his or her name
is being forced into some degree of complicity with them, silently
terrorized, threatened and co-opted, even as we go harmlessly
about our daily lives, bearing ill-will to no-one, working, shopping,
praying, fasting, caring for our children, sleeping in our beds. It
may be that only those committed heart and soul to the Greater
Jihad against the ISIS within can truly claim that, within that
deeper silence, they have taken *refuge in the Lord of mankind, the
King of mankind, he God of mankind, from the evil of the sneaking
whisperer, who whispereth in the hearts of mankind, of the jinn and of
mankind* [Q. 114]. These friends of Allah, the legitimate successors
of the *Ahl al-Suffa*, are absolved of all duties to the Dunya, unless
and until Allah calls them to active participation in it according to
His will.

Nonetheless, to insist that "silence is complicity" under all but the most extreme circumstances, or that externalism in religion is always tantamount to faithlessness, may simply be examples of the egotism and arrogance of the activist and the *batini* respectively. We can never claim that only those involved in heroic action, or else traveling an esoteric path, are acceptable to Allah. All He requires of us is that we remain faithful to the basic norms of *al-Din*, and that we fulfill our duties in life, large or small, according to our capacity, maintaining faith in Him and performing everything as an offering to Him:

> *Allah tasketh not a soul beyond its scope. For it (is only) that which it hath earned, And against it (only) that which it hath deserved. Our Lord! Condemn us not if we forget, or miss the mark! Our Lord! Lay not on us such a burden as thou didst lay on those before us! Our Lord! Impose not on us that which we have not the strength to bear! Pardon us, us absolve and have mercy on us, Thou, our Protector!* [Q. 2:286]

The "powers-that-be" in *al-Dunya* are just like the *Nafs al-ammara bi'l su'*, the "soul commanding to evil." They want to control everything in the world because they are afraid to die, and so meet Allah in the Night, and equally afraid to live, and so meet Allah in the Day; this is why we should never emulate them, even (or especially!) in the act of opposing them. Both Day and the Night belong to Allah—*His, whatsoever hath its dwelling in the night and in the day! and He, the Hearing, the Knowing!* [Q. 6:13]. But the powers-that-be want Day and Night to belong to them. They want the power to hide their crimes in darkness, and to throw light on whatever lies or disinformation they want us to swallow at any given time. This is why Allah will chastise them both by the Day and by the Night—and from Him there is no escape. So *Flee unto Allah!* [Q. 51:50]

Bibliography

Ibn 'Ata'allah al-Iskandari, *The Subtle Blessings in the Saintly Lives of Abu al-Mursi & His Master Abu al-Hasan*; Louisville: Fons Vitae, 2005.

——— *Kitab al-Hikam*, in *Ibn 'Ata'illah, The Book of Wisdom/ Kwaja 'abdullah Ansari, Intimate Conversations*; New York: Paulist Press, 1978.

Austin, R.W.J., *Ibn al-'Arabi, The Bezels of Wisdom*; New York, Ramsey, Toronto: The Paulist Press, 1980.

Burckhardt, Titus, *An Introduction to Sufism, The Mystical Dimension of Islam*; Wellingborough: The Aquarian Press, 1990.

——— *Letters of a Sufi Master: The Shaykh ad-Darqawi*; Louisville: Fons Vitae, 1998.

Chittick, William C., *Ibn al-'Arabi's Metaphysics of the Imagination: The Sufi Path of Knowledge*, Albany: State University of New York Press, 1989.

——— *Imaginal Worlds: Ibn al-'Arabi and the Problem of Religious Diversity*; Albany: State University of New York Press, 1994

Lings, Martin, *What is Sufism?*; Berkeley and Los Angeles: The University of California Press, 1975.

——— *A Sufi Saint of the Twentieth Century: Shaikh Ahmad al-'Alawi*; Berkeley and Los Angeles: The University of California Press, 1973.

Nicholson, Reynold A., *The Mathnawi of Jalalu'ddin Rumi*, vols. I–IV; Cambridge: E.J.W. Gibbs Memorial Trust, 1926.

Nurbakhsh, Javad, *Sufism*, vols. I–IV; London and New York: Khaniqahi-Nimatullahi Publications, 1982–1991.

——— *The Psychology of Sufism (Del wa Nafs)*; London and New York: Khaniqahi-Nimatullahi Publications, 1992.

——— *Sufi Symbolism*, vols. I–XV; London and New York: Khaniqahi-Nimatullahi Publications, 1997–2000.

Thackston, W.M. Jr., *Signs of the Unseen: The Discourses of Jalaluddin Rumi (Fihi ma-Fihi)*; Putney: Threshold Books, 1994.

www.ingramcontent.com/pod-product-compliance
Lightning Source LLC
Chambersburg PA
CBHW021357090426
42742CB00009B/898